D1596807

Evangelical Journeys

Evangelical Journeys

Choice and Change in a Northern Ireland Religious Subculture

CLAIRE MITCHELL & GLADYS GANIEL

UNIVERSITY COLLEGE DUBLIN PRESS

Preas Choláiste Ollscoile Bhaile Átha Cliath

First published 2011
by University College Dublin Press
Newman House
86 St Stephen's Green
Dublin 2
Ireland
www.ucdpress.ie

© Claire Mitchell and Gladys Ganiel, 2011

ISBN 978-1-906359-63-8 pb

All rights reserved. No part of this publication
may be reproduced, stored in a retrieval system,
or transmitted in any form or by any means,
electronic, photocopying, recording or otherwise
without the prior permission of the publisher

Cataloguing in Publication data
available from the British Library

The right of Claire Mitchell and Glady Ganiel to be identified
as the authors of this work has been asserted by them

Typeset in Scotland in Adobe Garamond,
Janson and Trade Gothic by Ryan Shiels
Text design by Lyn Davies
Printed in England on acid-free paper by
CPI Antony Rowe, Chippenham

Contents

Acknowledgements

This book has taken many years to come to fruition and our debt of gratitude is immense.

I (Claire) would like to thank John Coakley and all at the Institute of British-Irish Studies at University College Dublin where the work was begun as a Guinness Newman Post-doctoral scholar. The work continued when I came to Queen's University Belfast in 2003, and I would like to thank Mike Tomlinson for making further research resources available. I (Gladys) wish to acknowledge the Royal Irish Academy for funding much of my work for this book through its Third Sector Programme for doctoral research. This research was conducted in the School of Politics and International Relations at University College Dublin. When I took up my post in the Irish School of Ecumenics, Trinity College Dublin at Belfast in 2006, I received further support from Trinity's New Lecturer's Start-up Fund.

The academics and friends who helped shape this book are numerous. We would like to thank Jennifer Todd, as always, for her constant and sublime mentoring. Professor Todd supervised both of our doctoral dissertations and has been an important influence and inspiration. Katy Hayward's influence, as a brilliant academic and friend, is ever present. Grace Davie helped clarify our ideas at the beginning of the project. Gareth Higgins and Peter Rollins helped give advice and contacts. Niamh Puirséil helped enormously towards the end, when we needed an editing eye to streamline and pitch the book. Discussions with Liam O'Dowd, Matt Woods, Richard O'Leary, Frances King, Madeline Leonard, Myrtle Hill, Paddy Hillyard, Andrew Percy, Lisa Smyth, Vincent O'Sullivan, Jon Hatch, Jayme Reaves, Therese Cullen and Amber Rankin helped along the way.

For us, this book is about our friends as well as our interviewees. We see their stories reflected in the narratives of strangers. It is thinking about our communal journeys that inspired us to start this project in the first place. We would like to thank Kerry Anthony, Phil Harrison, Suzie and Nick Hamilton, Adam Turkington, Ali Fell, Wes Forsythe, Gemma Reid, Kellie Turtle, Esther Addley, Gail McConnell, Sarah Williamson, Ethel White and Chris and Janet

Morris for many conversations about our religious journeys over the years. I (Claire) would especially like to thank my partner Tim Millen, my parents Pamela and Ian Mitchell, and Tim's parents David and Renee Millen, not only for holding the fort while I wrote, but also for some of the most insightful discussions of all on the topic of religious journeys. I (Gladys) would like to thank past conversation partners at Ocean State Baptist Church in Providence, Rhode Island, Pilgrim Orthodox Presbyterian Church in Bangor, Maine, and Grosvenor Road Baptist Church in Dublin, and my students at the Irish School of Ecumenics, for their faithfulness and insights. This project also would not have been possible for me without the support of my husband, Brian O'Neill, our family, and my parents, Carl and Jennie Ganiel.

We would both like to thank Glenn Jordan and all at East Belfast Mission for giving us an opportunity to present and discuss work in progress with a variety of evangelicals. Likewise to Cheryl Meban and the Centre for Contemporary Christianity in Ireland and Lynda Gould at New Horizon. Special thanks to Sara Templer, who was everything we could have hoped for in a research assistant. And to Caroline Clarke at the Irish School of Ecumenics for her excellent proof-reading.

We are also grateful to the book's reviewers, John Brewer and Michelle Dillon, for helping us to vastly improve upon the original text. Barbara Mennell and all at UCD Press bore with us patiently while we clarified our thoughts.

Above all we would both like to express our gratitude to our interviewees, who gave so generously of their time and stories. We hope we have represented their journeys faithfully, and of course, any errors are our own. This book is dedicated to three of our interviewees who passed away during the course of the research.

CLAIRE MITCHELL
GLADYS GANIEL
Belfast, March 2011

Abbreviations

CCCI	Centre for Contemporary Christianity in Ireland
CU	Christian Union
DUP	Democratic Unionist Party
EA	Evangelical Alliance
ECONI	Evangelical Contribution on Northern Ireland
IRA	Irish Republican Army
NGO	Non-Governmental Organisation
NIMMA	Northern Ireland Mixed Marriage Association
NILTS	Northern Ireland Life and Times Survey
UDA	Ulster Defence Association
UUP	Ulster Unionist Party
UVF	Ulster Volunteer Force

Introduction

Our own religious journeys started in different locations: from an evangelical charismatic home in Belfast during the Northern Irish Troubles (Claire), and from a Bible-believing Baptist church in rural Maine (Gladys). Though thousands of miles apart, during our formative years we were shaped by many of the same religious assumptions, practices, biblical interpretations, songs and symbols. Evangelicalism filled our diaries with Bible studies, youth groups, morning and evening services, quiet times, summer camps and other social events. The religious teaching was serious business. There were strict social codes: making sure your close friends were evangelicals, not dating non-evangelicals; and moral codes: not having sex before marriage, not drinking alcohol. There were some differences too – cultural differences, and differing views on the Holy Spirit. But overall, we tend to see the similarities in our early religious experiences.

Now in our thirties, we have found that the people we grew up with have moved in radically different religious directions. A substantial number remain part of the evangelical movement. Some lead their own churches, others play in worship bands, or are missionaries overseas. Others are chaplains and Christian workers. Some have moved away from the strong evangelicalism of our childhood, but remain within the evangelical family. They have been questioning their faith, discarding some aspects of their theology and maintaining others. They now see themselves as liberal evangelicals, believing in God and participating in church, but in a different way than their parents believed and participated.

Others have come to question their faith in more radical ways, and are involved with the post-evangelical, emerging church movement. This group includes feminists, environmentalists, gay activists and those who are interested in exploring faith, but also want to transform its core assumptions. And there are friends who have asked so many questions of the faith they inherited that barely anything remains. They have made a decisive break with evangelicalism, and now consider themselves to be atheists or agnostics.

Because of our own experiences and those of our friends, we wanted to understand what prompted people to change in so many different directions. Why would one person want to become an evangelical pastor, whilst another is embarrassed about the religion of their youth? It is questions like this which motivated us to research and write this book.

On the surface there are a number of answers. Maybe it is that some people have gone to university and have questioned the ideas of their upbringing there. Maybe some people have closer ties to their family and childhood friends that help keep their faith alive, whereas others have a weaker relationship, enabling religious ties to be broken. Or perhaps it is that some people have experienced personal difficulties or traumas in their lives that have caused them to hold fast to the religious reassurances with which they were raised. In a divided society like Northern Ireland, could it be that some people have experienced violence or lost someone close to them, which has caused an entrenchment of strong religious and political positions?

All of these explanations are too simple. Many of us will know someone whose response to personal trauma has been to turn against God, rather than seeking comfort and reassurance. Whilst some who have experienced violence in Northern Ireland have clung to ultra-unionist and religious positions, others have found themselves compelled to forgive and explore liberal theologies. There is of course a relationship between going to university and questioning faith, but plenty of people emerge from university with their faith intact. In fact, from evangelical students at Queen's University Belfast to Muslim students at Bradford University, it seems that further education can at times make people's faith even stronger. There are no simple ways to explain why people's religious beliefs change.

In light of such questions and incomplete explanations, we explore how far people choose their own religious path, and how far certain types of religious identities are foisted upon them. In the process, we demonstrate that Northern Irish evangelicalism is a diverse and dynamic faith, in which people experience change and flux in their religious beliefs, practices and identities over time. We provide examples of that change, and demonstrate how it happens. This highlights the classic tension between religious choice and religious conditioning – in sociological terms, between agency and structure.

The heart of the book: evangelical journeys

At the heart of this book are people's stories about their religious journeys. We talked to 95 evangelicals and ex-evangelicals in Northern Ireland about how their religious ideas and practices had developed over the course of their lives.

Of course it would have been interesting to talk to people of all faiths, in a variety of different national contexts. But it is important to narrow the focus down when doing qualitative research, where the aim is to access as much depth as possible. We chose to keep the focus on evangelicals in Northern Ireland so that we could analyse processes of change within individuals, rather than across cultures. This allowed us to unpick the reasons why people who were raised in a similar social, political and religious environment could go on to make such different religious choices. Our focus on Northern Irish evangelicals gave our study depth, for which we no doubt sacrificed breadth of comparison. Having said this, we think that Northern Irish evangelicals have much in common with evangelicals throughout the world. There is a shared evangelical subculture, and this represents a global language and experience. This in part explains why Gladys's experiences in the United States resonate so much with Claire's experiences in Northern Ireland. Whilst we focus exclusively on evangelical Christianity in this book, we also think that its stories of family, romance, health, work and religious questioning will resonate with people of other faiths and none.

The result of our research has been that we have identified six varieties of religious journey among evangelicals in Northern Ireland. These journeys are converting (which we see as a long process, not a single event), a deepening of faith in a conservative direction, a steady maintenance of faith, moderating, transforming and leaving faith. These journeys are not to be likened to the empirical or ideal types used by sociologists. We are not constructing typologies into which we then slot people who have particular religious beliefs or engage in particular religious practices. Rather, our varieties of religious journeys are designed to further understanding about how individuals experience their religion over time in their everyday lives, in dynamic relationship with the religious, social and political structures around them.

Accordingly, we identify patterns of experiences and combinations of factors which push and pull people towards particular varieties of religious journey. This means that our accounts of religious journeys rely a great deal on rich descriptions of people's experiences: the everyday and mundane, as well as the dramatic and supernatural. These descriptions allow us to achieve a better grasp of patterns in social relationships, patterns over the life course, political factors, differences in the ways evangelicals engage with popular culture and experience crisis, and subcultural factors like the way evangelicals handle religious doubts and engage with their own churches.

We do not claim that our approach can predict the directions in which people will journey in a mechanistic way. Rather, we offer insight into the complexity of processes of religious change, arguing that individual choice should be granted a more prominent place in the sociology of religion.

Evangelical diversity and change

This book is about 'lived religion', and about choice and change in a specific evangelical subculture (see also McGuire 2008, 67–96). There are still many stereotypes alive and well in the media and in popular consciousness about Northern Irish evangelicals. These have been evident in some of the media coverage of evangelicals during the Iris Robinson sex scandal in 2010, and the controversy over creationism in the Ulster Museum.

But academic research has long established that evangelicals in Northern Ireland are a diverse group, and their subculture is home to people who believe and practise their faith in quite different ways (Brewer with Higgins 1998, Jordan 2001, Ganiel 2008a). Some evangelicals are biblical literalists whilst others interpret the Bible as allegory. Some see direct links between their faith and political unionism, whilst others believe that faith is a private matter, and others again believe that evangelicalism calls them to build peace rather than to protect their ethnic group. Many evangelicals in Northern Ireland are morally conservative, whilst a smaller number are exploring how evangelicalism relates to alternative sexualities and lifestyle choices. This diversity within evangelicalism provides us with an excellent opportunity to explore personal religious change. The subculture is broad enough that we are able to find people on very different religious journeys within it, whilst being contained enough to be recognisable, and to ensure that our study has coherence.

Further, while much important work has already been done on evangelicals in Northern Ireland, everyday life has not been a prominent feature in the literature. The bulk of research has focused on how evangelicalism intertwines with politics, whether by propping up ethnic and national divisions (Bruce 2007, Mitchel 2003), by providing religious interpretations for conflict (Akenson 1992, Miller 1978, Brewer with Higgins 1998, Mitchell 2005) or through its role in reconciliation (Liechty and Clegg 2001, Ganiel 2008a). This book takes this literature as a starting point, and asks what else we might want to know about evangelicals in Northern Ireland. We believe that the everyday, more mundane, aspects of evangelical life are equally as important as its political roles, and have not received much attention in the literature to date. In many ways, we are trying to emphasise the roles of individuals and individual choice in evangelicalism in Northern Ireland. So whilst we are interested in politics, we want to explore how individuals react to political change in different ways, rather than categorising types of evangelical beliefs. Through telling everyday stories of evangelicalism, including the stories of people who have left it behind, we hope to offer new insights into life in contemporary Northern Ireland.

Structure of the book

In the first chapter, we review the academic literature on religious change, locating our study within these debates. The second chapter describes the evangelical subculture in Northern Ireland, building on earlier work that has identified types of evangelicals but has neglected the more mundane, everyday aspects of evangelicalism. In the third chapter we review our methods and explain how and why we decided to study Northern Irish evangelicals. Chapters four to nine offer analysis of our six varieties of religious journey: converting, deepening in a conservative direction, maintaining a steady faith, moderating, transforming, and leaving evangelicalism. We provide examples of change and demonstrate how it happens. The interview-based chapters do not describe different subgroups of evangelicals, although we do show which subgroups people on religious journeys are more likely to fall into. Rather, these chapters provide a detailed perspective on how change happens for individuals, in ways that are not always fully explored in broader academic theories about religious change. In the final chapter we compare the patterns of experiences and combinations of factors that have prompted journeys in particular directions. We ultimately argue that Northern Irish evangelicals are choosing their religion, demonstrating a remarkable degree of creativity and strategic decision-making in this process. This underlines previous research about the diversity and flexibility of evangelicalism, while at the same time opening up new lines of research about what it is like to be an evangelical in a rapidly changing, post-conflict Northern Ireland.

Beyond the sociological analysis, we hope that the stories in this book resonate with readers. For non-believers, we think these stories can provide insight into what it is like to be religious in the contemporary world. For those who are evangelicals, we think these stories may help in the process of reflecting on their own religious journeys. We see aspects of our own experiences mirrored in the stories of these evangelicals, and think that readers may also be able to identify with some of the people they meet in the book. One of the hopes we have for the book is that people will be better able to understand those who have chosen a very different religious path from themselves. Whatever direction of journey, the interviews show us how complex, interesting, thoughtful and creative human beings can be. We hope that we have managed to do their stories justice.

CHAPTER ONE

Perspectives on Personal Religious Change

How do people experience religious change? As Ammerman (2003) argues, this question has received surprisingly little attention in the research to date. Some literature has focused on dramatic religious change such as conversion. But little has been said about how individuals construct, maintain and adapt their religious identity on a daily basis and over the course of their lives. That said, there are some strands of research that offer perspectives on the question of personal religious change. In this chapter, we argue that each of these approaches provides valuable insights into how change happens, but no one theory explains everything. Our approach resonates the most with those which acknowledge social structural constraints, while at the same time leaving plenty of room for personal religious *choice*.

Religious change across the life course

Life-course research is the study of people from birth through to old age. This uses longitudinal data, which involves tracking a group of people over time, studying them at various junctures in their lives. This is an excellent way to discover how people change over time. However, it is an expensive and extremely lengthy type of research, and there are very few studies of this nature about personal religious change. One exception is Dillon and Wink's (2007) impressive study of Californians in the twentieth century, which we talk about below. In addition to this, there have been some excellent studies that give insights into the importance of religion at key stages of life, from childhood through to adolescence, various stages of adulthood, and older age.

Increased religiosity, for example, has been found to correlate with older age. There is evidence that religious participation increases in older age as well as the tendency to ask existential questions (McFadden 1999, Ferraro and

Kelley-Moore 2000). This was the case for participants in Dillon and Wink's study, who found that people in their fifties to seventies increased their religiousness regardless of gender and denomination. Dillon and Wink (2007: 81) say this can be partially explained by the increased need in older age to cope with challenges such as 'health problems, spousal bereavement, death anxiety, and the lack of purposefulness that can characterise the post-retirement period'.

But older people are not the most religious group in society. Dillon and Wink's (2007) research confirmed earlier findings that the high point of religiosity is actually the teenage years, closely followed by early adulthood. When older people experienced an increase in religiosity they were usually reverting to an earlier higher level of religious involvement. For religious teenagers, the college years may mean a drop in religiosity. But this is often temporary, and people can bounce back rather quickly in their twenties and thirties to almost as high a level of religiousness (Baston, Shroenrade and Ventis 1993). Starting up a family is one of the main reasons why people resume their religious involvement. Having children often leads parents to increase their religious participation, out of concern for their children's socialisation or nagging concerns for their souls (Edgell 2006, Chaves 1991).

In contrast, the low point for religiosity is middle adulthood. Dillon and Wink (2007) found that the interval from middle to late adulthood was the nadir of religious involvement for their respondents, irrespective of gender or denomination. Similarly, Ingersoll-Dayton, Krause and Morgan's (2002) elderly interviewees, looking back on their lives, associated these years with a dip in religiousness. It seems that these are the years where one's career takes centre stage and where social networks are the most varied and robust, leading individuals to have less time and interest both in religious questions and in organised religion. Another pattern highlighted by the life-course literature is that people tend to make most changes to their religion in the years between adolescence and early adulthood, whereas they become more religiously stable by their thirties (Starke and Finke 2000). In Dillon and Wink's study, they found that only six per cent experienced 'dramatic change' after mid-life – evenly split between an increase and a decrease in religiousness (2007: 105–6). At the same time as showing that very dramatic change is not typical, however, Dillon and Wink are keen to emphasise the 'gentle ebb and flow' of personal religiosity over time (98). Nearly all of the participants they introduce to us have undergone personal religious change to some degree, at many different stages of the life-cycle.

Overall, the life-course literature is important in giving us indications about how we might expect personal religious change to intersect with changes in the life cycle. It highlights patterns, primarily relating to changing social roles, that open up and limit individuals' potential religious interest and involvement. But the patterns clearly do not apply to everybody. They are just general tendencies. Dillon and Wink found that a number of study participants were not influenced by social role or life transitions such as parenthood and ageing.[1]

Life-course perspectives are, by definition, better at highlighting big structural patterns of religious change than they are at explaining how individuals negotiate their experiences, and reach varying conclusions based on similar social conditions. Why does attending university prompt some people to question their religious beliefs, whilst reinforcing the faith of others? Why do some people reject the intensive religious socialisation of childhood, whilst it lays the groundwork for others' religious conversion in later life? This is where this book pushes further than the life-course research, because it asks how individuals make religious choices based on the social roles they find themselves playing. We ask not just how the life cycle correlates with religious changes, but how people interpret their place in life and why they feel certain social positions have led them to make one kind of religious decision over another.

Social psychological explanations

Another type of research about religious change comes from social psychology. This type of work focuses on social influences on the individual. As Baston, Shroenrade and Ventis (1993: 25) point out, 'what may seem to be a freely chosen and highly personal religious stance is in large measure a product of social influence'. This kind of analysis argues that all religion is socially learned, whether through families, schooling, religious institutions or wider culture. The type of religion a child associates with, the rituals they learn, the institutions they are familiar with and the moral norms they internalise are not random, nor divinely ordained, but reflect the culturally available options in a specific time and place. Over the course of a lifetime, individuals may change and alter their religious views, but these are not random choices. All religious decisions are made in the context of how people were raised, who their peers were, as well as in the context of their own physical and mental health.

This research has confirmed that one of the most important predictors of individuals' religion is, unsurprisingly, their parents (Hoge and Petrillo 1978, Spilka, Hood and Gorush 1985, Baston, Shroenrade and Ventis 1993). Moreover, the stronger the parents' religion, the more important religion tends to be for their children (Hunsburger 1976). Although as Roof (1999) found, this is not always the case – having extremely religious parents can provoke different religious responses, from following in the family's footsteps to rebellion. Dillon and Wink (2007: 91) also point out that while early childhood religious socialisation has a long-term influence, people can go different ways in later life – based on life-course changes, and social and historical events.

Education is also a key aspect of social influence and many studies have pointed to the effect that a university education has in reducing religious orthodoxy amongst students (for example, Feldman 1969, Orzorak 1989). Baston, Shroenrade and Ventis (1993: 41) conclude on the basis of these studies that 'the effect of college may be largely due to shifts in reference groups' and 'its liberalising impact is often temporary'. So friends and tutors that are influential during one's college years may become less important over time. Many people become more liberal or put faith aside at university, only to revert to their earlier friendship groups and traditional faith afterwards. Another way to look at the question of university is to examine people who have never attended. And what we find here is that people who have not gone to college tend to be more religious. Lower educational levels have been associated with the holding of more fundamentalist beliefs as well as the reporting of mystical experiences (Back and Bourque 1970).

Another aspect of individual religion that sociologists as well as social psychologists often focus on is the relationship with health and illness. They highlight the comfort and meaning that religion can offer in times of ill health or when facing death. Indeed, most studies find a positive correlation between religion and physical health, including a tendency to live longer (Ellison and Levin 1998, Koenig, McCullagh and Larson 2001, McCullagh and Smith 2003). However, ill health does not necessarily encourage individuals to turn to religion. Illness, adversity and facing death did not prompt some of Dillon and Wink's interviewees to waver from their lifelong aversion to religion. They describe how 'Jack' 'remained impervious to, and decidedly uninterested in, any personal comfort or meaning that religion might have brought him' through military life, alcoholism or distressing illness in later life (2007: 94).

Religion is often also associated with mental well-being, again particularly in later life. Dillon and Wink (2007), for example, draw attention to the role of religion in the 'healthy functioning' of adults. Sometimes religion helps people cope with almost intolerable psychological pressures, such as a fear of death, or losing a loved one, providing explanation and solace (see for example Kahoe and Dunn 1975, Kraft, Litwin and Barber 1987). When facing personal adversity, religion may offer comfort, ways of framing problems that ease individual anxiety, and solutions for the way forward. Smith, McCullough and Poll (2003), analysing 150 studies of religious involvement and depression, found a significant relationship between higher levels of religiosity and lower levels of depression. On the other hand, religion can stimulate dysfunction, if one is to use this language. It can be a key source of guilt, frustration and anxiety, particularly when there is a disjuncture between what an individual believes and how they live their life. In some studies religious people have been found to be more likely than non-religious people to experience tension, anxiety and guilt, including guilt about sex for members of conservative denominations (Rokeach 1960, Peterson 1964, Argyle and Delin 1965).

So clearly there are strong relationships between social influences and personal religion on the one hand, and well-being and religiosity on the other. These ideas play an important role as we analyse our interviews, and we examine what people say about their early religious socialisation, the influence of their parents, and how their faith fared during their college years if they attended. We also explore people's stories of health and illness and see what role religion has played in providing comfort, or sometimes in failing to provide comfort, during difficult times.

But social psychological approaches, like life-course studies, are much better at telling us about broad general tendencies than they are at illuminating what makes individuals go one way or another. They do not tell us, for example, why people react so differently to going to college, why some revert to an earlier form of faith, while some abandon their faith in these years and never go back. They do not tell us why one child rebels against their parents' faith whilst their brothers and sisters maintain a strong faith. They cannot tell us why one person seeks God's help to deal with their depression, whilst another person sees their depression as evidence that God does not care about them. In short, social psychological approaches cannot tell us much about individual differences and individual choices. They tend to see people as trapped into the roles that society has laid out for them. As Baston, Shroenrade and Ventis assert (1993: 27), individuals live out a Goffmanesque 'script written by society'.[2] Of course Baston et al. argue that scripts can conflict, as a 20-year-old man struggles to marry his new-found freedom at college with the expectations of his traditionally religious parents, which creates tension. But ultimately, they argue that it is difficult to escape the frameworks already put in place for us by society. In this book we analyse these social influences on religion, but we also explore how they play out differently for different individuals. We see the interaction between social influences and *individual choice,* as at the heart of understanding personal religious change.

Religion in times of social and political change

The research we have talked about so far documents general patterns of personal religious change. These patterns, relating to age, socialisation and health, could be at work in any time, in any place. But, as Gorski argues (2003), it is also important to focus on religion in specific times and specific places, asking how people's religious journeys can be affected by where and when they live. For example, we are all destined to go through the various stages of life from childhood through to old age, but where we live in the world, and at what time in history, shapes what it means to be a child or an old person. The assumptions and roles attached to childhood and old age will be different in an urban housing estate in the UK than in a rural village in Kenya.

Again we can turn to Dillon and Wink's (2007) work to highlight the impact of social and political change on personal religion. Studying Californians over the course of the twentieth century provided them with an opportunity to evaluate the impact of cultural change on religious orientations, in this case the counter-cultural change of the 1960s and 1970s. They found a rise in spiritual seekership, or a deconstructed search for meaning, after this time. Cultural change in big religious institutions can also cause personal religious change. Greeley (1985), Inglis (1998) and King (2007), for example, highlight the Second Vatican Council as crucial for the personal religious development of Catholics from the mid 1960s. The same goes for big political events. Some of Dillon and Wink's (2007) participants cited the Vietnam War as influencing their religious views. Mitchell and Todd (2007) highlight the ways in which conservative evangelicals in Northern Ireland have adapted their religious ideas to a changing political context – in some cases seeing the peace process as a sign of the end times.

One of the best studies of how evangelicals have responded to social and political change is Christian Smith's (1998) work on American evangelicalism. Drawing from social identity theory he argues that all humans feel a need to belong.[3] To satisfy this need they join social groups, and these groups maintain their boundaries by defining themselves against relevant out-groups. Smith says that religious groups have always adapted themselves to their cultural surroundings, and that evangelicals in particular have adapted well to late modern society. Whereas the evangelical enemy may once have been communism, now secular modernity and Islam have taken centre stage. While television and cinema were once anathema for evangelicals, now most have accepted the media's role in modern society and indeed use it for their own ends. In other words, American evangelicals have been able to creatively adapt to cultural, social and political change in the twentieth and twenty-first centuries.

But Smith's work helps us understand how evangelicalism has changed as a movement, rather than how individuals themselves have negotiated change. Whilst he draws on a massive 405 in-depth interviews and 2,591 telephone interviews, the book deals with finding out what evangelicals think in a particular time and place, rather than focusing on how individuals change over time. However, this, and Smith's wider body of work, is important in understanding how social and political change influence religious identity, the capacity for religious identity to creatively adapt to external changes, and the importance of religious belonging in uncertain, pluralistic, late modern societies. Drawing on Smith's insights, we also look at how wider social and cultural changes feed into our own evangelicals' religious journeys.

This brings us to the question of political conflict. As our book is based in Northern Ireland, it was important for us to consider how the very specific experience of conflict, and post-conflict transition, has impacted people's personal religious journeys. In our discussion of Northern Ireland's evangelical subculture in the next chapter, we explain how religion and politics have been inextricably linked. Building on this, we argue that the conflict has had some religious dimensions, which overlap with other ethnic, national and political divisions. This helps to create a potent cocktail of differences that can be used to justify violence.

Indeed, scholars have generally focused on how strong religions are used to justify violence or advance political goals. Far beyond Northern Ireland, ethnicity and nationalism have been identified as important in stimulating religious changes. Some researchers have described how politics and ethnicity can spark religious revivals. Sells (1998), for example, highlighted the role of Catholicism and Orthodox Christianity in the Balkans, where religious symbols were harnessed by Croats and Serbs respectively to explain and justify conflict. Sells argues that initially religion was being used instrumentally to garner support for political causes; however, he also says that '[o]nce militants had spilled blood in the name of that mythology they became dependent on it' (2003: 315). So Sells shows how using religion for political ends during a conflict can sometimes lead to religion becoming important in and of itself. We found a similar trend in the interviews for this book, where non-religious people who originally sought out strong evangelicalism to back up their political goals ended up experiencing genuine religious conversion.

Religion can also be important for people who need extra reassurance of their ethnic identities in peaceful societies, not just during violent political conflicts. By ethnicity, we mean geographical and historical questions of who the people are and where they are from. A good example of this is how migrants use religion in their new homes, such as Irish Catholic immigrants to the United States. Ebaugh's (2003) research shows how religion is used by migrants in America to prop up ethnic identity – through sponsoring community activities, helping people feel at home, and passing culture on through food and rituals. She says that, in doing these things, religion often becomes more important than people's original ethnic identity. This is similar to what Chong (1998) found with the Korean American migrants she studied. Chong's respondents initially began to attend Korean American evangelical churches for social and cultural reasons, to maintain social networks and 'keep up' their culture and language. However, their newfound participation led to genuine religious conversions. Pyong Gap Min's (2010) more recent book comparing Korean Protestants and Indian Hindus in New York is entitled simply *Preserving Ethnicity through Religion in America*. It also shows significant differences when it comes to religious practice and theology, underlining the idea that people who seek out religion to prop up other identities can end up taking religion seriously.

What we learn from this literature is that big political events and cultural changes can have a profound influence on individuals' religious journeys. We can see then that religion is not simply a matter of someone's place in the life cycle or how they were socialised. Rather, all of our religious journeys take place at distinct historical moments. Wars, conflicts, times of peace and technological advance, where we live and move, all impact deeply on our own private religious journeys. We also can gain from this research an appreciation for the importance of religion's relationship with ethnicity. Often people call upon religion to reinforce ethnicity, and sometimes to help explain troubling political circumstances or adjust to new social situations. In these cases, religion can become more important in individuals' lives than it was before. In this book we examine these intimate connections between culture, politics, conflict, ethnicity and religion in the lives of individuals. We have found few examples of this kind of approach in the literature to date. This book provides new insights into how and why people change their religious beliefs in relation to political as well as personal experiences.

Religion, identity and 'free choice'

In our review of the literature so far, we have seen religious change presented like it is something that *happens to* people, as they age, as they become socialised, as politics changes around them. But what role do we ourselves play in making change happen? As leading sociologist of religion, Nancy Ammerman (2003: 207) argues,

> As modern people have loosened their ties to their families and places that (perhaps) formerly enveloped them in a cocoon of faith (or at least surrounded them with a predictable round of religious activity), they can choose how and whether to be religious, including choosing how central religion will be in their lives. Religious practices and affiliations change over a complicated lifetime. [. . .] If religious identity ever was a given, it certainly is no longer.

But can people really choose whoever and whatever they want to be? How much control do people have over their own religious journeys? Recent research on the relationship between religion and identity explores these questions.

Interest in the concept of identity has been growing in the social sciences since the 1990s. Much of this comes from a social constructionist (also called a social constructivist) perspective, and tries to demonstrate how individuals create their religious identities in the context of late modern, or post-modern, societies. This work sees contemporary society as a large melting pot of people, interests, habits and opinions. It is often called a 'pluralistic society', a term which denotes the multiplicity of identity and lifestyle options on offer.

Whereas research on identity until the 1980s focused on how people were shaped by macro identities like class, gender and race, from the 1990s the emphasis began to shift to how people mixed and matched their own individual identities. Rather than stressing how people were constrained by the circum-stances of birth and social structures, social scientists and philosophers began to talk about how people might *choose* who they wanted to be. The fact that people had multiple identities, all at the same time, also came into focus. As Ammerman (2003) argues, because we all play so many roles in life (as a woman, a mother, a lecturer, a young person, an Irish person), we always bring our learning from one sphere into another. This means that many things that we do and experience in life can potentially feed into our religious ideas. Rather than being determined by how we grew up, our religious journeys become messy affairs, influenced by all the other roles we play and the things we experience.

Some post-modern theorists, such as Bauman (1998) and Lyon (2000), have taken this idea much further, arguing that identities are now freely chosen, that a core self no longer exists, and individuals haphazardly navigate a fragmented world where social influences and roles are thrown into chaos. In terms of religion, some have taken the position that religion is now a matter of free choice, and that given the choice, most people will conclude that religion is no longer necessary. Berger (1967, 1995), for example, argues that modernity brings individuals into contact with so many other perspectives that it makes it impossible to be sure that our own ideas are the right ones. A generation ago, sociologists predicted that this would inevitably lead to secularisation, where people would abandon religion en masse (see Bruce 2002).

While late modern living may offer much more potential for self-reinvention than any other age, to say we are totally free to be whoever we want to be is an extreme overstatement. Individuals do play an active role in the construction of their identities, but this freedom is never exercised in a vacuum. As Lamont and Fournier (1993) argue, macro identities such as class, race and gender continue to dominate how individuals categorise themselves and others. If I [Claire] wanted to radically change my identity – to be an Indian Hindu male for example – it would be all but impossible. Even if I could somehow obtain an Indian passport, other Indian people would be unlikely to accept my claim of Indianness. It would be possible to change my gender from female to male as the scientific expertise exists, but I would still face a significant battle to persuade other people in society to accept my choice. Whilst I am legally free to change my religion, my parents, wider family and friends might not support me, which in turn might influence my decision. Relationships with other people always play a role in our identity choices. We need to have our identities accepted by other people, and to a large extent, by society.

Moreover, as commentators writing in the 1990s and 2000s came to see that religion was not dying out across the world, they began to reframe their arguments about secularisation. Instead of saying people would freely choose to abandon religion altogether, they started to pay attention to the ways in which people appropriate, transform, resist, edit and use religion to make sense of the complexities of late modern societies. This allows us to appreciate how religion is both socially transmitted *and* a matter of choice. Neitz further argues (2004: 397) that an understanding of identity as relational helps us to bridge the gap between constraint and freedom. In her words, '[o]nce we look at selves as relational rather than essential, then structure and agency can be imagined as mutually constitutive rather than as opposed' (see also Somers 1994).

Ammerman (2003: 212) puts it well when she says '[a]gency is located, then, not in freedom from patterned constraint but in our ability to invoke those patterns in nonprescribed ways'. The dynamics of religious journeys include a mixture of social influences and individual choices.

Sociological research provides examples of how people balance traditional religious influences with new religious choices. For example, Thumma's (1991) gay evangelicals are compelled to try to balance their religious and sexual identities in inventive ways, for which there is no pre-existing blueprint. Harris (2006) provides an interesting analysis of the narratives of 'Christian Buddhists' who actively question the notion that they must choose between these two faiths. Neitz's (1987) work on Catholic charismatic conversion views changes in religious identity as a rational process in which individual reason plays an important role, as people test their religious ideas against reality. Ammerman (2007: 208) refers to this as 'active identity work' and 'intentional work'. In this way, the identity literature presents people as able to actively choose and construct their religious identities, but in the context of sometimes quite traditional structures, for example as gay people reshape what evangelicalism means to them.

We have found these perspectives on identity extremely useful in our work. We agree with those who argue that people are free to shape and mould their own identities, but we think that this shaping is also constrained by wider society and our relationships with other people. So our religious journeys are in our own hands – we decide what beliefs to accept or reject, and we can make creative changes to our religious practices over time. But the decisions we make are never detached from the types of social processes described above – relationships with our families, educational experiences, cultural and political contexts. We think that these perspectives on identity help us to take on board all the lessons about the importance of social structure discussed in the previous sections, whilst allowing more room to think about how and why individuals make different religious choices.

Conclusions

We have now spent some time describing how sociologists, political scientists, philosophers and social psychologists have characterised personal religious change. Each type of literature has thrown light upon one aspect of the puzzle of how religious change happens. The life-course literature has given us insight into how growing up affects personal religion, and the social psychological literature has shown us how society shapes our religious identities. From the literature on social and political change we see how our wider cultural context can impact upon our private religious journeys. The identity literature offers an added dimension to the debate by seeing religious change not just as something that *happens to* people, but also as a process that people play an active role in.

The analysis we offer throughout the rest of the book draws on the best aspects of these literatures. We have not chosen to follow one or the other of the theories, but rather, our work is informed by all of them, the strengths of one addressing the weaknesses in another. We use the work on religious identity and choice to help us understand why people react differently to the same changes in the life cycle and socialising influences. At the same time, we use what we have learned about the social and relational aspects of religion from social psychology to help us understand how people make religious choices in specific social contexts, rather than making these choices at random and without constraint.

The term we use to bring these ideas together is 'religious journey'. We think this captures the dynamic relationship between social structures, political context and individual agency, which shapes people's religious ideas and practices over the course of their lives. Taking cues from the literature outlined above, we consider in later chapters what our interviewees are telling us in relation to the research on, for example, family, health, ageing and experience of politics. And we identify some common experiences, and importantly *combinations* of experiences, that have pushed people's religious journeys in one direction or another.

CHAPTER TWO

Evangelical Subculture in Northern Ireland

When most people think about evangelicals in Northern Ireland, they think about the Rev. Ian Paisley. Although no longer at the centre of public life, Paisley's reputation as a larger-than-life figure, firebrand preacher and boisterous politician still reverberates throughout Northern Ireland's society. He has dominated many academics' and journalists' research agenda (for example Moloney and Pollack 1986, Bruce 1986, 2007, Smyth 1988, Southern 2005, Moloney 2008). Whether brandishing anti-Catholic placards at religious rallies in the 1970s, yelling 'Never, Never, Never' on the steps of Belfast's City Hall after the Anglo-Irish Agreement in the 1980s, or marching with the Orange Order in Drumcree in the 1990s, Paisley has often been seen as the epitome of religious and political dogmatism.

However, those familiar with evangelicalism in Northern Ireland know that this is a crude stereotype of the subculture (and even of Paisley himself). A number of significant studies now highlight evangelical diversity in Northern Ireland, and underline the many roles religion has played in peace as well as conflict. Work by Boal, Keane and Livingstone (1997), Brewer with Higgins (1998), Jordan (2001), Mitchel (2003) and Ganiel (2008a) has demonstrated that Northern Ireland's evangelicals come in many forms, with very different beliefs about the Bible, forms of worship, views on social integration and political attitudes. Baillie (2001) and Porter (2002) have underlined the significance of gender differences within the subculture. And journalists such as McKay (2000) have provided important insights into the differences between rural and urban evangelicals as well as variation along lines of social class.

In this chapter, we describe evangelicalism in Northern Ireland in more depth, demonstrating variety within the subculture as well as the ideas and practices that hold it together. We begin by reviewing what the literature tells us about evangelicalism and conflict, and about different evangelical subgroups – in general and in Northern Ireland. We then discuss some other – more everyday – aspects of the subculture that have featured infrequently in a literature which has tended to focus on evangelicals' relationship with conflict and reconciliation.

Evangelicalism, politics and conflict

Most academics do not consider the Northern Ireland conflict a religious conflict. We agree – up to a point. The conflict is not a holy war or a jihad. It is not about religious doctrines or creating a Catholic or a Protestant state. However, we believe that religion has played a much more important role in sustaining conflict than many commentators allow. We strongly dispute the argument put forward by McGarry and O'Leary (1995) that religion in Northern Ireland is merely an 'ethnic marker', seldom significant in and of itself. Instead, McGarry and O'Leary argue that the conflict has been primarily a dispute about ethno-national identity, influenced by other factors, such as economic inequalities. Hayes and McAllister (1999) have said that this represents an academic consensus about the role of religion in Northern Ireland.

Despite this, there is plenty of research that illuminates the role of evangelicalism in shaping the conflict in Northern Ireland. In his classic study of Paisley from the 1980s, Steve Bruce went so far as to declare that: 'The Northern Ireland conflict is a religious conflict' (1986: 249). Bruce argues that Protestants feel vulnerable in their British identity because they are aware that their values and ideals seem bizarre to many in the wider UK – and that the British may not actually want them. As a result, they rely on Protestantism to provide a secure identity. And evangelicalism is the strongest expression of Protestantism. Therefore Bruce argues that it occupies a special place within the Protestant community, even for those who are not themselves religious. As Ganiel (2008a) and Ganiel and Dixon (2008) have argued, this feeds into the idea that evangelicalism has been the most divisive brand of religion throughout the conflict.

Bruce is not alone in this focus on evangelicalism and conflict. Elliott's (2009) work, for example, explores the role of evangelicalism in formulating the 'origin myth' of Protestant unionism. Similarly, Akenson (1992) has focused on covenantal Calvinist ideas as the basis for some Protestants' self-conceptions as a 'chosen people' in a 'promised land'. Miller (1978) makes a link between Calvinism and Protestants' idea of 'conditional loyalty' to the British crown. Todd (1987) outlines the importance of evangelicalism in the formation of an

'Ulster loyalist' identity, while Brewer with Higgins (1998) focus on how the anti-Catholicism of some evangelicals contributes to conflict. Liechty and Clegg (2001) and Thomson (2002) claim that evangelicalism was especially important in maintaining boundaries between Catholics and Protestants, and Mitchel (2003) has argued that an evangelical ethos underwrote the unionist-dominated Stormont government from 1921 to 1972. Wright (1973) talks about the combination of these religiously informed ideas comprising a 'Protestant ideology' which can sour relationships with Catholics.

In our previous work, we have also argued that religion must be taken more seriously as a source of division in Northern Ireland. Mitchell (2005) has argued that religiously based ideas, informed by evangelicalism, are important even for Protestants who do not practise religion on a regular basis. Ganiel (2008a) has argued that evangelicalism had a privileged relationship with social and political power, especially from 1921 to 1972, which contributed to divisions between Catholics and Protestants. However, evangelicals' relationship with power has been breaking down throughout the conflict and the peace process, and this has forced evangelicals to change both their identities and their political projects (Ganiel 2006a, 2008a, 2008b).

All of these analyses have highlighted how aspects of evangelicalism have contributed to conflict in Northern Ireland. And indeed, evangelicalism's contribution to the conflict has been enormous. However, it is possible that clumsy or careless interpretation of this research can perpetuate two common myths about evangelicalism: that it is rigid and unchanging; and that it is preoccupied with politics. The consequences of these myths are that evangelicals look stubborn, backward, and mired in past grievances and conflict.

But there is another strong trend within recent research which shows how evangelicalism is changing and diversifying. We turn in a moment to these studies, so that we can better understand variety within the subculture. In fact, we find that the conflict is a deep source of tension amongst different types of evangelicals. Although some see their faith at the heart of their strong unionist beliefs, others engage with the political process to promote a cross-community, reconciliation agenda. Some withdraw from the public sphere and do not vote, while others seek to pragmatically engage with the political process to promote moral issues such as opposition to abortion and the extension of gay rights. Some continue to stress traditional religious arguments opposing power-sharing with 'unrepentant terrorists', whereas others engage with politics by running fair trade cafes in church buildings or carrying theologically inspired banners in protests against the Iraq war. The tendency to equate evangelicalism with division and conflict is not unique to Northern Ireland, nor is the more recent research agenda that recognises diversity and change within the movement in various parts of the world.

Evangelical diversity

There is a vast literature on evangelicalism, largely emanating from North America and concerned with the movement in the United States, although significant work has been done on Canada and Britain (Reimer 2003, Noll 2001a, 2001b, Bebbington 1989, Marsden 1980, Handy 1982) and increasingly on Africa (Ranger 2008). Evangelicalism has been of concern to historians, sociologists and political scientists, which has stimulated much debate about how to define it. One of the best-known definitions of evangelicalism has been developed by the historian David Bebbington (1989), who identifies four core characteristics of evangelicalism:

- One must be converted or 'born again'
- The Bible is the inspired word of God
- Christ's death on the cross was an actual historical event necessary for the salvation of the world
- Christians must exercise their faith through social action and evangelism.

These core beliefs are interpreted differently by believers, yet they will be recognisable to all evangelicals across the globe. It is important to begin with an understanding of basic, foundational evangelical beliefs, especially since evangelicalism as a movement places so much emphasis on individuals' intellectual assent to particular beliefs. Indeed, there is a danger that analyses of evangelicalism spend too much time analysing beliefs, while ignoring other important aspects of it such as everyday practices and immersion in a specific material culture.

That said, a variety of overlapping subgroups could identify with Bebbington's definition. These have been classified as types of 'conservative Protestants' in the historical and sociological literature, again emerging particularly from the United States (excellently summarised by Woodberry and Smith 1998, see also Greeley and Hout 2006). One body of research has focused on 'fundamentalists', who are best seen as a subset of conservative Protestants. They are characterised by an opposition to liberal theology that is not shared by all in the wider grouping (Kellstedt and Smidt 1991). In this sense, Tidball (1994: 17), not altogether helpfully, describes fundamentalists as 'evangelicals who are angry about something'. In her characterisation of fundamentalism, Ammerman (1987: 4–6) highlights a strict personal morality that forbids drinking, dancing and divorce, and includes separation from the world, dispensational pre-millennialism and biblical literalism.

More recent research has tended to use the term evangelical to describe an overarching constituency of conservative Protestants (Johnston 2000). Evangelicalism can be defined by its attachment to the beliefs outlined by Bebbington (1989), but outside of this, contains a variety of theological positions in attitudes to ecumenism, predestination, the role of the Holy Spirit and the appropriate relationship to the state. Challenging the stereotypes of American evangelicals as theologically and politically uniform, Greeley and Hout (2006) provide comprehensive statistical analysis that not only confirms diversity within conservative Protestantism, but also demonstrates that evangelicals are not all that different from mainline Protestants in a number of areas. Beyerlein (2004) argues that evangelical Protestants differ from fundamentalist Protestants with regard to their degree of engagement with society; the former group engage while the latter group withdraw. Woodberry and Smith (1998) argue that the term is best used to refer to a moderate grouping within a meta-category of conservative Protestants.

A third member of the family is Pentecostalism. It is best described as a close relative of evangelicalism that emphasises the gifts of the Holy Spirit, in particular miraculous healing, prophecy and speaking in tongues. Martin (2002: 8) describes Pentecostalism as a version of evangelicalism; however, he also highlights the social unacceptability of Pentecostalism, the 'loud-singing, groaning, bouncing and sighing' that can make some evangelicals uncomfortable. It is worth pointing out here that Pentecostalism is the fastest growing expression of Christianity in the southern hemisphere, so much so that it is probably now more accurate to describe evangelicalism as a smaller relative of Pentecostalism on the world stage (Jenkins 2002, Ranger 2008, Ganiel 2010a). Fourth, are charismatics, who share with Pentecostalists a focus on the gifts of the Spirit (Anderson 2004). However, whereas Pentecostals were often located on the social margins, charismatics in the United States have tended to be more middle class. Like Pentecostals, charismatics have not tended to be contained exclusively in particular denominations. They have spread through reinvigoration of older churches, as well as establishing new religious organisations, Martin argues (2002: 3), 'even displaying faint affinities with New Age "spirituality."'

Finally, the term 'born-again' is often used interchangeably with evangelical. Sometimes it is seen as a *belief* in, or an *experience* of, conversion rather than an *identification* per se (Jelen et al. 1993). Nonetheless, the Baylor survey in America shows that 'born-again' is the favoured religious label for those with ties to the evangelical Protestant churches in the US, as well as being the term that most distinguishes them from mainstream Protestants (Dougherty et al. 2007).

In practice there is a very large degree of overlap between these subcategories of conservative Protestants (Woodberry and Smith 1998). But these categories are important because they help to dispel myths and stereotypes about people involved with the movement – including the myth that conservative Protestantism is a monolithic, unchanging bloc (see also Greeley and Hout 2006). The subcategories also help to explain the various forms of social, political and religious activism that conservative Protestants, evangelicals, fundamentalists, or 'born agains' take part in.

Evangelical diversity in Northern Ireland

As in other parts of the world, it is not easy to pigeonhole Northern Irish Protestants into subcategories or types. Denominational labels such as Presbyterian, Church of Ireland, Methodist, Free Presbyterian, are not always useful when it comes to exploring diversity within Protestantism or evangelicalism. Indeed, in the interviews for this book, many respondents said they saw themselves as a fundamentalist and an evangelical, as a born-again evangelical, as a charismatic evangelical, or used another combination of labels. Mitchell and Tilley (2008) found that nearly twice as many Protestants in Northern Ireland identified with a combination of fundamentalist/evangelical/ born-again identities, as identified with just one of the subcategories. Jordan (2001: 20) also points to these overlaps in a Northern Irish context, saying that whilst nearly 'all fundamentalists are evangelical, not all evangelicals are fundamentalist'. We have chosen to use the term evangelical throughout the book, as it is the most inclusive term, and because it was the term used most often by the interviewees themselves. But as we talk about evangelicals, we bear these differences in mind, understanding how individuals can attach quite different meanings to the evangelical label.

Much of the recent and most significant scholarship on Northern Irish evangelicalism has been concerned with describing and analysing evangelical diversity. That research has gone a long way towards dispelling the myth that

Paisleyism equals evangelicalism. In addition to that, the research has sought to explain how different varieties of evangelicalism produce different social and political effects, especially when it comes to issues of conflict and peace. Some of those who have written on evangelicalism – such as Glenn Jordan, Patrick Mitchel, and Fran Porter – are internal to the movement and they present their scholarship as a means to push evangelicals in more reconciliatory directions.

The first research to hint at the diversity within evangelicalism, as well as the penetration of evangelicalism into mainstream churches, was Boal, Keane and Livingstone's (1997) survey of churchgoers in Belfast. Forty-four per cent of Protestants attended church regularly in 2008, more or less the same number, 43 per cent, as in 1998.[1] In their research, Boal et al. found that half could be classified as conservatives, based on their commitment to biblical inerrancy and their belief in the centrality of a conversion experience. A quarter of Belfast's Protestant churchgoers adopted neither of these commitments and were classified as liberals. A further quarter agreed with just one of the beliefs and were identified as 'liberal-conservatives'. Unsurprisingly, Boal et al. (1997: 96) found the highest percentage of conservatives in smaller denominations that are traditionally considered evangelical or fundamentalist: Baptist (83 per cent), Pentecostal (87 per cent), and 'other' Presbyterian churches such as the Free, Reformed, or Evangelical Presbyterian (94 per cent). Within the larger denominations, the conservatives were 38 per cent among Presbyterians, 27 per cent among Church of Ireland, and 43 per cent among Methodist attenders. This indicates that evangelicals are not just concentrated in the smaller denominations, but also integrated into the mainstream denominations (see also Jordan 2001, Mitchel 2003: 131, Ganiel 2008a).

Boal et al. do not single out evangelicals. But we do know from other studies, that Northern Irish evangelicals are very regular church attenders, with up to four fifths attending church at least once a week (Mitchell 2005, Mitchell and Tilley 2008).[2] In Ganiel's 2009b survey of laypeople on the island of Ireland, 69 per cent of self-identified evangelicals in Northern Ireland said they attended their main worship service four times per month, with a further 10 per cent saying they attended three times per month. In contrast, Mitchell and Tilley (2008: 743) found that just 35 per cent of weekly church attenders identified simply as Christians and as Protestants. Among Ganiel's respondents, 48 per cent of non evangelicals attended four times per month.[3] This allows us to conclude that a disproportionate number of Belfast's church attenders may be evangelicals. What we can draw from this is that the wider patterns of doctrinal diversity amongst Belfast's churchgoers are also likely to be reflected amongst evangelicals.

John Brewer and Gareth Higgins's 1998 work on anti-Catholicism was the first significant scholarly book to interrogate the evangelical and Calvinistic underpinnings of anti-Catholicism in Northern Ireland, which allowed for a more nuanced understanding of the varying political orientations of Protestantism. Of course Brewer and Higgins do not argue that all Protestants or evangelicals are anti-Catholic. Rather, they explain that where anti-Catholicism exists, it can take one of a number of forms. Brewer and Higgins are careful to point out that these forms are empirical rather than ideal types, where individuals may identify primarily with one mode or another, but may also incorporate elements of the other categories. These empirical types provide rich descriptions of the diversity within Protestantism, including the rather staggering range of theological resources that Protestants have at times employed to define themselves over and against Catholics.

For our purposes, the most important for understanding evangelicalism are *covenantal* and *Pharisaic* modes of anti-Catholicism.[4] Covenantal anti-Catholicism is informed by Old Testament biblical ideas of land and a sense of Protestants in Northern Ireland being a chosen people. It sees Roman Catholicism as evil, and theology and politics as inseparable. This appeals to the most conservative of Protestants in Northern Ireland, including those who describe themselves as fundamentalists or 'Bible Protestants'. Pharisaic anti-Catholicism is different in that is based more on New Testament understandings of faith by salvation alone through the person of Jesus, which Brewer and Higgins say has a wide appeal to evangelicals. Pharisaic Protestants are also deeply opposed to Catholicism, which they see as in doctrinal error. But unlike covenantal Protestants, they do not cut themselves off completely from Catholics, instead choosing to engage with them in order to evangelise. Another difference is that religious goals take precedence over political goals, so Pharisaic Protestants tend to be apolitical.

Building on this, Glenn Jordan's 2001 book, *Not of This World*, offers a six-fold classification of Northern Irish evangelicals. Like Brewer and Higgins, Jordan is careful to point out that these are not ideal types, that individuals may not fit neatly into any one category and may straddle several categories.

Jordan identifies *pietistic evangelicals*, for whom personal holiness is the most important issue in their lives. Sharing their faith with others is a priority. For pietists, faith is personal and devotional, it is not highly doctrinal, nor does it tend to be overly politicised. *Confessional evangelicals* are those who are most concerned with having a set of non-negotiable doctrines. He says that this group are inclined towards intellectual understandings of evangelicalism and are likely to be educated to degree standard. *Oppositional evangelicals*, Jordan argues, conceive of faith in non-intellectual, black and white terms. They are suspicious of liberal expressions of Protestantism, and accuse Roman Catholics of having a blasphemous faith. They value plain speaking, even when it offends others. In fact, oppositional evangelicals expect to be opposed by mainstream society, and see this as a mark of true faithfulness. Although confessionals and oppositionals may reject these labels – some of whom perceive them to be liberal value judgements – both of these groups contain those most likely to identify themselves as fundamentalists as well as evangelicals. It is also likely that this latter group contains many of Northern Ireland's Pentecostalists.

In contrast, Jordan says that *inclusivist evangelicals* see their faith as 'a tributary of the much broader river that is Christianity' (30). They value openness and engagement with other Christian traditions and feel that their evangelicalism must be constantly redefined. *Charismatic evangelicals* are somewhat different again. Like inclusivists they are open to ecumenical relationships, but the way they express their faith is different. This group emphasise religious *experiences*, feeling the Holy Spirit, and often take a less intellectual approach to evangelicalism than other groups. Finally, Jordan says that *cultural evangelicals* are people who participate in the subculture because it is familiar rather than having a well-thought-out relationship with faith. They are evangelicals by association.

Similarly, Patrick Mitchel (2003) emphasises diversity in his historical study of evangelicalism. But rather than constructing ideal or empirical types, he is concerned with evangelicalism's relationship with the 'national identity' of unionists in Ulster. To that end, he explores evangelicalism's relationship with the Orange Order, with Ian Paisley and the Free Presbyterian Church, with the mainstream Presbyterian Church, and with the organisation Evangelical Contribution on Northern Ireland (ECONI), which is now known as the Centre for Contemporary Christianity in Ireland. One of Mitchel's primary aims is to critique Northern Irish evangelicalism for what he sees as an unhealthy relationship with political power, and to urge evangelicals to adopt an approach like the 'evangelicals of ECONI' (260–98). The 'evangelicals of ECONI' would most likely be counted among Jordan's inclusivists.

Ganiel (2008a) also identified empirical types of evangelical identities in her book, *Evangelicalism and Conflict in Northern Ireland*. Her main concern is the roles evangelicalism has played in conflict and peacebuilding, so the content of her types is composed of very political matters such as the ways that different evangelicals conceive of the relationship between church and state, their attitudes towards religious and ethnic pluralism, and their attitudes about violence and peace. So Ganiel's *traditional* evangelicals believe in a covenantal Calvinist relationship between church and state, argue for a privileged place for 'right' religion within pluralist societies, and would justify political violence as a last resort. There are similarities here with Brewer and Higgins's covenantal anti-Catholicism and Jordan's oppositional evangelicals. Ganiel's *mediating* evangelicals argue for an Anabaptist-informed separation between church and state, celebrate pluralism as a fruitful context in which to live out their Christian lives, and advocate non-violence. Many of the interviews Ganiel conducted with mediating evangelicals were with activists from ECONI. And doubtless many of Jordan's inclusivist evangelicals would be found among her mediating evangelicals. Her *pietist* evangelicals advocate a withdrawal from society and politics, are not particularly clear on what they think about pluralism, and advocate nonviolence. This type resonates with Brewer and Higgins's Pharisaic anti-Catholicism and Jordan's pietistic evangelicals. Finally, Ganiel identifies a new (for Northern Ireland) type of *post-evangelicals*, who share many of the approaches of mediating evangelicals but are seeking to move beyond evangelical labels altogether. Ganiel's most interesting findings are that traditional evangelicals have given up on their ideal of a Calvinistic state (although they pay it rhetorical lip service) and are now playing by the rules of a pluralistic civil society, focusing on 'moral' issues such as opposing abortion and homosexuality legislation. Mediating evangelicals, on the other hand, have been at the heart of a process of religious change that has helped to bolster the peace process.[5]

We are often asked if we can quantify the different types of evangelicalism in Northern Ireland. First of all, in the 2001 census, 46 per cent of people in Northern Ireland identified as Protestants (Mitchell 2005). It is estimated that evangelicals comprise between 25 and 33 per cent of the Protestant population in Northern Ireland (ECONI 1995, Mitchell and Tilley 2004, 2008). Within that 25–33 per cent, the best estimate we are able to give is based on Mitchell and Tilley's (2004, 2008) analysis of various survey data. For example, in the 2004 Northern Ireland Life and Times Survey, respondents were asked if they identified with religious labels such as Protestant, Christian, fundamentalist, evangelical and born-again. About one-third of Protestants identified with some combination of the subcategories of born-again, evangelical and fundamentalist. In addition to being Protestant and Christian, six per cent said they were born-again only, three per cent said evangelical only, three per cent fundamentalist only, eight per cent born-again and evangelical, and eight per cent born-again, evangelical and fundamentalist (Mitchell and Tilley 2008). Among these respondents there was a strong belief that the Bible was the literal word of God together with conservative views about personal and sexual morality. From this, Mitchell and Tilley (2008) concluded that about one-third of evangelicals could be classified as 'conservative'. These would probably include Jordan's oppositional evangelicals and Ganiel's traditional evangelicals, as well as some pietistic evangelicals.

Mitchell and Tilley (2004) also isolated samples of evangelical Protestants from the 1991 Northern Irish Social Attitudes Survey and the 1998 Northern Ireland Life and Times Survey. They found that 43 per cent believed that the Bible was 'instructive but not always literal', while 54 per cent believed that the Bible was always to be interpreted as the literal word of God. They argued that the 43 per cent who believed the Bible is instructive but not literal would include 'liberal' and 'mainstream' evangelicals. In Jordan and Ganiel's terms, these would include inclusivist and mediating evangelicals, as well as some pietists. This hints that liberal evangelicals make up a significant portion of evangelicalism – which we, based on our years of research, guesstimate at up to one-third of the overall evangelical population. We would add that the liberal evangelicals are probably more likely to be found in urban areas in larger denominations such as the Presbyterian, Church of Ireland, and Methodist churches. The remaining third of evangelicals fall somewhere between the liberal and conservative poles we identify here.

These estimates resonate with the graphic representation of 'the spectrum of evangelicalism in Ulster' devised by Mitchel (2003: 131). He isolates three categories along the spectrum: fundamentalist (corresponding to our conserva-tive), conservative (corresponding to our mainstream), and liberal (corresponding to our liberal). Mitchel does not offer quantifiable percentages, but he maps spheres of various sizes on to the spectrum, that is, the largest sphere represents the 'Presbyterian Church in Ireland' and is located primarily on the conser-vative and liberal sections of the graph; the small 'Paisleyism' sphere is located squarely in the fundamentalist section, and so on.

An evangelical subculture

So what is it like to be an evangelical in everyday life? Moving beyond the definitions and the types presented previously, we now use the idea of an evangelical *subculture* to explain some further significant and distinctive aspects of the movement in Northern Ireland. In this we are influenced by sociologist Christian Smith's (1998) research on American evangelicalism. Smith demonstrates that evangelicalism does not depend only on intellectual assent to a set of beliefs. Rather, evangelicalism also relies on relationships and social networks, which together with beliefs form a subculture that encompasses people with distinct interests, behaviour, values and lifestyles. For Smith (1998: 118), evangelical subculture provides 'satisfying morally orienting collective identities' for its adherents. It allows them to be distinct from other sub-groups, but not so different that they cannot engage with the outside world. Smith argues that this dual distinctiveness and ability to engage is precisely why evangelicalism is thriving in America, and indeed across the globe. Jim Wellman's (2008) work on evangelicalism in the Pacific Northwest echoes this argument. For Wellman, evangelicals' religious ideas, networks and relationships produce spiritual capital which they then draw on to engage with a wider secular, plural culture. Further, Julie Ingersoll's (2003) exploration of the role of women within American evangelicalism elaborates on how encompassing the subculture can be, and the difficulties experienced by some women regarding their roles within it.

Because of the internal differences that have been identified above, it is necessary to ask what might hold an evangelical subculture together. In fact, most expressions of evangelicalism in Northern Ireland bear 'family resemblances' to one another. These resemblances are present in the religious ideas that evangelicals think are most important, in their social networks, and in their material culture. Whilst it is not defined by politics, this subculture has included ideologies and patterns of behaviour that created and reinforced boundaries with Catholics, and legitimated violence. But we want to move beyond politics, and argue that the evangelical subculture in Northern Ireland has six further significant features:

- Conversion experiences
- Advocacy
- Supernaturalism
- Existential questioning
- Social life
- Material culture

These features are prominent in evangelicals' narratives as they explain changes in themselves, the choices they have made, their relationships, and their place in the world. We briefly describe these features, so that non-evangelical readers may get a sense of everyday life as an evangelical in Northern Ireland.

Conversion experiences

We devote a chapter of this book to religious conversion, one of the six main types of journey we identified. But unlike the other religious journeys, *every* evangelical we talked to had some kind of conversion experience. The belief in the *necessity* of conversion, as well as having the *experience* of conversion, is crucial to Northern Irish evangelicalism.[6] By conversion we mean a process where people self-consciously perceive themselves becoming followers of Christ. They may repent for their sins, accept forgiveness and become 'born-again'. This is often talked about in terms of getting 'saved', becoming a 'new creation', or assuming a new religious identity. Some people converted as children, whilst others converted as adults. Some are able to pinpoint the exact time and date, whilst others experienced a series of smaller, cumulative decisions. But even for those who experienced a dramatic change at a specific moment, conversion is best described as a process rather than an event – in Lewis Rambo's (1993: 17) words, 'a series of elements that are interactive and cumulative over time'. Accompanying religious conversion is the tradition of telling one's testimony. This is essentially the story of how one came to be saved, and how God has changed one's life. Evangelicals repeatedly tell their testimonies to one other, formally and informally, so telling stories about a religious journey is actually central to the evangelical subculture.

We will not press the discussion of conversion here, only to say that it has several possible and important social and political effects. First, if evangelicals believe that someone must be converted to be a Christian, this can be a very strong mechanism for excluding those who have not been 'born again'. This can create a tendency towards division and polarisation, although this is not inevit-able. Second, because many evangelicals believe that conversion is essential for living a better life on this earth *and* ensuring their place in heaven, they may go to great lengths to evangelise or convert others. This means that evangelicals can be keen activists, trying to convince others of their point of view.

Advocacy

The desire to tell other people about faith, to spread the 'good news', can be seen in the aspect of the subculture that we call advocacy. In the chapters that follow, we often see the presence of an advocate – an individual, or sometimes an organisation – that encourages someone to convert to evangelicalism or, if already converted, to change their mind about particular issues. Many of the people we interviewed are advocates themselves. They actively seek to change people's ideas about faith, whether by the example they set in their own lives or more proactive proselytism. We often associate evangelism with traditional evangelical tent missions, revival meetings and rallies. But liberal and post-evangelicals also see themselves as advocates, fighting to get their interpretation of faith accepted, for example in their arguments that peace-making and social justice should be Christians' top priorities. The inclusion of advocacy in our description of the subculture emphasises the importance of personal relation-ships and networks. It also highlights the public and activist dimension of evangelicalism.

Supernaturalism

Most evangelicals see the hand of God in nearly all aspects of their lives. We call this supernaturalism, or a belief in God's Providence or agency in the world. Evangelicals talk freely about the way God or the Holy Spirit has intervened in their lives. This includes attributing political events to God, saying that God answers their prayers, or using phrases such as 'God has spoken to me' or 'It is God's will'. Such discourse can seem odd or jarring to people not immersed in the evangelical subculture. Some evangelicals interpret recent events in Northern Ireland in an apocalyptic light, seeing this as part of the events leading up to the second coming of Christ, as ordained in the book of Revelation. But supernaturalism is not only about God's role in the end of the world. Other evangelicals talked about the way God intervened directly in their lives to set them on a different path, for example pulling them towards ecumenism and peace-building.

Charismatic and Pentecostal expressions of evangelicalism focus most heavily on the supernatural, and on the power of the Holy Spirit. This can include speaking in tongues, receiving visions or prophecies from God and even casting out evil spirits or demons. This goes too far for others in the evangelical family, whose experience of the supernatural is more restrained – a quiet sense of God's power in their lives. Nonetheless, a belief in the power of an interventionist God is common to nearly all evangelicals, with the exception of only the most deconstructed post-evangelicals, or 'transformers' as we call them later in the book.

Supernaturalism can have significant social and political effects. For those who take a dismal, apocalyptic view of recent events it can be politically disempowering. If history is all in God's hands, as foretold in the Bible, it follows that there is really little one can do to change things. But for others, belief in God's ability to influence high level political events as well as the small details of their lives is inspiring. These people believe that God is on the side of justice. So if they work for what they see as justice in the world, God will help to influence the outcome of events in favour of it. Belief in God's guidance and intervention makes them feel secure that what they are doing is right, and will ultimately make the world a better place.

Existential questioning

The belief in an interventionist God means that many evangelicals are engaged in a process of nearly constant questioning. These questions range from trying to figure out God's will for their individual lives to attempting to ascertain how God's plan is unfolding throughout all of human history. A small number of evangelicals and ex-evangelicals in our study had abandoned belief in super-naturalism, but even those who had done so continued to ask questions about the 'meaning of life'. Though evangelicals are sometimes caricatured as sheep-like creatures following literalist interpretations of the Bible or charismatic preachers, questioning is actually deeply embedded in their subculture. Because Protestantism places a strong emphasis on personal responsibility – people cannot use priests to mediate between themselves and God – there is a widespread culture of 'finding out for oneself' and testing one's beliefs. Sometimes this manifests in rather an anxious culture where, as Weber (1958 [1915]) pointed out, people seek out reassurances that they are measuring up to God's expectations.[7] Even those whose faith had changed very little over time asked questions, and subjected their beliefs and behaviour to scrutiny. On the other hand, some people we spoke with had asked so many questions, that very little remained and they ended up leaving their faith.

The willingness of evangelicals to ask tough, existential questions may seem surprising to those who have assumed that evangelicalism is essentially rigid and inflexible. A by-product of the willingness to ask questions may be that evangelicalism is more open to change than is usually supposed.

Social life

The everyday social practices of evangelicals are also important in understanding the subculture. Most evangelical churches offer a staggering variety of activities. This gives people the opportunity to participate in something nearly every day of the week. Almost every Protestant church – especially congregations that are part of smaller evangelical denominations – will have at least two Sunday services, prayer meetings, Bible studies and 'cell' groups, in which people meet in each other's homes to pray or study the Bible. For those with more specialised interests there will be choir or worship band practices, mother and toddler groups, sports clubs and women's groups as well as a wide range of social activities – meals with fellow church members, even church summer holidays. Outside individual congregational activities, there are Northern Ireland-wide events like Mandate, Focus Fest, and New Horizon that bring evangelicals from different churches together. For children and teenagers there are more options again – youth groups, Sunday schools, children's Bible classes, summer schemes, Christian music gigs and festivals such as Summer Madness. All of this social activity is reinforced by private everyday practices, including daily personal prayers and Bible readings.

A congregation or extended religious network can come to feel like a family for some people, often replacing or structuring actual family life. These strong networks of relationships enable people to persevere in their faith. Moreover, doing things together such as singing, worshipping, praying and even eating with one another, builds a sense of togetherness. It creates strong social bonds, where evangelicals come to feel that they are at home with, and understand each other. This is not to go as far as Durkheim (1915), who argued that rituals create a 'collective conscience'. Rather, Warner argues (1997) that religious practices are usually ambiguous enough to unite the community whilst individual members can provide their own interpretation of them.

Evangelicals use their social networks and practices to develop their faith in different ways. For some, the practices of everyday life are a way to limit 'contamination' from outside, secular influences. For others, everyday participation in networks provides them with a safe space to ask tough, existential questions and critique their faith.

Material culture

The subculture also includes what Ingersoll (2003) has called 'material culture', or the objects and artefacts associated with evangelicalism. This includes books, CDs and ephemera available in Northern Ireland's evangelical bookshops, and the magazines published by various evangelical organisations (including the Centre for Contemporary Christianity in Ireland's *Lion and Lamb*, Evangelical Alliance's *Idea* and the Evangelical Protestant Society's *Ulster Bulwark*). Although evangelicals do not have holy objects in the way that Catholics do, the Bible and the symbol of the cross are found in most homes (King 2009). A plain cross may be worn as jewellery, or take the form of pictures or ornaments. Bible verses are often printed or embroidered for display in the home. Other material expressions include handmade signs posted on roadsides throughout Northern Ireland, with biblical messages such as 'the wages of sin are death', 'ye must be born again', or 'repent, for the kingdom of God is at hand'. For some, material culture includes adherence to dress codes. These codes vary widely – from suits, ties, dresses and hats in denominations such as the Brethren, Free Presbyterians, and some Baptists, to modern clothing such as jeans and t-shirts in some charismatic churches.

Many of these aspects of material culture reflect global, and in particular, American evangelicalism. This results in many cultural imports, such as praise and worship songs, television, books and DVDs, and even congregational forms such as the Vineyard charismatic churches. There are exports too, and many Northern Irish speakers and musicians conduct regular American tours. There are also many links with the developing world. It is common for churches to have a handful of people in the mission field at any one time – usually in Africa, Asia or Central America. Many Northern Irish evangelicals will engage with their colleagues abroad by sponsoring children, keeping prayer cards for mission families, receiving newsletters, raising funds at home and sometimes by going out to visit or work in the projects. So, rather than being insular, most Northern Irish evangelicals are accustomed to travel and the cross-fertilisation of ideas. What seems to be crucial in the development of people's religious journeys, as we shall see, is how far cultural experience is limited to evangelical circles only, or is extended to include outside influences.

We have developed the idea of an evangelical subculture to explain what is most distinctive and important about Northern Irish evangelicalism. The subculture itself is internally diverse. It has a number of internal features that encourage flexibility, and that can contribute to change, in a variety of directions. The features that we highlight are recognisable to all who call themselves evangelicals, although those who recognise and belong to this subculture may at times profoundly disagree with others located within it. Understanding conversion, advocacy, supernaturalism, existential questioning, social life and material culture helps us understand how evangelicals see themselves, what is important to them, and how they experience the world. Moreover, these are among the resources evangelicals use to negotiate their own religious journeys.

Conclusions

Evangelicalism has been heavily stereotyped, as well as criticised for its role in the conflict in Northern Ireland. Critique has come from outsiders and academics, as well as from scholarly evangelical insiders like Fran Porter, Glenn Jordan and Patrick Mitchel. They see their research and advocacy as helping to change evangelical identities, thus contributing to the peace process. This chapter has also described a Northern Irish evangelical subculture that is *not* solely defined by issues of politics and ethnic identity. And we have identified features of an evangelical subculture such as conversion experiences, advocacy, supernaturalism, existential questioning, social life, and material culture, which help us understand evangelicalism as a lived religion. We see this work as contributing to an emerging literature that is interested in the practices and experiences of everyday life in Northern Ireland (Todd et al. 2008).

This book is informed by previous scholarship on evangelical diversity in Northern Ireland. In the chapters on religious journeys, we refer back to the categorisations of evangelicalism outlined in the literature, highlighting how the distinctions detailed above play out for our interviewees. Our intention in this book is not to offer new categories of evangelical, but rather to explore the different sorts of religious journeys that evangelicals can experience over the course of their lives. In so doing, we find that different types of evangelicals are likely to be found on different sorts of journeys – for example people who could be categorised as Ganiel's traditional evangelicals are likely to be on a journey in which their faith is deepening in a more conservative direction, while Jordan's inclusivist evangelicals are likely to be on a moderating journey. But we are also interested in movement between the categories, for example in how traditional evangelicals *become* inclusivists, or come to leave their faith behind altogether. So there are not hard and fast relationships between categories of evangelicals and particular directions of religious journey. Rather, in the chapters on each variety of journey and in the conclusion, we explore the *patterns of experiences* and *combinations of factors* that push and pull people in various directions, and that prompt them to move between, and indeed beyond, orientations to evangelicalism.

CHAPTER THREE

Methods

In this chapter we provide details of how we conducted our study. We talk about why we decided to study evangelicals, why we chose to do the kind of interviews we did, and how we went about analysing the stories people told us. We also discuss the strengths and weaknesses of using the stories people tell in the present, to understand things that happened in the past. We provide enough information so that readers will be able to evaluate the reliability of our analysis in the chapters that follow.

Why we decided to study evangelicals

Given that our backgrounds lie within the evangelical subculture, we had a special reason for studying evangelicals. But aside from our personal histories, we are both living and working in a society where evangelicals are a strong and vocal group. Given that we both specialise in the study of religion and Northern Ireland, studying evangelicals in depth was a logical step. We also felt that studying evangelicals in Northern Ireland would help us understand something about evangelicals in other areas. As evangelicalism is a growing global religion, we felt our local study would help us connect to a global debate, and we thought we could add something to it.

It is worth noting at this point how our backgrounds in evangelicalism might have influenced our study. Many social researchers study groups that are familiar, or experiences that they can identify with. This can bring many benefits. Having intimate knowledge of a situation can mean that an insider researcher picks up on a lot more than an outsider. An insider may get more access to a group, and may be trusted more than an outsider. However, it can also be a weakness. Where an insider is so familiar with the context they are studying that they cannot think of it in new ways, they can miss things which they do not think are important, whereas an outsider might ask more awkward questions, revealing more insights about the group at hand (see Arweck and Stringer 2002). We brought a combination of insider and outsider characteristics to the study. Gladys is an outsider in that she is American, but considers herself to be an evangelical, so is a religious insider. Claire is an insider to the Northern Ireland context, but as an agnostic, could be perceived as a religious outsider (for further discussion see Ganiel and Mitchell 2006). During our research we used these different aspects of our own identities to interpret the interviews from a variety of angles.

Why we chose narrative interviews

We have done statistical research about evangelicalism before (Mitchell and Tilley 2004, 2008), but to answer the questions posed in this study – how and why religious beliefs change over time – the only option was to do qualitative research. Because we wanted to gain a sense of people's religious journeys over time, we felt that the best way to do this was through in-depth interviews with evangelicals and ex-evangelicals.

There are many different ways that researchers can approach interviews – from asking quite short, focused questions, to asking hardly any questions and just letting people talk. Since we were seeking an insight into people's life stories, we decided that narrative interviews would be the best option (Chase 2005, Bauer, 1996). These are interviews where we ask people to tell us the story of their lives, in their own words, but where we also ask some more focused questions. A typical interview lasted two hours. We began the interviews by asking people about their conversion experience and if religion played a part in their childhood. We then asked them to unpick how their religious journey unfolded over time. We asked people if there had been important turning points, events or experiences that impacted on their faith. We asked them if their religious beliefs or practices had changed at all. We did not intervene very much in this part of the interview, and let people tell their own stories in their own words. This meant that we were not over-influencing the stories at this stage with our own ideas. After this, we also asked follow-up questions, to clarify points and to test some of the theories about why religious beliefs might change over time. In this way we ended up with 95 stories, or narratives.

How we analysed the interviews

After we finished all the interviews, we transcribed them from the tapes. Essentially we had 95 life stories, typically about 20 pages each. We spent time familiarising ourselves with the transcripts, and began by trying to distinguish between types of religious journeys. In the interviews we asked people to begin by describing their faith in their own terms. After this, we tried to establish where they saw themselves within the evangelical spectrum in the past and in the present. Based on what people told us, we then arrived at our six types of journey. None of these six journeys perfectly captures everything about an individual's religious experiences. Journeys can comprise many episodes and individuals may have at one time or another journeyed in a number of different directions. Other people will move back and forth in different directions, or fall in somewhere between them. We could, in a sense, write 95 chapters, one for every single person, as everyone's story is unique. However, after many re-readings and discussions of the interviews, we believe that most people described a dominant journey and, at least at the time of interview, fitted more or less into one of the journeys described.

Each of these transcripts then contained a story about a religious journey, which was in turn made up of lots of smaller stories about events, thoughts and experiences. We devised a systematic way of analysing the interviews so that we could understand the wider themes. Based on the sociological literature on religion, identity and narratives we decided on a few central processes that we would pay attention to. One of these was religious turning points. We wanted to see how people described episodes that had changed the way they felt about their faith (for more on episodic analysis, see Flick 1998). These episodes were freely selected by interviewees, and this gave us a good insight into what they thought was important. Secondly, we looked at how people talked about their ability to choose their faith. We looked for people talking about how far they felt free to make changes to their religion, and how far they felt constrained by various factors. Thirdly, we looked at people's relationships with others. These could be family, friends, colleagues, people in their church and even strangers. We wanted to see what role other people played in individuals' journeys. Finally we looked out for how people talked about their place in wider society, which helped us to see how their religious journey might relate to wider cultural and political processes.

By analysing these processes of change, choice, relationships and place, we tried not to impose our own themes on the interviews at an early stage. We picked processes that were directly relevant to the idea of identity change, which was the puzzle we had set out to explore. But at the same time, the processes did not pre-determine what themes we should address. This made sure that we did not have our own pet theories that we, consciously or unconsciously, set out to prove. On a practical level, we both read the interviews, highlighting the processes above, and then compared our interpretations. As we both have different religious ideas and nationalities, we sometimes had slightly different interpretations of the interviews, but were usually able, through our discussions, to agree in the final analysis. We are also grateful to Sara Templer, our research assistant, who interviewed those who had left evangelicalism. Sara is a Zimbabwean from a Catholic background, and she added another perspective on interpretations of the stories. In fact we think that the debates between us resulted in a much better analysis than if we had been working alone.

Disclosing our biases

For those who believe that all things are ordained by an omnipotent God, it might sound heretical to say that human beings often change their religious views because of relationships and events in their lives. But it is not our intention to deny God's involvement in people's religious journeys. To write a book about evangelical Christians, leaving God out of the equation, would make no sense. But even if one strongly believes that God, not humans, determines the shape of our lives, there is still a case for exploring what else, apart from divine intervention, might help to form people's religious identities. As one of the most conservative of our interviewees told us during the research for this book, 'there are things that have happened that have had the effect of knocking me one way or knocking me another'. Although this interviewee sees God's hand as guiding every area of life, he is also able to retrace his religious journey and identify key moments and experiences that prompted personal change.

The two authors of this book write from quite different religious perspectives. I (Claire) was raised as an evangelical, but am now an agnostic. On the other hand, I (Gladys) consider myself to be an evangelical, albeit not in an identical form to the evangelicalism of my youth. Despite my agnosticism, I (Claire) do not rule out the existence of God and whilst my focus tends to be on the social aspects of religion, I do not disbelieve people when they tell me about their experiences of the divine. I do not write these off simply as social phenomena. Conversely, being a Christian, I (Gladys) am very interested in the spiritual aspect of life. I understand what people mean when they say they hear God's voice. My rural American evangelical background has many commonalities with rural evangelicalism in Northern Ireland, but I currently identify more strongly, in the terms of this book, with evangelicals on moderating or transforming journeys. Further, as I am also trained as a social scientist, I am acutely aware of how people are also shaped by the outside world, by their place in society and their relationships with other people. I do not write these off simply as spiritual phenomena.

Some evangelical readers will of course believe that the Devil, temptation and sin are the primary reasons why people move away from their faith over time. And where the people we interviewed talked about the Devil and temptation, we include these explanations. Our policy in this book has been to take what people tell us seriously. When we talk to people who believe that God plays an active role in their lives, and people who describe a supernatural dimension to life, we analyse their narratives on their own terms. It is not our role to question whether God really did this or that, or if someone really experienced God. If someone believes God has intervened in their lives, we accept their story in the knowledge that this belief has shaped their subsequent religious journey. Similarly, where 'backsliders' talk about their journey away from faith in human terms, we tell their story from their own point of view and do not seek to impose religious interpretations on their stories. What we have therefore tried to do is get inside people's shoes, to understand their religious journeys from their own point of view. And whilst offering a rigorous analysis of people's stories, we concentrate on what people have told us, rather than imposing our own view of what is *really* going on. We hope that this perspective will make the book accessible to students of sociology and religion, as well as curious believers and non-believers.

The strengths and weaknesses of talking about the past

Some of the people we talked to have moved on in their religious journey since the time that we talked to them. At least one of those people whose faith was stable at the time of interview has now 'backslidden'. Another person who had left evangelicalism said that the interview itself was his 'line in the sand moment', where speaking about his journey helped crystallise his new religious position. In this sense, the interviews capture people at a moment in time.

People may have been in a frame of mind on the day of interview that led them to put a particular slant on their story. How many times do we look back at an exchange and wish we had said something different? People also take cues from the interviewer's questions and reactions, which influence the story they tell. This echoes Holstein and Gubrium (1995) who conceive of interviews not simply as an exchange of information in which *what* is talked about is important, but as a particular form of communication in which *how* people 'frame' or tell their stories is important (see also Travers 2006, Watson 2006). People may want to present themselves in a certain light. People also tend to give a rather coherent version of events that does not always reflect the messiness of reality. There is a strong tendency to smooth out the story so that it makes sense to ourselves and others. For all of these reasons, we understand that our interviews cannot tell us everything about a person's story.

Just as importantly, by asking people to talk about the past, we have to accept that they are speaking from the perspective of the present. People constantly edit and revise their stories of the past, in relation to how they see themselves now. They may downplay elements that were extremely important at the time, and exaggerate others that were not so important. For example, someone who has left evangelicalism might be embarrassed about their involvement and want to downplay the strength of their belief, whilst a very strong believer may not want to talk about the extent of the doubts they once had. As Kathleen Blee (2002: 203) says, stories are both 'revealing and concealing'. Like Atkinson (2005) and Atkinson and Silverman (1997) we are not of the view that the aim of interview analysis is to uncritically reproduce the stories of participants, taking them at face value. Rather, we 'treat informants' accounts *as* accounts, that are performances through which informants enact biographical, self-presentational and explanatory work' (Atkinson 2005: 9). In other words, we cannot take stories at face value and assume that every event actually happened in the way it was described.

Quite apart from this, we are relying on people's memories which may be fuzzy, especially about things that happened many years ago. Many of us have recounted what we think is a well-worn family story, only to be greeted with howls of 'it didn't happen like that at all' from other family members. One way to get around this is to do interviews with the same group of people every ten years or so, as some life-cycle researchers have done. In an ideal world, we would love to have done this. However, no such study exists in Ireland, and if we started one ourselves, it would have taken another 50 years to write this book. Plus, even within longitudinal studies, all the above caveats about interviews still apply.

Despite the limitations of narrative interviews, we believe that they provide us with invaluable insights into people's religious journeys. There has been a lot of work in the social sciences over the last twenty years focusing on how important stories are for our identity (King 2003, Somers 1994, Riesmann 1993, Bruner 1987). We tell stories to make sense of our lives, and by telling these stories we reveal a great deal about how we understand the world. Our interviews are not factual reconstructions of the past. But they tell us about how someone on a particular religious journey perceives their life, what they highlight as being important to them, and what they leave out. For example, people who are strongly religious emphasise the role of the supernatural in their journeys, whilst people who have left evangelicalism give more human explanations for change. In this way our interviews help us to understand someone's *present journey*. Indeed, only some of the stories people tell are about the past. Many more are about the current strategies that people employ to support their religious positions.

So whilst we fully understand the limitations of our interviews, we believe that people's recollections of past events are useful in helping us understand why they have journeyed in one religious direction or another. We may all try to tell smoothed out, coherent stories about our lives, but we still select events and experiences that have been of great importance to us. Whilst we might not get all the facts straight, what matters more is that something has made an impact on us, we have remembered it and it has shaped who we are. By asking people what they feel has shaped them, we were able to identify clusters of themes that arose time and again within each type of journey. We were able to compare the arguments in the literature to the themes highlighted by our interviewees. We found some overlap, but our research also produced new insights, which we elaborate on in later chapters.

How we selected whom to talk to

The heart of this book is people's stories about their lives. If we had interviewed different people, it would have been a different book, with different people's stories. That said, we interviewed 95 people, which is a reasonably large number for a study like this. And after talking to so many people, the same themes came up time and again. This makes us confident that had we interviewed a different 95 people, we would have found similar *types* of stories and experiences.

Most interviews were conducted in 2001–5, with a top-up group of 14, mainly comprising people who had left evangelicalism, interviewed in 2008. The vast majority of the interviews were conducted by Gladys and Claire in the earlier period when we were postdoctoral and doctoral researchers in University College Dublin. After 2003, we were busy securing academic jobs, writing new lectures, publishing from our PhDs and generally being too overwhelmed starting our careers to devote the large amount of time needed to complete the present work. In 2008, we returned to the project with renewed energy, identified some gaps in the fieldwork and employed a research assistant, Sara Templer, to carry out most of the top-up interviews, using the same techniques as we had used before.

We used a snowballing method to find interviewees. This means that we started our search for interviewees with people who were known to us, significant figures in the evangelical scene and also some congregations that agreed to participate. We asked these people to introduce us to others who might be willing to be interviewed. We tried to ensure our initial contacts were wide and varied, from our neighbours, colleagues, friends, various churches and organisations, and even our hairdressers and local shopkeepers. Generally we did not follow a chain for more than one or two contacts, as people tend to suggest people who are similar to themselves. The criteria for being interviewed were simply that people had to be evangelicals now or at one time in their lives.

When we came to the end of the interviewing process in 2005, we had managed to recruit only a few people who had left their faith. People who had left evangelicalism were in fact the most hard-to-reach group we have encountered throughout over ten years of research and many hundreds of interviews in Northern Ireland. Partially this is because they are a hidden population, not organised around any central community or activity. Also, some people who had left evangelicalism – in particular those who joined the charismatic house church movement as teenagers or adults – were embarrassed that they had at one time been involved and were disinclined to talk about it. We tried again in 2008 to recruit more people who had left, using three different researchers' networks as departure points (our own and those of our research assistant). Whilst this method did generate some more respondents, we found after three months and seven interviews that we had hit a brick wall. We then placed advertisements in a number of local newspapers, which helped us to top up our sample.

We must be clear that we were not attempting to construct a sample that would be 'representative' of evangelicalism in Northern Ireland. Rather, we were trying to talk to people from all points on the evangelical spectrum, gaining in-depth perspectives on what it was like to be on various types of religious *journey*.

Our sample

Of our 95 interviews, 30 were women and 65 were men. Thirty-three lived in rural areas and 62 lived in urban areas, primarily in Belfast. Our sample was highly educated – 62 had third-level education whilst 33 did not. In terms of age, 23 people were aged 18–35, 41 were in the 35–50 age range, 20 were aged 50–65 and 11 were 65 or over. In the final analysis, we classified 17 people as deepening, 21 as on a steady journey, 34 as moderating, 11 as transforming and 12 as leaving. All 95 told stories of religious conversion, whether as children or adults.

We need to explain a number of issues that stand out in regard to the social characteristics of our sample, particularly in relation to gender, educational background, geographical location and the high number of people on moderating journeys.

Firstly, our sample is not balanced in terms of gender, with more than twice as many males as females. It became clear early on in the research process that a bias towards males was emerging, and we tried to contact a disproportionate amount of females to correct the imbalance. However, in the final analysis we failed to recruit an equal number of females. Fran Porter (2002) and Sandra Baillie (2001) have underlined the significance of gender differences within Northern Ireland's evangelical subculture. Indeed, similar to Ingersoll's (2003) study in the United States, Porter interviewed women whose faith had been informed by feminist ideas and theology, and who were chaffing against some of the male-dominated assumptions of the subculture. As Porter and Baillie have emphasised, the public, politicised face of Northern Irish evangelicalism has been almost exclusively male, from the Rev. Ian Paisley to the decidedly more moderate David Porter, the former director of the Evangelical Contribution on Northern Ireland/Centre for Contemporary Christianity in Ireland and member of the Eames-Bradley commission on dealing with the past.[1]

By interviewing considerably more men than women, we are aware that we may have reproduced the assumption of male dominance in Northern Irish evangelicalism, which Porter and Baillie have critiqued on the basis that at least as many women are active in the organisation of the evangelical subculture as men. There are a number of reasons why this imbalance came about. First, we encountered a certain amount of 'hidden-ness' amongst women as we carried out our fieldwork. Sometimes we would make contact with a household to enquire whether a family member would be interested in participating in the research. In many cases we tried to persuade female members of the family to participate and, despite some initial interest, when we arrived to do the interview, if a man was present in the house, the wife would push her husband forward as spokesperson for the family. We do not know whether this was related to childcare needs, or a lack of confidence or interest on the part of some women. This happened especially amongst conservative evangelicals (Jordan's oppositional or Ganiel's traditional evangelicals) so we would suggest that part of our difficulty in recruiting women was related to social conservatism and traditional gender roles in this group. Indeed of the many conservative evangelical events I (Gladys) attended, I found I was often the only woman talking to the men after the services. Most of the women were making tea and sandwiches and playing a background role. Whilst I tried to recruit these women as interviewees, I feel their deference in social situations led to their assumption that it was the men who should be spokespeople for the group. This was a shame because where we did recruit and interview conservative evangelical women, they were strong and vocal advocates for their faith.

We did not find this deferential behaviour among women who considered themselves liberal evangelicals (Jordan's inclusivist or Ganiel's mediating evangelicals). We did, find, however, that a number of these women, especially those who had demanding careers and high profile roles within their churches, had already been interviewed for other research projects. Anecdotally, one of these women told Gladys that she had probably been interviewed for every book on evangelicalism in Northern Ireland, and wondered where researchers might find some other women to talk with. This points to a lack of high profile women in evangelicalism. And indeed traditional gender roles in the evangelical sector helped contribute to the gender imbalance in our study. To find interviewees, we contacted a variety of people through para-church organisations, which we knew to have liberal or conservative leanings. Invariably the leadership of these organisations were men who were keen to participate, and we therefore ended up interviewing a disproportionate amount of them. The same pattern emerged when we tried to make contact with people through churches. All 11 of the religious ministers we encountered were male. Often ministers wished to be interviewed themselves before recommending us on to congregation members, and this also served to skew the gender balance. By the end of the process, we were turning down male contacts and attempting to recruit more women, but by this stage it was too late to correct the significant gender gap that had emerged.

Further to explaining why an imbalance occurred, it is vital to ask how it might have impacted on the analysis. We found that some of the women we interviewed were more open than some of the men. Perhaps this was related to the fact that the interviewers were also women. Most of the female interviews took place in their homes, whereas quite a number of men preferred to be interviewed in their place of work. This almost certainly would have affected some people's level of comfort and inclination to openness. However, even in their homes, some men preferred to focus on their changing doctrinal beliefs and were less keen to discuss their personal lives in detail.

A few other disparities emerged between male and female interviews. For example, women often talked about their partners, whereas men did so less frequently. Men did talk about other family members, however. Men were slightly more likely to tell stories about relationships and experiences in the workplace. Overall, though, we found that where people *were* comfortable talking about their personal lives, women's and men's stories had many more commonalities than they had differences. We think that both genders talked equally about family, parents, children, illness and loss, emotional, rational and spiritual experiences.

We also wondered whether the gender imbalance might reinforce the image of a muscular, politicised, male evangelicalism. Ongoing analysis of the Irish School of Ecumenics, Trinity College Dublin's 2009 surveys of laypeople and faith leaders on the island of Ireland by Ganiel and Christopher Morris found that evangelical men are the *least* likely to prioritise reconciliation in a variety of forms – including reconciliation between Catholics and Protestants and between ethnic groups. In the surveys, just 20 per cent of evangelical lay men had a 'high' view of all types of reconciliation, compared to 47 per cent of evangelical women, 46 per cent of non evangelical women, and 42 per cent of non evangelical men (Ganiel 2010b).[2] This was also the case for male evangelical clergy versus female evangelical and non-evangelical clergy, although the differences were not as vast. Ganiel and Morris's analysis shows us how more reconciliatory currents within evangelicalism may be carried by women and therefore hidden from outside eyes.

That said, we hope that the current study also shows a different side of male evangelicalism in Northern Ireland. Men do not emerge in this study simply at the 'hard' edge of evangelicalism. They are often found describing how their faith has moderated and liberalised over time. We find a loyalist male becoming converted and marrying a Catholic, whilst another discovers a Catholic birth family and changes his national identity to Irish. Many other men we interviewed worked in the peace and reconciliation sector. So although our study reproduces male dominance in terms of numbers of participants, we hope that it also challenges some stereotypes of evangelicalism in Northern Ireland as an aggressive, muscular religion, bound up with the politics of conflict.

Our sample is also imbalanced in terms of geographical location and educational background. These issues are connected, as people living in urban locations are more likely to have third-level degrees. The urban location and high educational attainment of our sample make it unrepresentative of the population of Northern Ireland as a whole, where only 33 per cent have third-level or higher education and 27 per cent live in the urban areas.[3] The main reason for this disparity is that we deliberately over-sampled people who were moderating, transforming, and leaving evangelicalism. All those who were leaving or transforming lived in urban areas, as did most people who were moderating. And people on these journeys also tended to be highly educated. Those who were deepening or on a steady journey were more representative of the general population of Northern Ireland in that a majority lived in rural areas and market towns. If more rural voices were included in the study, a different picture of evangelicalism in Northern Ireland would have emerged. But our focus was not on documenting *types* of evangelical, or assessing their numerical representativeness. Rather, we were interested in exploring a wide range of religious journeys in the book, even though the people journeying towards transformation or exit do not represent the mainstream of evangelicalism or of society in Northern Ireland.

With regard to education, it is important to point out that in Northern Ireland evangelicals are actually better educated than non-evangelical Protestants. Statistical analysis of the 1991 Northern Irish Social Attitudes Survey and the 1998 Northern Ireland Life and Times Survey by Mitchell and Tilley (2004: 591) demonstrates that these 'educational differences mainly apply to attainments in higher education', and that 'they are fairly large'. For example, they find that '40-year-old men in a professional/managerial job in 1991 with no qualifications are predicted to have a 25 per cent chance of being evangelical; similar men with a degree have a 68 per cent chance'. So although our sample contains a disproportionate amount of people with a third-level education, so does the evangelical population as a whole.

This is a surprising finding. At first glance it may seem to jar with Bruce's (1986) early work, which emphasised the lower social status of Free Presbyterians in both rural and urban areas. Nor does it confirm some American studies that find evangelicals have a lower educational attainment than non-evangelical

Protestants, although these studies tend to use 'fundamentalists' as proxies for evangelicals, which no doubt influences the findings (see Sherkat 1997).

Morris's (2010) research sheds some light on why evangelicals might achieve higher educational attainment – especially if we give due consideration to the presence of evangelicals within the mainstream denominations. Drawing on data from a range of surveys, Morris demonstrates that Presbyterians consistently have achieved higher social status than people from the (Anglican) Church of Ireland, a pattern that has persisted since the plantations of Ireland to the present day. Although the Church of Ireland ruling class initially discriminated against Presbyterians under the penal laws, Presbyterians' predominance in business and urban centres ensured that overall they were better educated and achieved a higher standard of living than the average Church of Ireland parishioner. Historically, evangelicalism has been stronger within Presbyterianism in Northern Ireland than in the Church of Ireland. So if Presbyterians are the largest Protestant denomination in Northern Ireland, as well as disproportionately richer and more evangelical than the second largest denomination, the Church of Ireland, this may be a significant factor in explaining the social class and educational attainment of people who identify as evangelicals overall – though more research is necessary to test this hypothesis. A further question that could be asked is whether Jordan's inclusivist and Ganiel's mediating evangelicals are more likely to be found in the Presbyterian, Church of Ireland and Methodist denominations than they are in the smaller denominations such as the Free Presbyterians, Evangelical Presbyterians, Reformed Presbyterians, Baptists, Free Methodists. In constructing his 'spectrum of evangelicalism in Ulster', Mitchell (2003: 131) suggests that this is indeed the case.

A final issue worth noting is the high number of people on a moderating journey in our sample, which further served to skew the social characteristics of our interviewees in the ways we have been suggesting. This disparity emerged for practical research reasons. Gladys interviewed the majority of people who were moderating during her PhD research, which focused on evangelical activism and peace-building in Northern Ireland. As she was turning her doctoral research into a book, she wanted to explore this group in as much depth as possible and followed whatever leads she was given. As a result, we ended up interviewing 34 people on a moderating journey. It did not then seem sensible to reduce the number of transcripts to match the numbers recruited for the other subgroups, as most of the interviews with people who were moderating were useful. Nor did we have the resources to increase the number of participants on other journeys. Therefore we decided to leave the sample as it was and simply to highlight this issue when it came to writing up the research. When interviewing evangelicals who were moderating, we came to the point where our sample was 'over-saturated', which means that we were hearing the same themes many times over. We think that we were able to achieve a similar amount of depth in our interviews with people on the other varieties of journeys. The issue is not so much to do with differing amounts of depth, as it is to do with the overall impact on the characteristics of the sample.

Characteristics of people on different religious journeys

This book is not about describing evangelical subgroups. It is therefore rather difficult to talk about the social characteristics of people on one journey or another. However, just as there are typical patterns of experiences amongst people on each journey, we can also identify some of the typical social characteristics of people who describe different kinds of journey.

First, we interviewed 17 evangelicals who described their faith as deepening in a conservative direction. Of these, six were female and eleven were male; five lived in Belfast, so the majority (12) lived in rural areas or the smaller market towns of Northern Ireland. Four had a third-level or higher education and the rest had a mixture of second-level education and no qualifications. It is difficult to pinpoint individuals' social class in a late modern context, but we can highlight typical professions amongst this group as police officers, security guards, office workers and an assortment of manual workers and those retired from similar jobs. One was unemployed. Two were church pastors and one was a freelance evangelist. In terms of religious background, only six grew up in conservative evangelical households becoming born-again at a young age. The remaining 11 had contact with evangelicalism in childhood, primarily through being sent to Sunday school, and became saved in later life. The denominations people belonged to included Free Presbyterian, Elim Pentecostal, Evangelical Presbyterian, Free Methodist, Baptist, Presbyterian and Gospel Hall – these being, with the exception of the Presbyterians, the smaller conservative evangelical churches of Northern Ireland. Many of the evangelicals on this type of journey resemble Jordan's oppositional evangelicals, or Ganiel's traditional evangelicals, and approach faith in a somewhat black and white way. Also on this journey were people whose beliefs resonate with Brewer and Higgins's (1998) Pharisaic Protestants. Whilst apolitical, they are primarily concerned with saving Catholic souls. Others were more like Brewer and Higgins's covenantal Protestants, who saw a direct link between their faith and politics in Northern Ireland, based on Old Testament ideas of a chosen people.

Many of those who described a steady religious journey could be seen as Jordan and Ganiel's pietistic evangelicals – people who have a private, devotional faith and who are not overly interested in doctrine or politics. Some others on a steady journey were more like Jordan's inclusivists, and Brewer and Higgins's Pharisaic Protestants, who said that they had always been this way. In total we classified 21 people as on a steady religious journey. Seven were female and 14 were male; eight lived in Belfast, and 13 lived in rural areas or the smaller market towns of Northern Ireland; eight had a third-level or higher education and the rest (13) had a mixture of second-level and no qualifications. Typical professions amongst this group were teachers, civil servants, shopkeepers and manual workers. One was unemployed. The vast majority of those on a steady religious journey had been raised in evangelical families, whilst just a handful were adult converts. Denominationally, the steady journeyers included Presbyterian, Church of Ireland, Baptist, Brethren, Pentecostal, Free Presbyterian, and one member of a charismatic house church.

Those on a moderating journey had generally come from conservative (traditional, Pharisaic, covenantal, oppositional and confessional) evangelical backgrounds. They are now akin to Jordan's inclusivist evangelicals, or Ganiel's mediating evangelicals, who see evangelicalism as part of a wider Christian family and who are open to engagement with people of other faiths. We classified 34 people as on a moderating journey. Of these, eight were female and 26 were male; most – 26 – lived in Belfast or Londonderry/Derry, whilst a handful – eight – lived in rural areas; 30 had a third level or higher education and a small minority, four, had second level or no qualifications. This group included religious ministers and people who worked for evangelical organisations that we deliberately contacted in order to hear stories from people whose views had liberalised. Apart from these, many of this group tended to be in professional occupations such as scientists, doctors, and senior civil servants. It also included people who worked for charities or NGOs, for example as youth, community and reconciliation workers. Denominationally, although they had often been raised in small conservative churches, people on a moderating journey were now by and large from the larger Protestant churches in Northern Ireland – Presbyterian, Church of Ireland and Methodist. There were also people who had been involved with the charismatic renewal movement in the 1970s, and who were now members of charismatic house churches.

People on a transforming journey are a tiny group on the margins of the evangelical family, with only a few hundred participating in activities through groups like Ikon.[4] Of the 11 people whose faith was transforming in a post-evangelical direction, four were female and seven were male. All 11 lived in Belfast, and all had university degrees. Two had PhDs. Two were over 50 and the rest were in their twenties and thirties. Despite their high level of education, only some of the transformers had traditional jobs – one was a youth worker and another was a researcher for a think-tank. Most were free-lancers in the arts, the media, in community and reconciliation work. This reflects the more fluid nature of professional work in the twenty-first century, at least in these sectors, and no doubt relates to the non-traditional views held by this group. Transformers have emerged from a variety of denominations, from Presbyterian and Church of Ireland to charismatic house churches.

Finally, we talked with 12 people who had left evangelicalism. For most people, identification with 'no religion' represents a change of identity, as only three per cent of people in Northern Ireland have been raised with 'no religion' (NILTS 2008). Of the 12 people we interviewed who had left evangelicalism totally, five were women and seven were men; nine had a third/higher-level education; three more had a second-level education. All lived in Belfast, except one who had moved to Dublin at the time of interview. Five had been raised in rural areas. There were no typical occupations in this group, which included a designer, a teacher, a waitress, an artist, a university student, a lifeguard, a university lecturer and some clerical workers. In terms of denominational background, leavers came from a variety of churches within the Protestant evangelical axis. Most had attended more than one church in the past. Five were raised in rather traditional Presbyterian churches, three of whom had moved on to a charismatic house church in their teens or twenties. Two were raised as Brethren, two as Free Presbyterian, two as Church of Ireland, one as Elim Pentecostal and one in the Gospel Hall. Some also had connections with Methodism. Their current religious identifications are as complicated as their past identifications. Four described themselves as agnostic, three as agnostic/atheist, one as atheist/nihilist, one as a humanist and atheist, and three continued to describe themselves as Christian, although in a looser and non-evangelical sense.

People on different types of evangelical journeys, then, do have quite different social characteristics and denominational backgrounds. These charac-teristics and backgrounds inform their experiences and life stories. But people on particular varieties of journey cannot be slotted neatly into the empirical types of evangelicalism previously identified by scholars. Although some directions of journey may resonate with particular types, there are no hard and fast relationships. As the stories in this book attest, religious change does not happen in a rigid or deterministic way. And going forward we are interested not just in connections between types of evangelicals and types of journey, but also in how people move *between and beyond* certain orientations to evangelicalism.

Conclusions

This chapter has provided an overview of our research methods, including reflection on the strengths and limitations of our study. We have spent some time explaining how we found people to interview, as well as how the interviews were conducted and analysed. The importance of telling stories about the past, as a means of constructing identities in present, has underpinned our approach. And it is through analysis of how people present themselves and others in their narratives, their agency and their constraints, as well as significant turning points, that we are able to unravel how personal religious change might take place. Our own orientations to our subject have also been explored, including some reflection on how our religious identities might have impacted on the work. Our aim has been to supply enough information to establish the rigour and reliability of the research, whilst being clear about its nuances and limitations.

In this chapter we have quantified how many of our interviewees we identified with each of our varieties of journey. We are aware that the sample we recruited is not representative of the population of Northern Ireland. This is partly because evangelicals themselves are not representative in some respects – such as their tendency to be more highly educated than non-evangelicals. It is also because we deliberately over-sampled evangelicals on specific types of journey in proportion to their actual size within evangelicalism – those who were moderating, transforming and leaving – who were much more urban and educated. The gender imbalance is partly due to traditional gender roles within evangelical families and workplaces, and partly a result of our snowballing technique which began, perhaps too often in retrospect, with contacting church leaders and evangelical organisations which were by and large male-dominated. These factors do not make our interviews inadequate for the task at hand, namely analysing religious journeys. But this information about the specificities of the sample will, we hope, leave readers better equipped to critically evaluate the analysis which follows.

CHAPTER FOUR

Converting to Evangelicalism

Conversion is a defining feature of evangelicalism. It is where someone adopts a new religious identity, or changes from one religious identity to another. Evangelicals believe that people must be converted in order to become Christians. Conversion experiences and narratives about conversions are key elements of Northern Irish evangelical subculture. We took converting as the starting point for our analysis of evangelicals' religious journeys, because it is a basic experience upon which all of the other journeys build.

In his book on religious conversion, Lewis Rambo (1993: 1) explains how it is a process, not an event. In his words, 'conversion is rarely an overnight, all-in-an-instant, wholesale transformation that is now and forever'.[1] Of course some people experience a sudden religious conversion, but nearly always, conversion takes the form of 'a series of elements that are interactive and cumulative over time' (Rambo 1993: 17). In other words, conversion is like a chain of events and experiences, with a variety of elements working together to produce the eventual transformation.

Throughout this chapter, we focus on the links in the chain of conversion. Often conversion is a process begun in early childhood, where people become familiar with religious ideas through family life and contact with church. It almost always involves relationships with advocates: other believers, whether these are family members, colleagues or friends, who introduce people to evangelical ideas and meetings. It also involves a deeply personal, religious dimension where individuals describe emotional and sometimes supernatural experiences that mark a religious turning point. Despite having these emotional elements, individuals often engage in very rational processes of deliberation when considering conversion, weighing up the pros and cons of making a life change.

This chapter is slightly different from those that follow, in that practically *all* of our interviewees described conversion as part of their religious journey. Most people we spoke to who had been raised in evangelical households experienced conversion in childhood, often before the age of ten. Their conversion narratives tended to be less dramatic, with some saying they could not remember the exact day and time when they converted and others claiming that they only gradually realised they had become Christians. Some experienced multiple conversions throughout childhood, as if topping-up each previous attempt. Other interviewees were adult converts, who had some religious reference points as children but no prior active commitment. We have drawn disproportionately on stories of teenage and adult conversion in this chapter, due to the fact that these people described a radical religious transformation from one religious identity to another. All but one of our adult converts had changed from a non-religious to an evangelical identity. The one exception is a former Catholic.

Socialisation: 'Even though it was all those years ago, it does stick'

Both the life-course and social psychology literature highlight childhood socialisation as a key influence on an individual's current religious beliefs (Baston, Shroenrade and Ventis 1993, Dillon and Wink 2007). Socialisation through family, education and early contact with cultural and religious institutions plays an enormous role in shaping our attitudes and behaviours in the present. We found that practically all of those who experienced conversion as adults were already familiar with evangelicalism, on account of their religious socialisation as children. As Rambo (1993: 61) points out, potential converts have to be intellectually available to convert – new religious ideas are more attractive when they have continuity with someone's previous viewpoint.

Parents do not necessarily have to be religious or to be church attenders in order for their children to be socialised into evangelicalism. A significant number of our respondents were sent to church, Sunday school and religious missions by only nominally Christian parents (Dillon and Wink also found this in the US context). For example, Jackie is a clerical worker in her thirties from a rural town in Northern Ireland. She was converted just one year before the time of interview. In her words,

> We were sent, and brought, to church every Sunday, whether we wanted to go or not. We were made to go to Sunday school. The youth Fellowship which would have been on the Friday night, we were allowed to go to that. The wee children's meetings up the street, we were allowed to go to those, but my

mother and father aren't Christians. That's quite strange, I think it's just possibly the way they were brought up, that they were brought to church, they were sent to Sunday school, they were made to go to these places, and it's just been carried on. It wasn't as if it had any bearing on the things that went on in the house, you just went, and that's all there was to it.

This represents very frequent religious contact, multiple times a week, for a child whose father, in Jackie's words, 'never ever went to church' in his adult life. For Jackie, these childhood encounters with religion, in her case the strong conservative evangelicalism of the Free Presbyterian Church, made a deep impression on her. She remembers at age eight or nine thinking that she needed to become a Christian, speaking to God and hearing him speaking back to her. Initially in her interview she presents herself as 'innocent' at this stage, a 'little child [who is] completely listening in the faith'. However, later she talks about this in slightly different terms saying 'the Bible was hammered into you' in Sunday school, and later again, speaking of her childhood, she says 'the Free Ps [Presbyterians] would be very much blood and thunder: you – are – going – to – hell. And that is all there is to it.'

Although Jackie stopped attending church for many years when she got married, she was very aware of the lasting impact of her childhood religious socialisation. She says 'even though it was all those years ago, it does stick. It goes in there and it does stick.' But in her interview Jackie did not make the connection with the voices in her head in later life who repeatedly told her that she was going to hell. She says that this was the first thought that would come into her head in the morning, 'you're going to hell', and when she went to bed at night. It would wake her up in the middle of the night. Jackie mentions a number of times that whilst she was worried about her own fate, she was even more concerned for her children – 'I wouldn't want to think that through something I'd done my children would end up in hell.' In fact, concern for children's socialisation and souls is a common reason for rediscovery of religion in adulthood (Edgell 2006, Chaves 1991). When Jackie spoke about her own upbringing she said the words 'you – are – going – to – hell' with gravity, as if every word was underlined. It seems that this message, learned in childhood, was to have far-reaching implications in Jackie's adult life.

A series of events led up to Jackie's conversion. First, she 'absolutely hated' her job and as a result was travelling to another branch of her office where she came into regular contact with a couple of evangelical advocates (see below, p. 60). This led to a process of questioning and seeking, culminating in her attendance at a religious mission, where she had an emotional response to the speaker whose message she felt was directed specifically at her. She said if it were not for this turn of events, she would not have been saved. However, it is also clear that many years of childhood contact with conservative evangelical ideas and a fear of hell laid the groundwork for her conversion in later life. This is despite the fact that her husband, her family and her husband's family disapprove of her decision. She says they tell their friends 'Jackie has got religion' as if it were a contagious disease. She says that now she is her husband's 'worst nightmare [. . .] one of the people he detests the most'. It is hard to say how Jackie's faith journey will unfold with such opposition from intimate family members. Studies, such as Galanter's (1980) research on the Unification Church (Moonies), show that no matter how much people may want to pursue a faith, strong emotional ties to spouses or family may prevent them from doing so. However, at the time of interview, it seemed that childhood reference points and religious conviction were proving more influential to Jackie's religious decision making than the current beliefs of her family.

Although our primary socialisation happens in childhood, Goffman (1961) shows that adults can be resocialised when they encounter powerful institutions in later life. Goffman made these arguments in relation to mental hospitals, prisons, and concentration camps, where new identities and behaviours are forced upon people and, in response, people develop a brand new sense of self. Although we are not implying that religion is usually forced upon people in this way in Northern Ireland, some aspects of evangelical life can be seen in this context – as an all-encompassing institution that offers an opportunity to entirely change one's life and assume a new identity. It is not surprising, therefore, that conversion is often referred to by believers as 'rebirth' or becoming a 'new creation'.

Diane's narrative is one of religious resocialisation. She is in her late thirties and works in the public sector. She is a devout Free Presbyterian and takes an active role in the religious pickets of Northern Ireland, protesting for example against abortion, gambling, and gay civil partnerships. Diane's family are originally from the Republic of Ireland, but they moved to England, which is where Diane grew up. Her family are Catholic, but Diane became born-again in her early thirties soon after moving to Northern Ireland. Some encounters in childhood may partially have stimulated Diane's conversion. She describes how as a child, she heard the gospel at an evangelical Sabbath school and how it made a deep impression on her, saying 'instinctively as a young child of 11, I knew that what I was hearing was true, despite everything else that I'd heard and been taught'. In contrast she says she watched her brother and sister take Holy Communion in the Catholic Church as children but that this made no discernable impact on their behaviour or lifestyle. After leaving home, Diane describes how she went travelling and had a string of chance encounters with Christians, of which she says, 'though I didn't realise it at the time I know now that the Lord was giving me opportunities'. Diane later moved to Northern Ireland and became saved shortly after that, after attending a theologically conservative Free Presbyterian church on the advice of a friend she met at work.

Diane's narrative is interesting in the extent to which she has been resocialised into the evangelical subculture. Since her conversion, Diane has assumed an entirely new religious identity. As we will see in chapter 4, Diane attends church at least seven times a week. She has completely rejected the Catholicism of her upbringing. She now equates the Catholicism of her family with heresy. In Diane's words, 'you cannot mix dark with light or truth with error, [. . .] I believe that certainly what I was taught as a child is contrary to the Scriptures.' She says that 'obviously [she has] a love for Roman Catholic people' in the context of her family, but also indicates that she struggles with '[embracing] that religion in the hand of friendship'.

This is a complete break with her childhood socialisation. Diane presents herself as a new creation even more than most, and has involved herself in an all-encompassing church network. This could have caused Diane a lot of anxiety as she struggled to equate her love for her Catholic family with her conviction that they were essentially damned. However, her mother has eased this potential tension for Diane by attending the Free Presbyterian Church when she comes to visit. Her mother says that she likes it, has met some people she asks after, and also thinks that it is good for Diane. Diane talks about her mother's approval of her religious choice on quite a number of occasions and it seems understandably important to her that her new lifestyle has been accepted. However, there are also indications that some tension remains. For example, when Diane talks about having to cut non-Christian friends out of her life because 'they drag [you] down', she says 'if I could just even put this over to my mum, if she could just see the extent of it'. This may indicate that Diane still feels that some of her religious views are not quite understood at best, or may in fact be disturbing, for her family. Despite this, Diane's story is more remarkable for her total immersion into a new, and almost total, world of conservative evangelicalism that goes against the grain of her Catholic childhood socialisation.

The advocate: 'Every conversation in the office always came around to faith'

Rambo (1993: 83) argues that 'a consistent finding in the study of conversion is the importance of establishing early a connection between the potential convert and a member (advocate) of the new group'.[2] Within evangelicalism, the advocate is basically an evangeliser, some might say a proselytiser, whose goal is to speak to unsaved people about becoming born-again. Sometimes advocates are missionaries, people appointed to spread the word of God. Given that a central tenet of evangelicalism is to evangelise, in many other cases advocates are simply ordinary people. The most influential advocates come from within the family circle, and we discuss the influence of family in more depth below (pp. 60–2). But in other cases, the advocate may be a work-colleague, a friend or can even be a stranger. All of our interviewees who experienced religious conversion as adults talked about the importance of an advocate. Of course, coming into contact with an advocate is not enough in and of itself to provoke religious conversion. It usually combines with a myriad of other factors. But the advocate is rarely absent.

Adam's story tells us a great deal about the importance of the advocate, as well as how conversion often grows out of personal adversity. Adam is in his fifties and comes from an extremely deprived part of Belfast. Growing up he was sent to church and Sunday school, but he found it boring and says he absolutely hated going. Adam was 20 when the Troubles were beginning in Northern Ireland, and became involved with the UVF, a loyalist paramilitary group. In just a few years he was arrested. Like many other loyalists, Adam experienced religious conversion in prison.[3] His parents had started attending a Methodist church around this time. They were 'devastated' about Adam's arrest, and were able to find some comfort in the church. Soon, the minister of the church began to visit Adam in jail.[4] He gave Adam a copy of the New Testament, which he initially studied because he knew the minister might ask him questions on his next visit. After a time, though, what Adam was reading began to resonate, and he 'asked Jesus to come into [his] life'. He says 'there were no bolts of lightning'; it was not emotional, but rather a gradual and simple acceptance of God.

Just as the early prison visits from a Methodist minister were an important catalyst for his conversion, visits from another evangelical friend, sustained over the next twelve years, helped to cement Adam's faith. His friend, who was involved with the charismatic renewal movement, brought in religious books and tape-recorded sermons, which Adam said influenced his way of thinking. Interestingly, Maruna, Wilson and Curran's (2006) research shows how religion offers people in prison narratives of redemption, which help to explain their lives and offer hope for the future (see also Thomas 2006). While these elements were important later on in Adam's religious journey, at the time of his arrest and imprisonment it was the steady visits from religious advocates, people that were interested in his welfare as well as his soul, that kick-started his conversion process.

Then there is Jackie. Her conversion, heavily influenced by religious socialisation in childhood as discussed above, also highlights the key role of the advocate. She describes the role of two work colleagues who talked to her continually about becoming born-again, leading to her conversion. She says of her colleagues, 'they like to talk about their faith. And every conversation that was had in the office always came around to faith and religion and Christianity and Lois used to tell me that I really would need to make myself right, and that this would affect the rest of my life.' Over a period of some months, her colleagues would bring the subject up nearly every time they saw her. Initially their message would simply wash over Jackie, but soon she could not remove thoughts about the afterlife from her head. Eventually, Jackie promised one of the colleagues that she would go to church to hear her sing. It was later that week that she was converted. Jackie's story shows once again how important advocates are in people's journeys to conversion. Religious advocates are never the only reason that people become born-again; however, their persistent conversation about faith often catches people at moments when other things in their lives are pointing towards conversion. Advocates can then have a great influence, not only in setting someone's conversion in motion, but also in the direction that their religious journey takes afterwards.

Family advocates: 'He became an evangelist at home'

One of the most compelling features of the conversion stories was the influence of family members on individuals' religious journeys. This confirms studies, such as Stark and Bainbridge (1980), which find family networks to be a key factor in the process of conversion. The majority of our respondents had at least one family member who was born-again before their own conversion, and who introduced, or reintroduced, evangelical ideas to them. Sometimes this was an immediate family member, and often these people had the most impact on an individual's decision to become born-again. But for others, these were aunts, uncles, sisters-in-law and the like.

Hugh's conversion was stimulated in no small part by the conversion of two of his brothers. Hugh is an Elim Pentecostal pastor in his forties who was raised in a non-evangelical Protestant home. Hugh's story is fairly typical in that he describes having non-religious parents who nonetheless sent him to Sunday school, providing him with early religious reference points. When his brothers became saved, his parents were deeply unhappy and this led to many debates and arguments in the household. Hugh says his eldest brother 'became an evangelist at home'. The fact that he had previously been a staunch atheist made a deep impression on him. Hugh says,

> I heard my brothers talking to each other at home. The younger one was being helped by the elder one with any questions he had. And this began to get in my mind, and then this realisation came to me that there is something wrong in my heart, there is a distance between me and God.

When he realised this, Hugh asked to go along to church with his brothers. This was an Elim Pentecostal church, very different from the liberal Presbyterian church he was sent to as a child. Initially Hugh says 'I joined [the church] by accident because my brothers were going there'. But he soon came to prefer the simplicity of the worship and the strong gospel teaching that he found in the Elim, staying there until mid life when he himself became a pastor. Hugh's parents still do not attend church, and he reflects that whilst few peers of his own age were in his new congregation, 'I had a lot of mothers and fathers I suppose', whom he says he plagued with questions about his new faith. Overall, Hugh's story shows us how early religious socialisation and the influence of family members can work together to stimulate religious conversions. It also shows us how church can feel almost like a family to new converts.

In quite a number of cases, parents were brought to church by their born-again children, which ultimately resulted in their own religious conversion. Victor describes how his conversion 'rubbed off' on his parents, both of whose conversions followed just a few years after his own. They were impressed by the 'radical change' to his life. Or take the case of Billy, a security guard in his fifties. He comes from a medium-sized town in Northern Ireland and had been saved for about a decade at the time of our interview. Billy's mother was not a church attender, but she sent Billy to Sunday school anyway when he was a boy. Billy found church 'very boring', however, and stopped going in his teens.

Although he said he did not have 'a clue what they were talking about, there were other times that yes, something registered, and that part that registered always stayed with you'. When Billy was having serious marital problems later in life, his daughter, who was born-again, talked to him about her faith and eventually persuaded him to go along to a local Pentecostal church. She said it would help him 'get away from problems [and] to get things right' in his marriage. This is one of many examples from our interviews where children influenced their parents' beliefs – a process highlighted also by Sherkat (2003) in an American context. In fact, Billy's other two children joined suit and also became born-again shortly afterwards. Religious conversion had a domino effect in Billy's family.

Active deliberation: Choosing between the church and the nightclub

Billy's conversion story is interesting for other reasons too, including the way in which he talks about considering various options and making personal choices. Billy describes how he felt 'a draw towards the church' after attending with his daughter and said 'that there must be something to all this that everyone's speaking about'. But it took quite a number of visits to church before Billy made a commitment. His decision to become born-again was made slowly and only after a long period of rational deliberation. On the one hand he says that in church his 'spirit started coming alive', he would feel a 'tremendous heat [. . .the] presence of the spirit' which was an 'absolutely gorgeous, beautiful' experience. On the other hand Billy says he was afraid:

> Even though I knew I was supposed to hand myself to the Lord, there was still this part of me – you know you can't do that 'cos once you do, you'll not be able to go out here, you'll not be able to go out to a nightclub if you want, you'll not be going out for a few drinks and all if you do that. And, what are your mates going to say at work and all; they'll laugh at you and all.

Around this time, Billy met an advocate. Billy was working as a handyman, and after his work partner retired, an evangelical man came to help him out for six weeks. This man sat and 'read his Bible every day at dinnertime' and also in the van while Billy was driving. Billy describes how he used to go home at night and compile lists of questions to ask his work partner the next day. Usually these questions would revolve around what he would and would not be allowed to do if he were to become born-again. This is a fascinating insight into how individuals deliberate and come to religious decisions. Billy had to balance whether his feelings of warmth and of his spirit coming alive were worth the sacrifices he should have to make in his lifestyle. Eventually Billy decided that the sacrifices were worth it and he describes the final decision to become born-again as an uncharacteristically emotional experience. Although he did not 'hear any trumpets blowing', a change in him took place 'that was a great turning point'. Billy's conversion combines a number of elements, including his socialisation, current family influences, and contact with an advocate. But the process was also characterised by choice, involving both rational and emotional elements. Billy is an active agent in the construction of his own religious journey.

This resonates with research on Scientologists by Straus (1976, 1979), who found that people actively managed their own conversions, as well as Neitz (1987) who finds Catholic charismatics rationally working through their religious options. Rambo (1993) and Richardson (1985) convincingly argue that converts are not usually passive agents in their religious changes. Whilst in some contexts, for example colonialism, conversion is forced, this was not typical in our study. Many of our respondents present their conversion as an active decision where they weigh up the consequences of becoming born-again. Like Billy, Colin said the prospect of conversion was 'scary' because he 'didn't want to leave the old life behind'. Jackie explained that she was very concerned about what people would think if she were saved, but that ultimately it was 'the only decision that was left to make'. This reflects the narratives of some of Dillon and Wink's (2007) participants, who also took a 'deliberative approach' in making religious choices. However, for Dillon and Wink's Californians, religious decision making often seemed like religious 'shopping'. One individual says his friend 'investigated many faiths [and] selected the one she wants', another tried out many different options from Congregationalism and Unitarianism to Baha'i before settling on paganism (2007: 64, 127–30). Although few of our respondents described a similarly eclectic process of deliberation, limited as they no doubt were by a lack of cultural options and social influences, they nonetheless indicated a high degree of personal choice in their decision to convert.

People also spoke about the benefits that justified the costs of salvation – although they did not put it in these terms. They mentioned feeling comfort and acceptance, having assurances about the afterlife and being able to put temporal concerns in God's hands. Fiona, for example, is a teenager from a loyalist housing estate in Belfast. She became converted three years prior to our interview, and now attends a Pentecostal church. Fiona describes life before conversion as difficult and uncertain. Social life revolved around drug and paramilitary culture, and several of her friends had been killed. In contrast, church provided a sanctuary for Fiona – she uses words like 'home', 'safety', 'trust', and 'welcome' to describe her new Christian community. This is a long way from the danger that defined her early youth.

Given these active deliberations, it might on the surface seem that the rational choice theorists are correct, that individuals make cost-benefit calculations about religion and often decide that the benefits outweigh the sacrifices. Indeed, these kinds of deliberations are certainly part of the process. However, our interviews indicate that this is only part of the process, and that conversion has a messier, more emotional, and much less calculated side. These processes exist in tandem with one another, and are significant for different individuals in different ways.

Emotional aspects of conversion: Going with your gut

While many people described a rational weighing up of the pros and cons of religious conversion before they made their decision, often the moment of conversion itself was much more emotional. Jackie recounts how she 'cried her eyes out'. Billy, whose deliberations we have seen, describes how at the moment of conversion he felt emotional – 'not like [him]self'.

Colin's story also highlights the emotional as well as the rational dimensions of conversion. He was 22 at the time of the interview and became a Christian when he was 19 and a university student. His uncle and then his mother had recently become born-again and he had started to attend a small, conservative, independent evangelical church when he was 17. Colin listened to the preaching at church, but says he 'wasn't interested in it'. However, he began to feel convicted after six months, in the last three of which he could not sleep. He started to think about his life and 'knew [he] had to be saved', but put it off as he felt it would mean making too many personal sacrifices. The following year, things were not going well for Colin, especially romantically. He had split up with his girlfriend, and then things ended badly with another girl he had started to date. After an argument with her in his local nightclub, Colin stormed off to go home. It was about three o'clock in the morning and Colin said he was 'absolutely drunk – I could hardly walk never mind talk'. Instead of going home he decided to go to his pastor's house, rapped on the door, woke him up and told him he wanted to be saved. He did get saved that night, and attended church for a short time afterwards, but ultimately says 'I was still drunk. I never stuck at it.' However, less than a year later he decided that he needed to 'get himself right' and again went to speak to his pastor. The pastor told him that if he repented his sins he would get a clean slate, which he did, and has been following an evangelical path ever since.

For Colin, then, conversion was both a rational and an emotional process. He listened to sermons and weighed up the pros and cons of becoming born-again, but he also felt deeply convicted and knew that something was not right. Eventually his conscious decision to 'put off' becoming born-again was overridden by his sudden drunken urge to make a commitment. Unsurprisingly, his conversion under the influence of alcohol proved fragile. But Colin continues to describe this as a turning point in his life, and it was a precursor to his less dramatic religious conversion less than a year later. Colin's story tells us something more about gut feelings and emotions, and how they relate to more rational deliberations, in the conversion process.

In fact, conversion sometimes occurs despite an individual initially not being interested at all. There is no gradual process of active deliberation, nor calculation of the benefits of salvation, although of course this may take place afterwards. Take Arthur, for example, a travelling preacher in his forties who lives in a rural part of Northern Ireland. He was saved in his late teens at a tent mission but describes how initially he attended the mission 'reluctantly' with his family and how he 'just couldn't wait to get out [. . .] to get home, to get away from these meetings'. However, halfway through a service, after listening to the preaching, Arthur felt deeply convicted and ended up attending the mission every night that week until his eventual conversion at the final meeting. He said he felt he 'had touched something that was supernatural', that 'God was actively speaking to [him]' and he also felt 'extremely disturbed' as a 'fear [of hell] came on [him]'. Of course if we think about Arthur's biography prior to his conversion – regular church attendance, the death of a father which left him with questions about mortality, a previously saved but backsliding mother – we can see that the foundations and reference points of faith were already in place. However, Arthur's story is illuminating in terms of how lack of interest in salvation can become replaced by a dramatic conversion in a very short space of time – Arthur describes it as 'a total about turn'. He does not describe his conversion in emotional terms – for him it is more a process of realisation of the truth of the Scriptures. But Arthur's narrative is nonetheless one of an all-encompassing gut reaction rather than a story involving a slow and conscious weighing up of the pros and cons of conversion.

These stories highlight the messier, more emotional and uncontrolled sides of conversion. These often accompany, and sometimes override completely, the deliberative decision-making process. Indeed the feeling of 'conviction' was something many of our participants spoke about, which they described as if it were an encompassing gut realisation of their sinfulness and their need for conversion. The fact that this feeling of conviction would wake people up at night is testament to its powerful emotional impact. This is underlined by the descriptions of conversion as accompanied in so many cases by tears, relief, joyfulness, warmth, excitement and peacefulness – emotions that may fade over time but which continue to be associated with conversion as individuals look back over their lives.

Existential questions: 'If I died in this state would I go to hell?'

Some people may have personalities that incline them to ask existential questions more than others. Some individuals question the meaning of life to a greater degree after a personal tragedy, while others have been preoccupied with these questions from a young age. But as we saw in chapter 2, existential questioning is an important element of evangelical subculture. Our participants often described their conversions as prompted by questions about the meaning of life and fears about death. Asking these types of questions does not necessarily lead to conversion. They are usually combined with other, often social, factors before they prompt individuals to become born-again.

Rachel, a recent convert and full-time mother in her early thirties, says that she has 'a fear of dying, an awful fear of dying, right from a young child'. She describes herself as feeling paranoid that the world was coming to an end, and says that these questions started her thinking about becoming a Christian. For her religious socialisation, Rachel attended church occasionally as a child but it was not a big part of her life. The only person she had been close to who had died had been her grandmother, and that had been ten years prior to the interview. She was bullied by a teacher at school until she had a nervous breakdown which she speculates could have fed into her fear of dying. In her interview, Rachel kept bringing the conversation back to her fear of dying, which seemed to be her primary motivation for becoming born-again. This gave her 'peace' and 'certainty' and 'answers to questions that [satisfied her]'.

Before converting, Rachel had considered psychiatry and had consulted a fortune teller a number of times because she 'wanted some answers'. The fortune teller ended up telling her that her marriage would end and this 'scared the life clean out of [her]'. After her religious conversion Rachel says she still fears death, but that this is 'not as bad as it was'. In fact, she says she cannot imagine what life would be like now if she did not have church, and that it would 'really scare [her] to go back [to the way she was before]'. Rachel has a few evangelical family members, and lives in a rather religious rural area of Northern Ireland, both of which pushed her in the direction of evangelical Christianity. But it is her questions and fear of dying that ultimately seem to have been the motivation for her conversion. Indeed Dillon and Wink (2007) found that people who believed in an afterlife yet were not religiously active were the most afraid of dying, probably fearing for their own eternal fate. In contrast, the deeply religious held least fear of dying. In this sense Rachel's decision to become born-again may well help buffer her from a debilitating fear of death (for more on this point see Wong (2000)).

In contrast, others described a different kind of existential questioning. These individuals were much more concerned with the meaning of life than with the fear of hell. 'Meaning of life' questioning was more common for people who were already converted or felt secure in their faith, so it was prominent in interviews with people whose faith was moderating (chapter 6) or transforming (chapter 7). But for a few, questions about the meaning of life were important for solidifying their conversion. Redmond, a family doctor in a rural area, said that he was 'born into a Christian family' but that during his days at university in Belfast he went 'through a questioning period'. He said he was concerned about the presence of good and evil in the world, wondering how a good God could allow both. He credits his study of botany with convincing him that there was a God who was good and in control of the universe: 'believe it or not it was the study of botany, cell structure, which made me say to myself that some influence had to create this. This is not chaos.'

For a majority of our participants, the fear of hell was not prominent in their conversion stories. Even so, it seems as if the fear of hell is alive and kicking for a significant minority in Northern Ireland. This is reinforced by elements of evangelical material culture, such as gospel tracts that warn people that they will go to hell if they do not repent. In rural areas it is common to see handmade signs on the roadside admonishing people that 'the wages of sin is death' and 'ye must be born again'. Rachel was by no means the only person who talked about this fear as an impetus for religious conversion. After the death of his father when he was eight years old, Arthur was left questioning 'eternal issues'.[5] Although he said he had a happy childhood, he describes how he became aware of death, including the 'realisation of [his] own death', and it gave him a fear of God. Arthur said that during a tent mission in his teens 'I became very well aware that I was literally lost, that if I died in this state I would go to hell.' Helen, whom we introduce in the next chapter, also cites a fear of hell as a major motivation for conversion. We could add multiple names to this list – Jackie, Colin, Billy – in fact most of those people who describe their faith deepening in the next chapter articulate a fear of hell. Perhaps this is therefore a particular type of existential question that thrives in the conservative evangelical heartlands of Northern Ireland, in the independent evangelical churches and Gospel Halls, as well as in Free Presbyterian circles. And conservative evangelicalism, it seems, is very effective in providing reassurances about death. Most of these interviewees now fear the consequences of death for people who are unsaved, but actively look forward to their own life after death.

It's supernatural: Hearing the voice of God

Many people we spoke with described supernatural experiences around the time of their conversion. Again, supernaturalism is a prominent feature of the evangelical subculture and is reflected in the everyday language of many evangelicals, who use terms such as 'God told me', 'It's God's will', or 'The Lord provided for us.' People also mentioned 'hearing voices in your head'. For Jackie (above) and Helen (chapter 4), these voices repeatedly told them that they were going to hell. For others, like Andrea, the voices were gentler. For example, Andrea talks about God as if he is a real presence in her life, speaking with her and acting on her behalf on a daily basis. She converted at age five in a Sunday school class when she 'realised I needed Jesus as my saviour so I asked him to come into my life'. She says that at such a young age she 'didn't understand very much about it', but her faith solidified as she made Christian friends at school and she began to perceive God acting in her life. Andrea said she came to understand that God 'had a plan' for her, and 'he encouraged me. If I prayed and it was within his will then I was content [with what happened] [. . .] in terms of exams and things.'

Others described much more dramatic supernatural experiences. James says that before his conversion, he 'might have gone to the extreme of saying that I didn't believe in God'. All that changed one evening when he was taking a walk. A group of paramilitaries approached and compelled him to carry a pipe bomb to its intended target, threatening that they would harm his family if he did not. The bomb exploded before he reached the destination and he was injured badly. James says that he was immediately considered a paramilitary and a suspect rather than a victim, and that some people in the village where he lived turned against him. He lost his job and received death threats from republicans. When he returned from hospital he was arrested by the police and put on trial. He describes his experience in his jail cell after his arrest:

> I was sitting in that police station in a corner in a cell. It was quite an old police station, dingy and all the rest. And this was one of the things that brought me to faith to be quite honest with you [. . .] Whenever I sat in that prison cell I prayed, and I prayed that God would help me [. . .] And he did, he just simply came into my life.

Although James was not converted in the jail cell, he credits God with helping him make bail. When he was awaiting trial, he and his wife were befriended by a Christian couple. They treated James kindly, having him and his wife over for dinner and socialising with them when many others in the village would not. Three months after the explosion, influenced by his new friends, James says 'I asked God to forgive me for all my sins'. James's experiences of the supernatural continued after his conversion. He says God gave him a sense of peace heading into his trial, so that 'my frame of mind was, well if I go to jail here it's where God wants me to go'. He describes praying before his testimony in court. When he went into the box, he noticed a triangular-shaped window above the judge's head. He says that:

> As soon as I prayed, and this is the truth, the sun shone through that window. To me, that was God saying to me, alright James, I'm here with you. And not only that, the triangle window seemed to stand for the Father, the Son and the Holy Spirit [. . .] Whenever that happened my whole body got goose pimples and I knew that everything was going to be grand here.

Andrea's and James's stories highlight a belief in an interventionist God who is in control of the universe, concerned with both the dramatic and mundane details of individuals' lives. Supernatural experiences, and discerning God's voice, are common for Northern Irish evangelicals and can be especially important for individual conversions. This is just the sort of information that many social scientists dismiss, ruling out supernatural influences and arguing that what such people experience is really something else – such as a psychological problem. We disagree with that approach. Supernatural activity can be neither proven nor disproven by social scientific research. But what can be discerned is that people who perceive themselves to be influenced and guided by an interventionist God may act in particular ways, which then have religious, social and political consequences.

Personal adversity: Turning to God in times of trouble

Rambo (1993: 44) argues that 'some form of personal crisis usually precedes conversion'. Sometimes the crisis is existential, such as Rachel's growing fear of hell. In other cases personal crisis is dramatic and rooted in events in this world, such as James's experience with the pipe bomb and his subsequent imprisonment and trial. In Dillon and Wink's study, some people who converted as adults did so in response to personal adversity, such as chronic pain and illness, bereavement or other traumas, for example a parent whose child became involved in the Californian drugs scene (1997: 106). We also found personal adversity to be a key factor that catalysed some of our respondents' religious conversions, from the illness of a child, to the break-up of a marriage, to experience of violent conflict. It seems that in times of stress religion can provide emotional support (Ellison and George 1994). For some people, adversity encouraged them to think about evangelical Christianity almost for the first time in their lives, but, for most, experiencing personal difficulties reactivated former religious sensibilities. In other words, they may have been born-again at some point, then fallen away from their faith, or 'backslidden', only to recommit again at a later stage. Alternatively they may have had evangelical reference points from childhood, which took on new meaning in times of stress in adult life.

One example is Alan, a police officer in his late forties from a rural part of Northern Ireland. He said that when he was growing up family life was 'just centred around the church'. He became saved at a Christian meeting when he was 11, but by his mid teens says he began to 'dabble'. He does not say what he dabbled in, but suggests that he was not keeping Christian company. By the time he was 18 he had joined the police reserves and said he 'backslid for those years' because he 'wanted to be one of the boys'. At the age of just 20, Alan experienced a serious trauma that was to reactivate his religious involvement. One of his colleagues was murdered in a booby trap car-bomb during the height of violent conflict in Northern Ireland. Alan was put in charge of taking his friend's body, which had been 'blown apart', out of the shattered car, putting the parts in a plastic bag and taking them to the morgue. This was a devastating event for Alan, who describes the smells and sights of the bomb's aftermath in graphic detail.

The bomb also catalysed a dramatic religious turning point for Alan. It left him with questions about the possible fate that lay in store for his unsaved colleague in the afterlife. He describes feeling incredibly guilty that he had not spoken to his colleague about salvation, despite having had plenty of opportunities. Alan also explained how this incident brought him face to face with his own mortality, making him think about the 'frailty of life' and the fact that 'you could be gone tomorrow'. Facing up to death in this way, Alan felt the religious ideas of his youth took on a new significance. It was only a few months after this that he went to a gospel concert, where he ended up 'trembling' and 'shaking' and 'just knew that [he] wanted to go back to the Lord again'. He recommitted his life again that night. In view of Alan's very religious upbringing and family, it might have been expected that he would himself follow a religious path in later life. However, plenty of religious families have non-religious members, and it is clear that his deeply traumatic experience catalysed a quick and decisive re-conversion from which he has never looked back.

Both James's and Alan's conversions were sparked by violent and tragic events related to the Northern Ireland conflict. But for both men, there were other factors that came into play, including the influence of advocates, Christian parents, or being sent to Sunday school as a child. James and Alan present their God as one who is in control of those terrible situations, eventually turning evil into good. They believe that God intervened on their behalf to convert them, and that God continues to help them through difficult times.

Political conversions: 'I went to church to hear a political message'

Beyond the direct experiences of violence recounted by James and Alan, political events in Northern Ireland also provided the catalyst for some religious conversions. As we saw in chapter 1, previous research indicates that sometimes when individuals use religious symbols or rituals for political reasons, this may stimulate a revival of religion itself (Sells 2003, Raj 2000, Chong 1998). This was the case for some of our participants who initially saw religion as a political accoutrement, but once they started to utilise religious meanings and practices for their own ends, they became genuinely religiously convinced.

John, for example, describes himself as immersed in Protestant tradition. He is a civil servant in his fifties from Belfast. He says that when he was growing up he was 'steeped' in the Orange Order, its parades and paraphernalia. But whilst the Protestant tradition was 'in his blood', John says the evangelical element took on significance only in 1969 when he became saved. John's family had been active in the Church of Ireland, but he says growing up 'I really got nothing out of it.' When political violence erupted in Northern Ireland in 1969, John says, 'I began to look at Paisley and what Paisley was saying politically, and I thought I must get into that. I went [to church] to hear his political message – that was the only thing, I had no interest in the gospel at all.' However, beneath the surface, things were changing in John's family. In 1966 his mother had become born-again through hearing Billy Graham on television, and although she did not initially tell her family, by the early 1970s it became clear that 'the balance in the family was tilting' towards evangelicalism.

In any case, John kept attending Paisley's church. He says,

> I remember going a couple of times and there was hardly any politics, and that was a bit of a disappointment to me. I remember thinking the hymns were strange, they were all gospel hymns. I went back a couple of times, and got lifts there. I didn't go back that often at the start, maybe every month to begin with, hoping that maybe this time I will hear politics mentioned. But then it began to arrest me that there was a clear challenge to my standing before God.

It was out of this political context that John finally became born-again. He says that 'in the end because of my leanings towards Paisley and the Paisley political message, I was quite happy to marry in the evangelicalism with the Protestantism', going on to say that in the Free Presbyterian Church he was attending that 'was quite an easy thing to do'. John initially describes the start of the Troubles and him hearing the gospel at church as 'coincidence'. But as he reflects on the next few decades of his life, he remarks 'the more I'm talking the more I see how the political and religious bounce with each other'. He adds, 'in times of extremity the Gospel can reach out to people'. Here John is describing a classic sociological as well as religious proposition – that religion helps people to make sense of troubled situations.

Politics continues to be important in some religious conversions in contemporary Northern Ireland. On one occasion we were invited to join in as three new converts were being interviewed for an evangelical magazine. The magazine interviewer wanted to talk to the three working-class men in their thirties about their conversions from a violent loyalist subculture to born-again Christianity four years previously. The men described their lives growing up in a semi-rural area of Northern Ireland as involving Sunday school and Youth Fellowship activities. This was followed by their rebellious teens and twenties, where they told many stories about driving around looking for trouble, fights, riots, drunken vandalism and loyalist paramilitary feuding. However, through these years they always had, in Tommy's words, 'respect' for evangelicalism. Questions about the Bible and salvation sometimes arose in drunken discussions. When making banners to take to loyalist protests, the men described how they would use images from the Bible instead of secular images because they imagined that this would be more offensive to Catholics. So evangelicalism was in many senses familiar terrain and was sometimes used for political purposes.

What led to the three men's conversions in the end was a tent mission in their local town. At least one of them, Tommy, was drunk at the time, although four years later continues to be a committed evangelical Christian. He said that the choice for him was between becoming saved or joining the paramilitaries. The men maintained that very often evangelical missions were strategically placed beside loyalist political events and protests in order to attract their attention. In fact, they described how seven out of eleven of their loyalist flute band became saved that summer. Their conversions were 'the talk of the pubs' and although the men received some 'slagging' (verbal abuse), they also felt that they were given respect for their decision from their peers. Now the men say all their friends are born-again and that they spend a lot of time sharing the gospel, giving out tracts and giving their testimonies at other missions. What we see here is not so much a political event catalysing religious conversion, as with John above. But rather, we see how far evangelicalism is interwoven with a loyalist political subculture in some parts of Northern Ireland. Religious symbolism is often used for political ends, political events are targeted by evangelicals for proselytising opportunities, and religion represents a viable alternative to a paramilitary lifestyle. The religious conversions of these 'hard-men' of Ulster are inextricably linked to a cultural mixing of evangelicalism and politics. This cultural mixing includes a lingering respect for religious ideas that can be expressed emotionally, and sometimes even drunkenly.

Conclusions

No two conversions are identical. Yet a number of broad patterns can be observed. Firstly, all of those who converted as adults (even our one convert from Catholicism) had some familiarity with evangelicalism from childhood. When they encountered evangelicalism in later life, this was not radically new information. Seeds of ideas had already been planted in childhood that would germinate in adult life.

Of course not all of those who have experienced and rejected evangelicalism as children are destined to convert in later years. A variety of other elements need to be present also. One of these elements is some form of relationship with other believers. Often 'advocates' initiate conversation with potential converts. As we have seen this relationship is very often with a friend or family member. Sometimes work colleagues and strangers can be the point of contact. In our study, in a western Christian democracy, religious missionaries were not often highlighted as advocates, the way they might be in the developing world. However, many of our interviewees became saved as a result of contact with church leaders and pastors. Sometimes this was at an event, such as the tent missions common in rural areas, or special festivals for teenagers such as Summer Madness. At other times a church figure would take the potential convert 'under their wing'. This underlines the central importance not just of social relationships, but of deliberate and strategic conversations initiated by other people – friends, family and strangers – in people's inner religious journeys.

In addition, our research echoes Rambo's emphasis on crisis and quest as important elements of the conversion process. When people experience some kind of crisis, large or small, it can prompt them to seek out answers. Experiencing trauma, reflecting on the death of family or friends, the break-up of a relationship – all of these can provoke a tipping point, where someone who has perhaps been contemplating conversion will take the final step. Crises may also come suddenly and prompt a more rapid process of seeking out answers and finding a solution in faith. Other people may of course turn away from God in the face of personal crisis. But we find that religious conversion is a serious option when other factors – such as the presence of an advocate and early religious socialisation – are also present.

In such a way, the actual turning point can come fast or slow. Sometimes people spend a long time weighing up the pros and cons of conversion. In other cases, people are overtaken by an emotional gut reaction, and they make an immediate conversion, sometimes with little prior reflection. Often the moment of conversion is a deeply religious experience, where people hear the voice of God, or feel that they have accessed a supernatural dimension. In most cases we found that conversion had both rational and emotional dimensions, in different degrees for different people. This demonstrates how individuals exercise a great deal of agency in the construction of their religious journeys. Even where conversion takes place in a dramatic or emotional way, it seldom occurs without a great deal of prior active deliberation on the part of the potential convert.

Finally, the political dimensions of religious conversion in Northern Ireland provide an interesting example of how cultural context influences personal religious change. Experience of political conflict in Northern Ireland brought some people into contact with evangelicalism who were only looking for a political message. Once they had begun to use religion for political ends, they came to experience genuine religious transformation. Political motivation alone did not produce religious change, but it acted as an important trigger for conversion. This provides an example of how internal religious changes can be catalysed by external events and broader political developments.

CHAPTER FIVE

Deepening Evangelicalism

In this chapter we explore the stories of people whose religious beliefs have become more deeply conservative. We focus on cases where religious practices, lifestyle choices and related attitudes have become more traditional and where individuals see their religious beliefs as becoming more important over time. In other chapters, of course, we see individuals describing a deepening of faith that has moved them in liberal or radical directions. But this chapter is concerned with the fifth of interviewees who said their faith was deepening in a conservative direction. They include travelling preachers, business people, supporters of the Rev. Ian Paisley's Democratic Unionist Party (DUP) and working mothers. They share a pessimistic unionist analysis of Northern Ireland politics.

The term conservative is our own. When we asked our interviewees to locate themselves on a conservative to liberal continuum of evangelicalism, some rejected our typology and said that there was no such thing as a liberal evangelical – as Wesley, one of our interviewees, said, this is 'a contradiction in terms'. They believed there was only one strong biblical position on evangelicalism, and all other interpretations were misguided or blasphemous. Quite a number of individuals in this chapter identified themselves as fundamentalists. Many could be described in Jordan's terms as oppositional evangelicals: people who conceive of faith as black and white, who value plain speaking and are often suspicious of formal theology. A smaller group in this chapter are more like Jordan's confessional evangelicals, or Brewer and Higgins's Pharisaic Protestants, for whom detailed study of biblical doctrine was paramount. And ever-deeper immersion in the Scriptures helped intensify their faith. Some are like Ganiel's traditional evangelicals, or Brewer and Higgins's covenantal Protestants, who value Calvinistic interpretations of the relationship between church and state. Some people whose faith was deepening described themselves as 'right-wing conservatives', 'traditional', 'saved' and 'born-again'. This language is reflected throughout the chapter.

We highlight a variety of patterns of personal change in this chapter. Some people have been saved since childhood and describe a gradual process of faith deepening over time. A significant number of people whose faith was deepening were actually adult converts, who describe their subsequent religious journey as one of increasing traditionalism. Others have found that personal crises and sometimes political events have catalysed their faith journey in a more conservative direction. In many cases, people described the strategies they use to promote a deeper faith. For example, they are very strict about whom they socialise with, because they believe this protects their faith from contamination from liberal Christians and secularists. We also explore how individuals talk about their ability to *choose* a more conservative religious path, as well as how they present the social push and pull factors in this direction.

Surrounding yourself with godly people: Church activity as a way of life

Evangelicalism is a very busy faith (Smith 1998, Jordan 2001). Most evangelical churches offer an enormous variety of social as well as religious activities that people can become involved with every day of the week. This gives evangelicals the opportunity to totally immerse themselves in church activities, and there is no need for a social life outside the church. Understandably, this usually has the effect of reducing individuals' contact with non-evangelicals, which in turn can strengthen their faith. In this sense, the people in one's church can come to feel like family for some people, as they build their lives around church activities, meals and camaraderie.

Diane, the civil servant from Belfast whom we met in the previous chapter, attends her Free Presbyterian Church at least seven times a week:

> Currently I would go to the Tuesday morning prayer meeting, on Tuesday evening I would do the outreach with the church, there's a Thursday morning prayer meeting that I would go to, and Thursday evening we have a prayer meeting, and then Friday afternoon I would go, if I'm not working I would go with some of the congregation to [a picket in] X street. We would hand out gospel tracts and literature concerning the issue. On Sunday I would go to the early morning prayer meeting and then I would attend the services on the Lord's Day.

Another Free Presbyterian man, Wesley, describes his weekly routine, and shows how this religious immersion structures family life and is passed on to the next generation. In Wesley's words,

Sunday is a special day, obviously [. . .] So there is Sunday school, church in the morning, often a meeting in the afternoons and church again in the evening. And as [the children] get older, they will be at youth rallies and things like that after church on Sundays. On a Monday evening the children go to the children's meeting in the Gospel Hall just down the road. And they are having a special week this week, so they are going every night. On a Wednesday evening it's our midweek Bible class and prayer meeting, and one or other of us will be at that. On a Friday evening it's the children's meeting, which I lead in our own Church. So we all go to that as well. So that is the pattern of the week. It's a way of life, very much so.

Wesley's children also attend a small faith school. It is clear from his description that faith is the main focus of family life and that church activities take up practically all of their spare time. This total immersion in church was described by quite a number of participants whose faith was deepening, and it was usually accompanied by a regulation of social relationships outside the church as well.

The regulation of friendships: 'You don't pull people up as quickly as they pull you down'

Who we spend our time with has an important influence on our attitudes. We also often feel more at ease in the company of people who we know share our views (see Asch 1956). The precedent for believers to surround themselves with other like-minded people is established in the Bible, for instance in passages such as 2 Corinthians 6: 17 ('Wherefore come out from among them, and be ye separate . . .') and Hebrews 10: 25 ('Not forsaking the assembling of ourselves together . . .'). Due to these and other biblical admonitions, social networks are understandably a key concern of many evangelicals – both in the discouragement of secular social networks and the provision of faith-based alternatives. Evangelicals tell each other that they must choose friends and partners that are born-again. Often this message is targeted at young people, to keep them out of trouble. Converts to conservative forms of evangelicalism are reminded that their past lives were filled with sin, and that they must avoid contact with their former friends, to avoid contamination (Rambo 1993, Heise 1967). A number of studies have found that when religious believers' ideas become more intense, their need for support from other like-minded individuals increases (Galanter

1989, Staples and Mauss 1987). So there is a chicken and egg relationship between the regulation of social networks and the deepening of religious belief.

The regulation of friendship was an important theme for those whose faith was deepening. People who talked about this made the, quite logical, assessment that it would be easier for them to maintain their faith if they surrounded themselves with like-minded people. In many cases this entailed actively cutting unsaved former friends out of their lives. Often this was a painful process, but over time, this became habitualised. Turning down party invitations initially would be a source of guilt and embarrassment, but eventually the invitations would stop coming, which lessened the need to make difficult social decisions.

Diane tightened up her social networks almost immediately after becoming saved. At this time she shared a house with two other women who were 'nice' but 'worldly', and whom she considered to be 'good friends'. Initially Diane said she wanted to keep them as friends, and decided that she would simply not do certain activities with them, such as going out for a drink. When she was faced with their weekly Friday night outing just two weeks after being saved, Diane describes herself as having a dilemma. She considered going out and not having a drink; however, she ended up not going at all that night, nor ever again – because she soon 'realise[d] that this was not going to work'. She says 'I realised being in that company that, especially when drink starts to flow, that I'm in company where God is being dishonoured and his word is being dishonoured.' She says that she has learned as a Christian that 'you don't pull people up as quickly as they'll pull you down', and now she does not even consider going anywhere where the 'Lord is dishonoured'.

Billy, a security guard in his fifties, puts this in similar terms, saying 'bad company corrupts good character if you allow it to be that way'. Both Diane and Billy actively choose to prevent themselves from being with people who have different beliefs to them. On the other hand, spending time with fellow believers reinforces people's faith. In Billy's words 'when you are with people that believe in the same thing as yourself and you start to speak about it, there's a desire [for God] that starts to rise from up in your spirit [. . .] We have in common, you see, because we are of the one spirit, of the living God.'

Sydney focuses less on the potential corruption by the unsaved and concentrates instead on the positive and affirming role that other evangelicals play in his faith life. In his forties, Sydney is an elected DUP representative from a predominantly Protestant town, and has been saved since he was nine years old. He says that over the last number of years his evangelical and Reformation convictions 'have grown because [he] has become more aware about them and informed about them'. When asked what prompted this deepening, Sydney repeatedly singles out a small group of like-minded friends who are all members of a conservative evangelical organisation. For him this has been 'a big influence' and says it is 'one of the most enriching experiences that I have had'. Sydney left school with few qualifications and presents himself as somewhat intellectually uncertain. He often refers to himself as 'indecisive' and says whilst his friends can produce written documentation to back up their faith, he 'could not write a thesis on it'. It is in this context that he talks about his friends and colleagues as a 'sounding board', and says these associations have helped him become 'more grounded in what [he believes]'. The regulation, or Christianisation, of social networks, then, is a double-edged strategy. It helps people avoid temptation and corruption whilst giving them like-minded friends who reinforce their beliefs. It is no surprise that this process often goes hand in hand with religious deepening.

Social networks take on extra significance in times of upheaval or change in one's personal life. Leaving home is often a crucial moment in opening up opportunities to meet new people and to think and behave in new ways. John, a civil servant in his fifties, initially had some trouble settling into university life when he moved to Belfast, describing himself as a 'desperate home-bird'. He soon began to meet new people, including his future wife, and began to see university as an 'amazing place' and 'an exposure to this amazing world'. However, John did not leave his social network formation to chance. He gathered up a number of Christian contacts, given to him by a conservative evangelical minister, and says that after that, he found a circle of friends quite quickly, all of them born-again Christians. This was immediately followed by John becoming involved in DUP politics, a scene which was full of 'good folk' who were not involved in the typical student drinking culture. At the time he was attending Ian Paisley's Free Presbyterian Church twice a day. John, like Diane and Billy, presents himself as proactive in his choice of friends. He says '[I was thinking] that I'm a fundamentalist evangelical Protestant and I'm not going to get involved in this.' He goes on to say that 'because I was surrounded by friends with similar views, I was nurtured and protected'. A similar regulation of reference groups in order to protect one's beliefs has been found in other studies, for example Hammond and Hunter (1984), and Christensen and Cannon (1978).

Ray, a Belfast student, agrees that in university it is difficult to make friends because 'there's very few people who wouldn't go out and get drunk every night'. He says if he hung out with them he would 'get jacked back to the way [he] was' before he became a Christian, so he chooses not to. For Ray, regulating his social networks at university is a form of 'self-defence'. In contrast, he has some friends in his church whom he describes as his 'support group'. He says 'we help to keep each other upright and [. . .] strong in what [we] believe'. Again, Ray is aware of the consequences of his actions and he presents himself as actively choosing his friends with religious goals in mind. This is interesting because it runs counter to the popular notion that strong religions lure people in and brainwash them. Whilst there may be an element of social control in many churches, people also choose to limit their social relationships to other evangelicals, fully aware that this will help them strengthen their faith.

Spiritual dimensions: Allowing God to take control

Thus far we have focused on social aspects of religious deepening. But we also identified specifically religious – our interviewees would say spiritual – factors that contributed to the deepening of their faith. One significant process was a shift in individuals' perception of control over their own lives. People described themselves as moving from a position where they made their own decisions and coped with their own problems, to one where God was called upon to direct decisions. They attributed life's struggles to God's will and/or the power of the Devil. They described a psychological reorientation where they began to surrender power over their own lives and put their trust in the power of God.

This can be seen in the way Diane talks about cutting her old friends out of her life. She presents herself as an agent who is free to make her own choices about this. Initially she felt she had a dilemma, and she agonised over what to do. She says she consulted other religious people and finally came to a decision that she would not go out when others where drinking. Initially the decision, to choose whether to go to bars or not, is very much Diane's own. But over time she says she has realised that there are negative consequences to going her 'own foolish way' where she would 'lose out on God tremendously'. She thinks her own potential choices are foolish and God's will is superior. She goes on to say that this 'makes you then start to be very cautious, I wouldn't now make the decision, even little decisions, I don't make the decision before I pray to the Lord whether it's to do with my time or whatever, I put things before the Lord and he never ever fails'. Although Diane decides what issues to pray about, she does not now make any decision without consulting God. In this way she presents herself as having handed her agency over to God.

Another example that Diane gives relates to purchasing a house. She says,

> When I moved to buy this house I had asked the Lord, I put out a fleece and I said to the Lord 'look, you provide the house you want, and one of the signs that I would like is that I buy it from Christians'. And [. . .] as soon as I walked in and I met the lady of this house I knew, I said 'this is the house'.

Diane bought her house in a predominantly Protestant area, and it would have been likely that a variety of houses she viewed would have belonged to evangelical Christians. Added to this is the very human tendency to prefer one's own group, and to believe that they are more honourable. In fact Diane's methods of house buying are quite logical, but she presents them as a process of testing and confirming faith. Although the agency was Diane's in the determination of search area and criteria for buying, she attributes the success of the venture, and therefore the agency, to God – as an answer to prayer.

Allowing God to take control was a common strategy for dealing with life's difficulties as well as in decision making. Indeed, people who described their faith as deepening in a conservative direction seemed to articulate a different approach to dealing with adversity than individuals on other types of religious journeys. When bad things happen, or life seems difficult, these people are inclined to see this as a divine test, rather than as God letting them down. More than this, many of these individuals used occasions of struggle and hardship to strengthen their faith.

For example, Billy describes his bumpy journey through Christianity, where doubts and fallow periods often plague him. He says,

> I had more obstacles than enough to my faith, sometimes when I did depart from the faith a bit, I felt everything eased off, the problems seemed to stop and every time I seemed to come back in they started to grow again.

Although Billy correlates periods of faith with times of having more personal problems than usual, he does not interpret these difficulties as meaning that the Christian faith is not for him. Instead he says that 'this is all part of the plan of the Devil to take your eyes from the Lord and look at the problems'. This echoes Diane's handing of her agency over to the Lord. In this case, it is the

Devil who Billy says is responsible for his difficulties. He goes on to say that 'Christianity is not an easy walk and I would never tell anybody it is a simple walk, it is one of the difficultist [*sic*] walks to walk'. The difficulties he describes are mostly around resisting temptations, political concerns and doubts about the existence of God. He goes on to describe how 'the deeper you get into the Bible and the more praying that you do and the more sacrifice you start to give, the harder that the problems come at you'.

However, for Billy, these difficulties are worth it because since his conversion he has 'had [his] own happiness from within'. He says,

> I mightn't be necessarily at times content with things, but deep within I'm still happy because I know that when you die that there is a living God that is going to be there. And you will be [. . .] in heaven – there is no crime, there is no disease, there is no pain of any kind, there's nothing but love and nothing rusts or nothing wears away – it's there for eternity.

The belief of better times in the afterlife is what keeps Billy going through the hardships of this earthly life. The idea that religion helps people take their mind off the terrible things in this world is most famously associated with Marx (1844), who called religion the 'opium of the people'. We do not have to be atheists like Marx, however, to point out that religion *does* help many people to cope with life, as the literature on religion and mental health makes clear (see Koenig ed. 1998). Certainly Billy's story echoes this. He says he often thinks 'please come back today Lord' so that his troubles will come to an end as he enters the next life.

Personal struggles and supernatural battles

For some whose faith was deepening, struggle and hardship have a supernatural dimension in this world as well as in the afterlife. Arthur, a travelling preacher from a rural part of Northern Ireland, explains how experiencing what he calls 'personal failure' eventually helped him to deepen his faith. He says that God uses 'experiences in our lives, whether it be grief, or whether it be disappointment, temptation and failure or conflict to strengthen us'. Arthur's father died when he was a child, and his mother died when he was in his thirties. He suffered with ill-health and depression which led to his dropping out of Bible College. These experiences, or 'personal failures' (a phrase which he repeats several times), brought Arthur to 'a crisis in [his] Christian life'. In his words, 'I couldn't understand genuinely why I was experiencing these failures. And I didn't want to fail, but it was happening.'

Arthur responded to these perceived failures by turning to the Scriptures and reworking some aspects of his beliefs. He says he was introduced to the concept of 'spiritual warfare', a charismatic/Pentecostalist belief that supernatural battles between 'principalities and powers' influence events on earth. Arthur came to see the hand of the Devil and demonic powers playing a role in his life, to the point where he describes how 'through a whole string of events God clearly showed me that it was not purely depression, which I did have as a condition, and required medication, but on top of that there were spiritual powers operating as well'. This spiritual dimension, for Arthur, explains why for a long time he was unable to come out of his depression. When he heard a voice in his head telling him to go and see a spiritualist for help, Arthur says he suddenly realised that 'something sinister was going on'. After consulting and praying with others in his church about this, Arthur says that the Lord then began to 'teach me how to actively resist the Devil'. In fact, he has come to a point where he believes that God used his illness, as well as the death of his father, to strengthen his ministry, and helped him to identify with and be able to comfort other people. He concludes that 'those things, God has used in a very clear and definite way'.

But more than this, Arthur's growing awareness of demonic forces allowed him to push past his own sense of personal failure. Arthur says God brought him to, in his words, 'a place where I was completely willing to do whatever God wanted me to do and my life was completely available to him'. He says he 'gave [himself] wholly to the Lord', a state which he describes as 'being yielded', and says that 'for the first time the Holy Spirit had complete control'. In fact, Arthur handed control of his life over to God to such an extent that he and his family 'live by faith'. In other words, they have no fixed income and rely on money donated to them for their ministry. This is an extreme example of someone surrendering their agency. For Arthur, the consequences have been positive. He says this decision to give up his own power 'totally transformed [his] life'. He began to see supernatural occurrences in his life, and good things would spontaneously happen, whereas before he was 'always trying, but failing'. The words he now uses to describe his life are 'satisfaction' and 'joyousness'.

When we asked Arthur why he thinks his personal struggles deepened his faith, whereas they may have inclined others to turn their back on God, Arthur returned to the theme of the demonic, saying that he had encountered another dimension of life and that he became acutely aware of 'the Devil's tactics'. He goes on to say,

> Far from driving me away from God, it drove me to God because I experientially became aware that these powers are very real, and no one can convince me otherwise because I have literally felt things that could only come from the underworld, totally abnormal, totally supernatural.

Arthur's conviction of the existence of the supernatural was one of the elements that contributed to the deepening of his faith. But it is possible that thinking about the supernatural dimension of struggle also helped Arthur to deal with his feelings of failure. He was no longer the author of his destiny, and those hardships that he did encounter came to be seen as only those things that God 'permitted' to happen to him, and were intended to strengthen his faith. Moreover, in God he had a powerful ally, as, in the spiritual warfare being waged, the Holy Spirit 'is able to outwit the Devil in every way. Anything the Devil attempts to do against us, the Holy Spirit is much more powerful.'

Arthur says that God only permits things to happen that he knows 'we will be able to endure'. Whilst Arthur perhaps felt as though he could not endure his troubles on his own, in God's hands, by definition, he knows he will be able to endure any suffering – because it will be what God has intended for him and will be 'for his own good'. In fact, whilst Arthur's story reads on the surface like someone who has very little agency, having handed control of his life to God, in fact he has rather a lot of control. By viewing his experiences through a supernatural lens, Arthur has arrived at a place where he has much more strength and happiness. Arthur's story echoes previous studies that highlight the positive role religion can play for people coming out of depression (Smith, McCullough and Poll 2003, Koenig ed. 1998). In one of Dillon and Wink's interviewee's words, after his depression he decided to 'do what [he] could do to control the situation' by leaving the balance up to God, which took a 'great weight' off his shoulders (2007: 109). Finally, and without wanting to over-interpret his story, Arthur refers to God on a few occasions as a 'caring father', which in the context of the early death of his own father, may also help explain why he feels much more secure allowing God to take control (for more on God as a substitute parental attachment see Kirkpatrick and Shaver 1990).

Overall, then, an important theme for people whose faith was deepening in a conservative direction was handing control of their lives over to God in relation to making decisions and dealing with adversity. This underlines the supernaturalism that is so prevalent in Northern Ireland's evangelical sub-culture. Whilst the conservative evangelicals here present themselves as having handed their agency over to God, we can read their stories on another level as well. Individuals often give logical reasons why they feel better knowing that their fortunes are in God's hands. It can reduce personal stress and feelings of failure, it can provide a blueprint for making decisions and help justify decisions as divinely ordained. Not only can attributing control to God help explain suffering in this world, but it also offers hope for a better life after death. This in itself can be interpreted as a clever and creative strategy for dealing with life's difficulties.

Political catalysts I: 'We were wanting to hear Paisley's views on politics, more than the gospel'

There was a strong connection between many of the deepeners' religious and political journeys. In fact, across most types of religious journey we found that politics played an important role in provoking and shaping religious change. But for those whose faith had deepened, political factors loomed particularly large.

As we saw in chapter 4, some of our interviewees became interested in evangelicalism and became born-again in the late 1960s to early 1970s. They attributed their initial point of contact with conservative evangelicalism to the political rallies of the Rev. Ian Paisley. Some of our other interviewees, who were already saved at this time, described the role that the intense political climate of the early Troubles played in pulling their faith in a more conservative direction. One example is Renee, a 70-year-old from a working-class Belfast family, who had been attending the Church of the Nazarene for 15 years by the time the late 1960s came about. This is a small denomination in the Wesleyan tradition which is well known for its emphasis on personal holiness and evangelism. Renee describes how her husband and she became disillusioned with the church because of in-fighting, and how this led to a process of 'church shopping'.[1] This was, in Renee's words, 'just about the time Mr Paisley was coming to the fore with the political situation'. They attended Paisley's Free Presbyterian Church the first time, Renee told us, for political reasons: 'we were wanting to hear his views on politics, more than the gospel'. There had been a series of IRA bombs in the early 1970s and Renee maintained, 'I wanted to hear somebody who [I] knew was going to tell [me] the truth about the situation.' But once they started going, she found that she enjoyed the services and the preaching and they have been attending the Free Presbyterian Church ever since. This was an important turning point for Renee who has continued on this conservative evangelical trajectory. She now regularly attends pickets on issues such as abortion and homosexuality around Northern Ireland, and continues to espouse a strong mixture of religious and political beliefs.

John, who is what Jordan might describe as a confessional evangelical, also notes the connections between his religious journey and his orientation to the political situation in Northern Ireland. It is difficult to say precisely how his religion and politics influenced one another, but John himself makes the connection saying, 'the more I'm talking the more I see how the political and religious bounce with each other'. The first overlap was his involvement with DUP politics at university. This was in the 1970s during the height of political violence in Northern Ireland, and John soon came under attack, receiving threats on his life. He says, 'I loved all this' and also 'I think that my faith was strengthened and my crusade was strengthened, politically and spiritually.' John talks about university as if it was his heyday, and says he tells his children stories of 'daddy getting into scrapes here and there'.

After university, John describes himself as becoming 'spiritually re-formed'. He presents the Reformed tradition as containing 'the hard-men of evangelicalism', and became attracted to this position as he began to read seventeenth-century Puritan literature, and joined a small Paedo-Baptist, separatist, conservative evangelical congregation (he was formerly attending the Free Presbyterian Church). Interestingly, this move of theological and denominational position occurred after John stepped out of DUP politics. After university John had been working full-time for the DUP, but soon funding dried up and he no longer had a job. He says this was 'a completely amicable departure' with 'no animosity whatever', but that it unsettled him and he 'went through a freefall of lots of different ideas'. John presents this change as 'a seminal moment in terms of my growth and my own direction'.

In some ways, this change may have reflected a desire to explore the connections between religion and politics outside the DUP–Free Presbyterian nexus. However, John continued to believe that 'Christians should be out there getting [their] hands dirty and that the struggle in Northern Ireland had a peculiarly millenarian aspect to it and [. . .] was a struggle of God's people.' Although he says that many in his church are more pietistic than himself, he says that now 'I suppose I've really returned to my roots politically [. . .] if anything, I've probably gone back quite a bit to a traditional evangelical

Protestant position, both politically and spiritually, my attitudes would be much more robustly conservative, than they were 20 years ago anyway.' John proceeds to outline the ongoing difficult political situation for Protestants in contemporary Northern Ireland, as well as his efforts to engage politically and change the situation. It seems then as if the change in John's personal fortunes prompted a religious rethink, but that ultimately in the context of the Northern Ireland conflict he was drawn back into religious and political activism. It is of course difficult to establish causality – have John's religious beliefs driven his political ideas or vice versa? But John is right to point out the way that religion and politics have 'bounced' off one another as his personal journey has unfolded, something that was common among people whose faith was deepening.

Political catalysts II: The peace process in Northern Ireland as a sign of the end times

If the political situation in Northern Ireland in the 1970s had the effect of pulling individuals towards religiously driven political activism, this did not appear to be the case for many in the 2000s. However, religion and politics did continue to intersect in interesting ways for some people. There were indications from our interviews that the 1998 Good Friday Agreement provoked a conservative religious response. Helen, whose story is discussed in more depth below, became born-again just after the approval of the Agreement. In chapter 4 we introduced a group of three working-class men who had been on the fringes of loyalist paramilitarism but had become born-again in the late 1990s, and who described the summer of 1998 as one full of loyalist conversions. They spoke about how seven out of eleven members of their loyalist flute band were saved that summer. Paralleling their story was the assertion of a revivalist preacher in a different county who talked about the conversions of 1998. The minister of a Free Presbyterian church in Belfast claimed his church had an influx of converts after the Agreement, so much so that they had to build an extension.

In the early days of interviewing, this led us to surmise that there was perhaps some connection between the political changes of 1998, so negatively received by many Protestants, and the apparent flurry of religious conversions. We hypothesised that experiencing such a dramatic change in political circumstances, seen by many as a devastating loss, had led to a religious reawakening. We thought some Protestants were perhaps despairing of the political climate and were seeking religious answers.

As we continued with our fieldwork it became clear that there was an important relationship between political and personal religious change since 1998, but it was not in the direction we thought. When we asked other people, including religious ministers and pastors, if they had observed a rise in religious conversions around this time, most said they had not. Instead of stimulating new religious conversions, we found much more evidence of a deepening of faith amongst those who were already saved. In particular, there was a belief in conservative evangelical circles that, due to unfavourable political circumstances, the 'end times' were drawing near and that saving souls was now more important than trying to change earthly society.[2]

For example, Billy became saved in the mid-1990s and his story is typical of religious deepening after 1998. Billy's politics were staunchly unionist throughout the Troubles. He liked the DUP's 'hard line' and at times played an active role 'hitting back' at republicanism. In fact he joined the 'Third Force', a pseudo paramilitary grouping in the 1970s, and 'would have marched around the street in balaclavas'. He says 'I even considered doing time to kill; Gerry Adams was the man I wanted.' However, since his religious conversion, Billy's ideas have changed considerably. Now he feels sorry for Gerry Adams because he is 'lost', and that for him 'living for the Lord is more important than a silly political end'. This change for Billy did not happen overnight, but was rather a 'gradual' process where he 'trained' himself to think differently. In his words, 'this oul body, this flesh was used to being one way, of doing one thing on its own, because you are born in the spirit of the Lord then, it takes a while for you to start to train it not to be doing these things'.

For many of those whose faith was deepening, global developments also pointed to the immediacy of the end times. Global warming was cited as a fulfilment of biblical prophecy. Helen tells us the Bible says that in the last days 'vile poured out and men's flesh would be scorched and the world will become warmer'. Helen lists earthquakes, famines and floods as pointing to Armageddon whilst Billy lists developments in Afghanistan, India and Pakistan. They both agree that events in Israel are a good barometer of biblical prophecy. For Billy, the foot and mouth disease that devastated cattle in the British Isles in the 2000s was a modern day plague, similar to the plague that affected cattle in Egypt in the time of Pharaoh and Moses. He says 'these things come as a warning, it is like warning signs from the Lord – it's like saying just give me a shake up, wake up and see what is happening here'. A shopkeeper in his fifties, Jeremy agrees that the recent extreme weather is a marker of the end times and he also talks about the growing influence of the Anti-Christ. Arthur too says he firmly believes that we are coming to the 'last days', of which a sign for him is the 'spiritual darkness' of our society, the increase in sin. From Arthur's point of view one of the 'prevalent problems' of our times, 'as in the days of Lot', is homosexuality.

It is perhaps unsurprising that developments in Northern Ireland would also be interpreted in this apocalyptic context. Helen is a policewoman in her forties. As she sees it, in the last days 'you will have tribulation and there is no doubt about it, not only is it getting harder, I'm talking about the Protestant tradition, it is getting harder as a Christian'. She says the 'green [nationalist] victory' in Northern Ireland is 'a sign of the times'. For her, the presence of 'murderers' in the Northern Ireland Assembly ties in with predictions in the biblical book of Revelation that in the last days evil men will rule the earth. Billy says that 'providential circumstances are being created in Northern Ireland to bring about evangelical testimony'. Indeed the majority of individuals discussed in this chapter felt that things were becoming more difficult for evangelical Protestants in Northern Ireland, who had to endure constant challenges to their faith as well as their culture.

It is interesting that this sense of political loss has not resulted in an outburst of political activism amongst these conservative evangelicals. In fact, at the time of the interviews in the early 2000s, it seemed that the opposite was happening. Many described how their faith was deepening in response to the end times, but said that their political interest was waning. Helen and Billy were interviewed separately, but at a later stage happened to be in the same room when the tape recorder was running. This exchange between them is very revealing about this shift to a deeper, more private faith. Helen was at one time extremely politically active and vocal. Now she says,

HELEN: That's why politics – it is nothing. It certainly doesn't fire me up any more, I mean X said to me why don't you get involved with politics, speaking out for us. I have absolutely no desire for it at all. The only desire now is to warn people, that Armageddon is definitely coming, that the apocalypse is not far off [. . .] the fact is that Christ is coming back, he's going to come back and sort out this mess [. . .] That belief becomes stronger with each passing day. There is not a morning I don't get out of bed and, I think Billy's exactly the same, when your feet touch the floorboards, your first thought is Christ – whether he is coming back.

BILLY: That's what I said, even though at times the political situation can change here and it makes you feel angry what's going on, but then you say –

what's the point? We have to concentrate on the Lord, so my tendencies towards the political end is not the same – sometimes I get annoyed, of course – but I mean that is just our old flesh – that is just my old flesh crying out again.

HELEN: So really, as regards to the political arena we have nothing to offer any more. I actually feel more and more that the real believers are separating themselves even more. You watch the news and see what's going on, you mightn't agree with it, I just look at it – you get annoyed [and think] I couldn't let them away with that and then after a while you don't worry about it because you know, it's not the end of the road.

INTERVIEWER: You can't change it, no?

HELEN: You can't change it – it's all foretold. This is prophecy being fulfilled.

On one level this shows the impact of politics on people's private lives. The political situation has changed so drastically that some conservative Protestant evangelicals have given up hope. They feel powerless to change their situation. On the other hand we see individuals coming up with creative responses to change. Their lack of political activity is a highly rational adjustment to the post-1998 context where an evangelical political position is unlikely to be successful. The DUP are now in the Northern Ireland Executive and Assembly, with Peter Robinson holding the post of First Minister. But this has not been without serious compromises on the DUP's part and their entry to power hardly signifies the evangelical utopia that many had wished for (Ganiel 2008a). Many evangelicals are devastated that the DUP now work side by side with Sinn Féin, seeing this as an 'immoral' compromise with 'terrorists' that the Lord will surely judge. In another arena, the DUP is required to uphold European and British law relating to the rights of same-sex couples – which many find difficult to stomach. It is not yet clear whether the emergence of the ultra-unionist and religiously conservative Traditional Unionist Voice under Jim Allister might re-inspire this section of evangelicalism (Ganiel 2009c). In the early to mid 2000s, however, the perception was that the battle to save Ulster had been lost on a multitude of fronts. This pushed some people's religious beliefs in an ever more apocalyptic direction.

Take Helen, for whom the second coming of Christ is an all-encompassing belief. Her response, to withdraw from politics, is not matched by a withdrawal from arenas of life other than evangelism. Helen is a keen home decorator, and although she says that now if she is doing anything in the house she will 'hurry up and get something picked' before Armageddon, she continues to be enthused by home improvements, saying she is 'absolutely mad into it'. Whilst we should not make more of this comment than was intended, it is interesting that Helen continues to improve those temporal things around her that she has control over, such as her home, and does not attempt to change things in areas of life where she feels powerless, such as Northern Ireland politics.

If we have paid a lot of attention to politics in this chapter, it is because many of our interviewees also chose to dwell on political issues. Again, this is not unusual in Northern Ireland, where evangelicalism and unionist politics have historically been so intertwined. Whilst we did ask for people's views about politics in each interview, in practically all cases people on a deepening journey raised political issues themselves when talking about their religious journeys. Of course this heightened relationship must be seen in the light of political violence and the peace process in Northern Ireland – both of which represented dramatic moments of political change that deeply impacted on individuals' sense of well being and security. However, simply because these processes are rendered more obvious in times of political crisis does not necessarily mean that they are insignificant in times of relative political calm. All modern societies have political tensions relating to race, class and security, and in some cases religious tensions per se, that may catalyse these types of religious feelings. Given the current rise of conservative forms of religion in many modern societies, we believe this is an important aspect of personal religious change that has not received much attention from either academics or journalists.

Conclusions

The people whose stories we explored in this chapter described their faith as deepening in a conservative direction. Some had been raised as evangelicals, and had experienced personal conversions as children or as adults. Some did not have an evangelical background, but became saved in later life and felt that their journey was characterised by a strengthening of faith. Some people in this chapter had backslidden, or fallen away from the faith, for a period of time, but had returned and become stronger than ever.

There seemed to be three complementary groups of factors that pushed and pulled our participants in conservative directions. People shared similar views and experiences of social contact, the spiritual dimensions of life, and political analysis. These factors seemed to work in combination with one another, to varying degrees for different individuals. Firstly, most people in this chapter highlighted the regulation of social networks and immersion in religious life as playing a vital role in buffering their beliefs. This emerged as both the cause and effect of a deepening faith. It echoes earlier research findings that the stronger one's beliefs, the more one needs confirmation and support from social groups who believe the same thing as oneself (Baston, Shroenrade and Ventis 1993, Festinger, Riecken and Schachter 1956). In this sense the importance of social contact would seem to support theories within social psychology about the importance of social influence. But what is most interesting about conservative evangelicals' regulation of social contact is the way that they talk about it as a thought-out strategy, as something that they *choose* to do, fully self-conscious that the likely effect will be to protect and deepen their faith. This points, therefore, both to the role of relevant others in shaping beliefs, as well as to the role that individuals play in choosing whom to use as reference points. It is an example of how social influences intersect with individual choice to produce personal religious change.

Secondly, people had similar ways of conceptualising the power of God vis-à-vis the power of humans. They spoke about God as an all-powerful figure who controlled all aspects of life. Indeed, participants whose faith became more conservative often described a process of allowing God to take control of their lives. Although they are often attributing agency to supernatural forces, we see in their stories how they have themselves *decided* to cede control over their own lives to God. This is an interesting example of individual agency – at once a deliberate choice and an abandonment of control. Sometimes, people's faith deepened in response to personal problems, and attributing control to God helped to relieve the pressure on them, echoing the literature on religion and mental well-being (Dillon and Wink 2007, Smith, McCullough and Poll 2003, Kraft, Litwin and Barber 1987).

Finally, the impact of political change on personal religious identity was significant. All of these participants were DUP voters and share, to a greater or lesser degree, the view that political change in Northern Ireland is harmful for Protestants and evangelicals. This political disillusionment has strengthened their religious identity. This involves an increased focus on religious belief as well as a tendency to withdraw from the political sphere. Some focus on the belief that, due to unfavourable political circumstances, the 'end times' are drawing near and saving souls is now more important than trying to change earthly society. This chapter therefore shows how inner religious changes are profoundly influenced by external social and political developments. As we see in subsequent chapters, other evangelicals responded to the same political events in very different ways – some opening up their religious ideas and becoming interested in reconciliation. But in these cases, there were very different *combinations* of factors and experiences at work in individuals' lives. For people whose faith was deepening, processes of closing down non-evangelical social interactions, handing one's agency over to God and interpreting political change in a negative way worked together to push their faith in a deeply conservative direction.

CHAPTER SIX

Maintaining a Steady Faith

The evangelicals featured in this chapter, about one fifth of those we spoke with, say their faith is steady and has not changed very much over time.[1] Their religious beliefs and practices as adults in mid or later life closely resembled their beliefs and practices as teenagers and as young adults. Rather than exclude this group because they did not experience significant change, we felt it was important to explore *how* people maintained their faith in a fairly consistent way. Whilst on the surface it may seem that we might have little to say about this as a religious *journey*, once we unpick people's stories, we find a range of ingenious strategies that they use to maintain their faith. In fact, people whose faith is relatively stable over time think and behave just as creatively as people on more dramatic journeys. We do not agree with Iannaconne's (1990) characterisation of the inertia of religious choices. Maintaining a steady religious journey is also a choice. Accordingly, we explore a whole range of religious choices and changes that usually take place below the radar.

People on a steady religious journey highlighted a number of different ways in which they had maintained their beliefs. All mentioned going through a period of finding out about faith for themselves, rather than simply accepting what they had been taught without question. For one person, this meant subjecting his faith to extreme scrutiny by studying religion from the perspective of social science. Most others preferred to protect their faith from intellectual challenge, for example by not studying certain subjects at university or only reading books that confirmed their faith. Others simply chose not to dwell upon any difficult questions that arose. In this way, many people who described a steady religious journey resembled Jordan and Ganiel's *pietistic* evangelicals, for whom faith was personal and devotional, rather than being overly focused on doctrine.

We also find cases where people have maintained a steady faith through very difficult personal circumstances, some of which relate to the conflict in

Northern Ireland. As with pietistic evangelicals, most people who described a steady religious journey did not tend to be overly politicised. Talk about the conflict arose insofar as it had impacted on people's personal lives, which is very different from the all-encompassing political analysis of some of those on a deepening religious journey. One person who described a steady journey was a charismatic evangelical, who also tended to focus on personal experience rather than doctrine. And a small handful of others could be described in Jordan's (2001) terms as oppositional evangelicals, with overtones of Brewer and Higgins's (1998) Pharisaic anti-Catholic views.

Overall, we conclude that steadily holding onto your faith is just as much hard work as changing or leaving it. People have to *choose* to stay in the same religious place, and to do so they devise creative ways of protecting their faith.

Stories of stability: A 'slow and steady' journey

Jim describes himself as a 'middle of the road evangelical'. A shopkeeper in his fifties, he comes from a medium-sized town, grew up in the Church of Ireland and attended a Brethren Sunday school as a child. Although he had a wide circle of friends at school Jim says he kept out of trouble, did not drink much alcohol and tried to 'live a good life'. Whilst Jim felt 'convicted' throughout his childhood, it was not until he was in his twenties, when his son developed a serious illness, that he eventually experienced religious conversion. In hospital, he met the elder of a local church, who told him that God was calling him. Jim began to study the Bible and soon made a commitment. He describes his journey ever since as 'slow and steady' and says that he is a 'run of the mill Christian'. Jim says he has never experienced any doubts about his faith, and never felt he was in any danger of losing his faith. He says 'it's all to do with surrendering'. Before he became saved, Jim was an active member of the Orange Order and the Royal Black Preceptory. But, unlike those in the previous chapter for whom religion and politics went hand in hand, Jim left these organisations when he became a Christian. His 'whole life became the church'.

Douglas's story provides another typical example. A pastor of a small church, he is in his sixties and describes himself as a conservative evangelical. Douglas became born-again when he was twelve and has had a 'personal walk with the Lord' ever since. His parents were born-again and they attended church regularly. Douglas says although he accepted what he was taught about evangelical religion in Sunday school and children's meetings, he did ask his own questions. At one point he came across a book called *Remarkable Answers to Prayer* which encouraged readers to 'put God to the test'. Douglas said after doing this that he definitely felt that God had answered his prayers. Other than these early questions Douglas says 'I never ever doubted God and was never involved in what people refer to as worldly things.' After school Douglas worked on a farm and enjoyed his quiet times, speaking with God in the fields, and reading the Scriptures. Later, he spent some time abroad as a missionary before returning to Northern Ireland to be the pastor of his conservative evangelical church. Douglas identifies a number of important moments in his religious biography, such as his conversion and his decision to be a missionary, but none of these resulted in any significant personal changes in religious beliefs or practices.

Some people who became saved later in life talk about their religious journey in terms similar to ageing. They say that at the time of conversion they were like babies. Many people are actually children when they become converted (see chapter 4), but adults use this terminology to talk about their spiritual growth over time. Mervyn says that when he was saved, it was a 'new birth', he was 'like a new child' that 'had to learn to walk and talk'. Hannah says that at the beginning of her life as a young Christian she was 'only given the milk of God's word', but that over time, she has grown into a strong and steady faith. Growing out of spiritual babyhood is an interesting way to think about the small-scale changes that characterise a steady religious journey. There are no dramatic moments of religious crisis nor change, instead a slow, almost imperceptible, process of religious growth over time.

Finding out for yourself: 'You have to know why you believe it'

Most of the people we spoke to were raised in evangelical homes, and as a result our study contains numerous stories of childhood conversions. This results in people feeling as if they have *always* been evangelical, and whilst people may identify significant moments in their religious journeys, these moments do not mark a change in ideas or practices.

Connie, a teacher in her forties, says evangelicalism 'is all I have ever known'. She was brought up in the Free Presbyterian Church and became saved at age ten while at a children's meeting at a gospel hall. Her story is one of religious consistency over her adult life, after a deepening of faith in her teenage years. In contrast to those adults who experienced religious conversion, whose stories we explored in chapter 4, Connie describes a situation not of changing her beliefs but instead '[finding] out *why* you believe it'. She says that when you are young, 'you probably believe certain things because that's what everybody in the house believes. But there comes a point when you have to know why you believe it.' She describes how the debate about evolution flared up when she was at school, and says that whilst this never caused her to doubt her faith, she needed to find answers. Like Douglas, Connie was trying to find out about her childhood faith for herself. She did not want to follow any other path, but she had to go through a process of asking questions and finding answers that made sense to her. Douglas and Connie probably received the answers they expected, answers that confirmed rather than challenged their faith. Even so, they show us how as children they tried with the resources at hand to explore their faith for themselves. This shows a level of enquiry not always associated with children from religious families who 'choose' to become saved.

Connie also points out that becoming saved at such a young age did not really make a dramatic change in her life. She compares herself to people who have had dramatic conversions after having a 'wild life', and postulates that in her case 'probably outwardly nobody [could] see a change'. However, even though there was no great alteration of beliefs or practices, Connie is keen to point out that this does not 'lessen the effect of the miracle that was done', because she was just as much a sinner as anybody else. So, although our characterisation of the individuals in this chapter is a journey of stability, this is not to downplay the moments of religious change that are significant to them, even if these are less dramatic than they are than for others.

Sandra, in her late twenties, also talks about a process of finding out about faith for herself. Sandra is a newly qualified doctor and, after moving away for university, now lives in the medium-sized town where she grew up. She says that as a child she attended church multiple times a week, and knew what the Christian faith was all about. In her words, 'I'd heard all the theory but as I've grown older I think that I claimed faith for myself. It's not that my faith has changed or my ideas have changed, it's just that I've claimed it for myself.'

Like Connie, Sandra went through a process of asking questions about her faith, particularly around the time she did a Religion 'A level' course in school. Initially, dissecting the Bible like an ordinary piece of literature, Sandra says she felt confused, as she had always assumed that the Bible was simply true. She began to wonder how parts of the Bible such as Daniel and Revelation can be taken literally and, if they are not literal, what about the other parts? Sandra goes on to say 'I can't answer those questions. I was confused by the "A" level and I still don't know the answers.' To an extent Sandra resolves this tension by concluding that 'there are things that we will never understand while we are here, we were just never meant to. But some day we will understand it all.' She chooses simply to leave these questions unanswered, and overall her story focuses on how faith gives her great comfort and happiness. This is an interesting example of how some people are content to live with grey areas in their faith. Certain questions and doubts can be shelved, allowing them to focus on the things that can be understood. This echoes Jay, a lifelong American Presbyterian on a steady religious journey, interviewed by Dillon and Wink (2007: 98), who says, 'I don't have to understand it, totally, to believe it . . . I accept it more or less on blind faith because it's not worth it for me to spend that much time [worrying about it].'

Amongst those with a steady faith, Daniel subjected his faith to the most intense period of questioning. A full-time church worker in his fifties, he describes himself as an evangelical who is conservative about 'the basics'. Unlike Paul (see below), Daniel did not shy away from studying subjects at university that would challenge his beliefs. Quite the opposite. He studied sociology, and took a course on the sociology of religion. The course was taught by a Marxist professor, and Daniel says,

> I found my world being taken apart in a very articulate kind of way and also discovered that so much of what I had taken for granted and as read was actually part of a whole subculture that could still be seen as part of one subculture among many, as opposed to actually any great bastion of God's truth in the world.

Taking the course was a difficult experience for Daniel, who says 'at that stage I didn't really know who I was and what I believed, and it was making you face all the stuff, like do you believe this because you've believed it or do you believe it because it is true?' When attending his Baptist church during this period, Daniel describes looking at the services through the eyes of his classmates. He says the Sunday service provided a 'classic illustration of everything that we were talking about in our sociology text books'. Moreover, Daniel had always felt a calling to full-time Christian work, and doing the course made him question his assumptions about his future.

But rather than cause Daniel to abandon his religion, intellectually scrutinising his faith helped him achieve 'clarity'. He concludes that the course was 'a profound experience and probably was spiritual for me'. Daniel describes how he resolved his new-found questions like this:

> I felt that so much of my life and church life and experience is part of my subculture and actually the tools of sociology are very useful in understanding how it works, and I need to take that on board. I mean that's good working knowledge – that actually tells me a lot. But it doesn't help me unpack the key issue, of what I believe about who Jesus Christ is, so that's basically how it resolved and gave me a much clearer, sharper focus on what I actually believe as a Christian.

So Daniel felt that the sociology of religion did not address one central question – *who Jesus is*. As he pondered over the evangelical beliefs of his childhood, he says the person of Jesus stood out to him, and this became a 'core issue'. The course helped him to 'strip down to the basics of what I actually believe'. Daniel came to see that the things he learned on the course were useful and that he could apply them to his own life going forward, but that the sociology of religion was inadequate when it came to answering deeper theological questions. In fact Daniel later went to Bible College to study theology, to search for the answers he needed. Having put his faith through the crucible at this early stage, Daniel says that afterwards his journey was 'straightforward' and that 'what is important to me about being a Christian didn't really change' after that.

The stories of Connie, Sandra and Daniel help us understand how people who have been raised as evangelicals develop their own faith. They do not unthinkingly accept the beliefs that they were raised with, but try, to different degrees, to make up their own minds about what they believe. Daniel took this process much further than most, by directly engaging with ideas that challenged the bedrock of his faith. Whilst some of the people in later chapters radically changed or abandoned their faith when confronted with intellectual challenges, Daniel experienced more clarity. He incorporated elements of his studies into his analysis of his own evangelical subculture, but ultimately concluded that social science had little to offer him on the 'core issues' of faith. He then studied theology to find these answers. Sandra has not been able to resolve her questions so satisfactorily, but she is happy to live with an element of uncertainty about key theological questions, because her faith is otherwise a source of comfort and joy. Connie says she had no doubts, but asked questions anyway, to confirm that what she believed was true. But whilst the level of questioning differs, we see here a common process of finding out for oneself. Although people's faith stays relatively steady on the surface, behind the scenes people are actually working hard to achieve stability.

Protecting your faith from harmful ideas: 'University can be a dangerous place'

The people above tested their faith against *outside* criticisms. However, others choose to verify their faith from *within*. Examples of this are where people read evangelical literature that confirms their religious position, rather than trying to answer the questions posed by secular or liberal Christian literature. Henry, a rural businessman in his fifties, spent hours showing us his extensive array of religious books and pamphlets. He had bookshelves in every room of the house that contained many well-thumbed volumes. Many of these were extremely anti-Catholic, including works by the Chick publications founder, Avro Manhattan, whose work on the evils of Catholicism is well known. There was even a book by Einstein on the ills of the Catholic Church alongside works produced by religiously conservative evangelicals. Many small tracts were in the collection, some of which were left on the interviewer's bed at night for discussion at breakfast the next morning.

Henry says that his religious beliefs have not changed much over time. Despite some 'disappointments and losses' and a period of 'backsliding' in his twenties, Henry's story is another journey of relative religious stability. Henry relates nearly every event in his life through a religious lens, and accompanies each story with a reading from the Bible. It seems Henry has developed an almost encyclopaedic knowledge of Scripture and conservative evangelical literature. But all of this literature is of a similar nature, and all serves the purpose of confirming his faith and justifying a conservative evangelical position. No books on the shelves provided a counter-argument and Henry gave no indication that he had ever explored alternative challenges. Study, then, can play an important role in maintaining faith, just as it can in provoking religious changes (as we see in chapters 7, 8 and 9), depending on the type of reading one decides to pursue.

The strategy of buffering one's faith by shutting out influences that one knows will be challenging appears to be effective in helping some individuals maintain their faith. Many of our participants adopted these strategies, fully conscious of their likely effects. It is as if they decided that they were happy with their current religious position and did not wish to expose themselves to any unsettling influences. This is yet another example of the active role of individual agency in shaping religious choices. Even where the choice is to retain the status quo, this is often an intentional choice.

An example of this is provided by Colin, a conservative evangelical in his early twenties, when he talks about his strategies for surviving university. We saw in chapter 4 how the regulation of social networks is an important way in which religious individuals protect their faith in university. But Colin also articulates a keen awareness that some academic disciplines may pose a greater intellectual challenge to religion than others and, as a result, has avoided these disciplines. He believes that how a young Christian's faith fares at university has a lot to do with the subjects they study. He says that 'university can be a dangerous place if you're a Christian', and in particular, that subjects like philosophy can 'mess with your whole beliefs'. He goes on to say,

> You are taught to think in university and investigate and look at things from a different point of view and what you have to be careful not to do is transfer that onto your Christian beliefs [. . .] because you are constantly taught to question and you could start doubting it.

Colin continues, saying that 'you have to be careful not to be caught up in it, let it overtake you, you have to try to control it'. He says that even the way theology is taught can promote this kind of harmful questioning. Having attended universities in Northern Ireland and England, and recently graduated, Colin has had to utilise this strategy of not transferring questions from his academic life onto his faith life. And of course Colin is correct in his analysis, as we see from Daniel's story above. Daniel's faith did survive intellectual scrutiny at university, but not without a period of deep uncertainty.

Indeed, plenty of the conservative evangelicals we spoke to had attended university. Evangelicals have a slightly higher level of education than non-evangelical Protestants in Northern Ireland (Mitchell and Tilley 2008). So we are certainly not arguing that people who maintain traditional evangelical beliefs do not engage with ideas, or are unable to think for themselves. In contrast, Colin's story shows us that maintaining one's faith in university is a very active process. It does not just happen accidentally but, rather, people carefully select their friendship groups and actively buffer religious beliefs from outside challenge. This compartmentalisation is done in a very self-conscious way, and Colin for one is fully aware that this strategy will help to keep his faith strong.

Culturally updating your faith: 'I must not smoke nor drink nor chew, I must not stand in a cinema queue'

Some people said their faith was essentially unchanging over time, but described how they had changed their attitudes on what they considered peripheral issues. For example, fifty years ago, evangelical teachings about lifestyle were extremely strict, as exemplified in the adage my (Claire) grandmother taught my father, 'I must not smoke, nor drink, nor chew [gum]. I must not stand in a cinema queue.' At the beginning of the twenty-first century, it seems that things are changing. Jason, for example, says he has retained 'the basics' but has liberalised his views on whether women should wear trousers and whether Christians can consume alcohol. Alexander continues to identify as a 'traditional evangelical', but he now allows his children not only to work in a cinema, but to work on Sundays as well. In fact, a large group of people, including those whose faith was deepening as well as those with a steady religious journey, talked about how they culturally updated their faith. They held fast to what they considered important issues, such as an opposition to homosexuality, abortion and divorce. But they compromised on things like working on the Sabbath, watching television and films, or having an occasional alcoholic drink.

Daniel says that his way of being a conservative evangelical is 'very radically different' from that of his parents. He says,

> Everything about it is probably different. I remember the first Sunday I wore a blue shirt to church, oh wow, they made me take it off. So our model was you dressed a certain way to go to church, and that was always a white shirt under a suit and that would have been taken as part of what mattered. Now the Church I go to has no dress code, people could come as they come and that's up to them [. . .] Alcohol is another issue, cinema going is another issue, all of those kind of things. They are just not issues any more so yes it is very radically different.

This is a highly rational strategy for people who want to maintain their faith. It underlines Christian Smith's (1998) research, which finds that American evangelicals have managed to update their faith in relation to the changing world around them, so that they can be culturally relevant. In other words, evangelicals are able, slowly and over time, to adapt the social and moral issues that define them in order to engage effectively with the current debates and to prevent them from becoming truly countercultural. In such a way we can see how young evangelicals appropriate some forms of popular culture such as music and fashion, whilst adapting these to fit their own needs. They are able to 'fit in' to an extent with the rest of society while retaining a distinctive religious view of the world.

Again here we see how people who experience a relatively steady religious journey over time make small adaptations to their religious beliefs, in line with cultural change. This echoes Atchley's (1999) emphasis on people's capacity for religious adaptation. Atchley argues that many adults develop fairly stable patterns of thought that allow them to accommodate quite a lot of changes in circumstance and experience without having a crisis or radical change in religious beliefs. However, religious stability does not mean that people remain exactly the same over a lifetime. Rather they quietly review, update and revise their beliefs, and this actually helps them to retain a strong faith.

Drawing on faith in times of trouble: I am weak but He is strong

In the previous and in subsequent chapters, we encounter a number of people whose experiences of the political conflict in Northern Ireland have led to dramatic changes in their religious journeys. Amanda's story is different. Of all our respondents, Amanda's life was one of the most affected by violent conflict. But throughout all her troubles, her faith has remained steady. Brought up on a run-down Protestant housing estate, a teenage Amanda fell in love with a Catholic boy she met on holiday. Against all the odds, their relationship continued and they were married some years later. Although the area Amanda was raised in was staunchly Protestant, the couple decided to move back there in the early 1970s because social housing was readily available. Obviously, being married to a Catholic, life was by no means easy on the estate. Their lives were threatened many times, their house was continually attacked and they were eventually 'put out' of their house by paramilitaries. When she became a community worker in the area, Amanda's children were targeted by paramilitaries, and posters and graffiti accusing her of being a traitor were plastered around the estate. On top of this, a close family member of Amanda's was arrested, accused – falsely she says – of paramilitary activities, and jailed. This was devastating for Amanda and her family. On the day her relative was released from jail, Amanda's father was diagnosed with a terminal illness and died soon afterwards.

Amanda was not attending church regularly after she was married. But after her family member became a born-again Christian in jail, Amanda found herself increasingly drawn to faith and followed suit. Her husband became a

Christian some years later, and after attending separate Catholic and Protestant churches for a while, they found a charismatic church where they could worship together. While Amanda's story of her personal life is full of trials and heartache, the story of her religious journey since her conversion is one of stability. Although she has experienced times of doubt – for example on the day her father was diagnosed she says she felt 'so angry with God' – Amanda nonetheless trusts that God knows what he is doing. She says,

> Ultimately I just have to believe that even things that don't make any sense to me make sense to God, and ultimately God does know what's better, better than I do. So even if life doesn't make any sense or when life is really hard and difficult I still can't imagine what it would be like to live without God.

Similarly, the morning she discovered the poster campaign against her, Amanda says,

> I remember sitting in my house saying God I have never felt so frightened in my entire life [. . .] and I remember hearing God saying to me, I remember actually distinct, I said, God I've never felt so weak ever in my life, and God saying that's all right, because I'm strong.

Not only does Amanda trust that God is looking after her life, she also has been empowered by her faith. Throughout her struggles, the Bible verse she has drawn upon is 'I can do all things through Christ who strengthens me.' She says that to live and engage in community work on the estate is her 'calling' from God. Moreover,

> When God calls you to a place and you know very clearly that it is God, it makes all the difficult times make sense. Or it makes all the difficult times copeable because you think that this is where God called me to be, and if God wants me to do this job then he'll give me whatever I need to be able to do it.

Amanda's story helps us to understand how people maintain their faith in times of trouble. Rather than questioning why God would allow her to have these difficult experiences, Amanda believes that God has chosen her to do his work on her estate, and if God has planned this, he will look after her. Although Amanda herself must deal with life on the estate, she believes that God is working through her. By putting her faith in God's strength, Amanda feels she has the ability to overcome any troubles that come her way. This helps explain why Amanda's faith is not shaken when bad things happen. It echoes Wink and Helson's (1997) work, which also finds people turning personal adversity into an opportunity for spiritual growth. In Dillon and Wink's words, spiritual growth can be boosted by 'emotional pain and the ability to positively learn from and integrate that pain' (1997: 131).

Before moving on from Amanda's story, it is also interesting to note that she, like others we meet in subsequent chapters, is angry with the churches in Northern Ireland. Primarily Amanda is angry because she feels the churches ignore working-class communities. Unlike many others, Amanda has not decided to leave the church, but to work to change it from within. Amanda's feelings are strong – she says she feels 'very let down by the church', and that the churches' lack of social action is 'one of [her] biggest frustrations', and that she 'couldn't even begin to tell you how angry it makes me' that Christians are not more socially aware. She says the churches 'don't want to know kids that are out there smoking dope, thirteen-year-old girls that are pregnant. The Christian church isn't interested in them at all.' Whilst other people we spoke with share this sentiment, Amanda stands out for her ability to maintain a strong personal faith despite her anger. This shows how different people process similar frustrations in different ways. Amanda's overarching trust in the power of God helps her work to change the church, whereas others who come to doubt God as well as the church may radically alter or abandon their faith altogether.

Highs and lows: 'I've been up and down to be honest with you'

Some people we talked to said that they had never experienced any doubts about their faith. We do not know whether these people really *never* experienced doubts, or if they simply could not remember any doubts, or if they did not wish to talk about them. Henry, for example, mentions a period of backsliding in his twenties but refuses to go into detail, glossing over this chapter of his life as insignificant. Others, whose journeys were characterised by relatively unchanging religious belief, do talk in more detail about moments of doubt. But interestingly, people talked about doubting *themselves* rather than doubting God. In other words, they questioned how far they were able to live up to the standard set by the Bible, rather than questioning if the Bible itself was true.

Jason's story captures the ebb and flow of self-doubt. Jason is a chemist in his early thirties, a Baptist from a rural area. He begins the interview by saying,

> I have to confess something, I'm not, I'm not a perfect example of somebody living the life, following his faith. I think this week I realise again that I could do better, you know, make more effort.

Throughout the interview, Jason talks about trying to be more Christ-like. He scrutinises his own behaviour, evaluating how far he is living up to the standards he believes evangelicals should live by. In his dealings with other people, he agonises about whether he should have spoken or acted differently. He asks if he could have put 'love thy neighbour' into practice more often. He admits that sometimes he misses church because of his obsession with mountain biking. Although someone from the outside could look in at Jason's life and see all the hallmarks of a devout evangelical – well versed in the Scriptures, sings gospel music in church, is a teetotaller – Jason is harder on himself. He is frank about the highs and lows in his religious journey. In his words,

> I've been up and down to be honest with you. Sometimes you're more active and conscious of God and more wanting to follow God; sometimes you're not really and you're sort of dormant and then something comes along and you're up again, you know. It can seem like being on a rollercoaster.

In the final analysis, Jason, like Amanda, finds great comfort in his faith. Prone to worry, Jason says that when looking for jobs, he feels reassured when he remembers that everything is in God's hands. He says,

> Maybe I could have got through without God, people do in a way – you see them walking the streets. But I wouldn't have liked to have gone through without God, you know, I wouldn't. It is a big bonus now to have faith in God at times like this. It's good to know somebody's there basically.

When Jason is having a religious low he reads the Bible and finds reassurance in its words. Although his commitment level may ebb, Jason says the fundamental messages of faith are always at the back of his mind. He never questions the fact that evangelicalism is the right path for him.

Hugh is less prone to agonising over his faith than Jason. He also has much less pronounced highs and lows. But Hugh also talks about the role that self-doubt plays in an otherwise steady faith journey. Hugh is the Elim Pentecostal pastor whose conversion we discussed in chapter 4. Reflecting on how his faith has developed over time he says,

> The idea of something that fundamentally crashes in on your faith and raises questions, I suppose, about the whole foundation of your faith, I couldn't honestly say that that has ever happened. I would say that there are times when you go through periods of self-doubt about the genuineness of your own experience. But that's something that should be there in every Christian because the Bible tells us to examine ourselves, the Bible tells us that that should be present.

Hugh says, for example, that when he hears a particularly gifted preacher talking about holiness or sin, this causes him to evaluate his own progress. He wonders whether there are areas of his life in which he could be serving God better. But for Hugh, it is 'a healthy thing to examine your faith', and the 'periods of self-doubt' do not cause him to redefine or change his beliefs. Like Jason, Hugh never doubts that evangelicalism is true; rather it is his own performance that he occasionally doubts.

Jason and Hugh's stories show how even ostensibly steady journeys are prone to highs and lows, times when people feel they are doing better at their faith than others. This demonstrates how people who appear on the surface to have an unchanging faith actually work quite hard to maintain it. Jason and Hugh never question the fundamental tenets of faith, but rather their ability to live up to the evangelical ideal. This is what distinguishes Jason's 'rollercoaster' of self-doubt from the more radical doubts about God experienced by the transformers and leavers in chapters 8 and 9. Unlike those on a steady journey, they question the whole foundation of faith, not just their ability to live up to the evangelical standard.

Conclusions

Having a steady religious journey does not mean that a person experiences absolutely no religious flux over the course of a lifetime. Whilst some people said they have never had any doubts, many others have had highs and lows. They have run into questions about their faith that are difficult to answer. But what is common to the people we have met in this chapter is their ability to get themselves back onto a steady religious trajectory. Moreover, the core tenets of their belief do not change much over time. They may need to ask questions and test out their faith for themselves, but they rarely doubt that their faith is true, or that evangelicalism is the right path for them. Doctrinal detail, for those on a steady journey, is rarely a priority. They may culturally update their faith over time, but their central evangelical beliefs do not change.

People that have a steady religious journey engage in a number of strategies to maintain their faith. One is to compartmentalise questions about their faith. For some this involves shelving difficult questions and choosing to focus instead on what is positive and tangible. Others try to ring-fence their faith from outside challenge, avoiding books and learning that might contradict evangelicalism. This does not apply to all on a steady journey, however, some of whom have intensely scrutinised their faith. When confronted with the counter-arguments, they also chose to compartmentalise the criticism, on the basis that it was interesting but did not have any bearing on the mystery of faith. What is common then, is that they *know* that evangelicalism is not the only way of looking at the world, they *know* that scientific and philosophical critiques of their faith exist, but they *choose* to bracket off these critiques to protect their faith. People must *work* to maintain a steady religious identity, and they respond creatively to life's experiences in order to regulate challenge and nurture stability. This gives us further insight into how individual agency shapes religious decision making. Although people on a steady religious journey might on one level appear to adopt the kind of evangelicalism they have been born into, this belies the important identity work that they continually carry out in order to protect and maintain that religious identity.

Indeed, there are many reasons why people would want to have a steady religious identity. Evangelicalism brings many of our interviewees comfort and happiness. While we meet people in later chapters who have felt angry and let down by evangelicalism, this is simply not the experience of those on a stable religious trajectory. Instead, people who steadily maintained the faith of their childhood or early adulthood focused on God's love, feeling secure, the warmth of religious community, and the inspiration of the life of Jesus. Their stories show how faith provides a well of strength in times of trouble, and offers reassurance that people are not on their own – their problems are in God's hands. All of those on a steady journey we spoke with talked about these positive aspects of faith. In this sense, protecting and nurturing that faith is a highly rational strategy.

CHAPTER SEVEN

Moderating Evangelicalism

The people whose stories we tell in this chapter described themselves as 'liberal evangelicals', 'progressive evangelicals' or 'followers of Jesus', whilst some preferred simply the term 'Christian'. Some said that they are 'charismatic evangelicals', while others said that they are uncomfortable with the term evangelical, especially in Northern Ireland, as the word is so heavily associated with Paisley. Many of the people interviewed for this chapter could be categorised as Jordan's *inclusivist* evangelicals, or as Ganiel's *mediating* evangelicals. Many were frustrated with their churches, but most remained members of congregations and continued to attend church. All had experienced a moderation of their faith, even as they maintained focus on the teachings of Jesus and held to the idea that the Bible was the inspired word of God. People on a moderating journey commonly emphasised religiously inspired conceptions of social justice, peace and reconciliation. This had led many of them not only away from their conservative evangelical upbringings, but also away from strong forms of unionism, loyalism and Orange Order politics. In fact, a significant minority of people on a moderating journey had come to see themselves as Irish. This is highly unusual, as just two per cent of Protestants in Northern Ireland identify themselves as Irish (Northern Ireland Life and Times Survey 2003). Jordan's (2001: 172) research hints that a significant number of that two per cent may be evangelical, highlighting a growing tendency among younger evangelicals to identify as Irish, even nationalist. As explained in chapter 3, we talked with 34 people on moderating journeys, making them overrepresented in our research.[1]

People on moderating journeys explained the changes that they had experienced through stories of developing real friendships with Catholics, engaging in an intense internal evangelical dialogue about what it means to be a Christian in Northern Ireland, and finding meaning in social and political activism. Some talked about how their faith had changed by interacting with popular culture through books and music, living abroad, and communing with

God in their everyday lives. These factors overlapped and reinforced each other, interacting in different ways in the stories of different people.

Crossing the divide: 'Accepting my Catholic friends as fellow pilgrims'

'Some of my best friends are Catholics',[2] has become one of the superficial truisms of life in Northern Ireland. We found that many evangelicals on a moderating journey had progressed beyond this and established deep relationships with, and genuinely positive attitudes about, Catholics. Rather than holding on to the strong religious unionism with which they were raised, and seeing Catholics as hell-bound sinners, their faith has become more open and inclusive. This change generally came about when evangelicals had the opportunity to interact with Catholics beyond the short and polite encounters that define most Catholic–Protestant relationships in Northern Ireland. Sometimes this was at work or in their social lives. In other cases, evangelicals met Catholics through ecumenical events or through the charismatic movement. Catholics were sometimes part of the extended family circle as a result of mixed marriages. So people on moderating journeys began to see that, rather than being the enemy, Catholics were actually 'fellow pilgrims'.

This is what happened for Timothy, a Presbyterian in his fifties who had what he calls a quiet conversion experience at the age of 21. He said that in the past he identified with the religiously conservative elements of evangelicalism, but that his faith had moderated over time. In his words,

> When I look back then to those early evangelical days in my early twenties and where I am today, I'm not worshipping the same God – or at least I'm not worshipping the same vision of God. How I've understood God has changed. God is still God, but I'm viewing God from different perspectives and just understanding how big and non-denominational and inclusive that God is.

Timothy goes on to say he is 'very thankful for all the people who have helped' him on this religious journey, especially Catholics. As an adult, Timothy's first meaningful interaction with Catholics was when he worked in the shipyard in Belfast. He says he seemed to naturally gravitate towards his Catholic workmates:

> My first job was in the shipyard here in Belfast. And I really found myself, just as an ordinary human, gravitating towards men who were marginalised by

others. So I found myself having my lunch almost every day with a Catholic guy who was one of the few Catholics that worked in the place. Our bonding was actually over liking football, eating sandwiches together.

When he left the shipyard, Timothy became involved in conflict mediation work. This took him to the prisons in Northern Ireland, meeting with both republican Irish Republican Army (IRA) and loyalist Ulster Defence Association (UDA)/Ulster Volunteer Force (UVF) prisoners. But rather than simply go into the prisons to preach *at* paramilitary inmates, Timothy describes how he gradually built up relationships with them, and how this challenged his stereotypes of both Catholics and republicans. Timothy had already been travelling in a moderate religious direction to have become involved in this kind of mediation work. Many within the evangelical subculture would not have gone anywhere near prisons and would have viewed interaction with 'terrorists' as compromising with 'sin' or 'evil'. But when Timothy started to build relationships, his own religious ideas began to change even further. He says 'I met Jesus in those prison cells in a way that I was not able to do in my church.' In his words,

> Those guys in the Maze, particularly the Provos, and their small group discussions around faith and politics and violence. They turned out their best. They led me into the cell which was designated a kind of living room, which was really nicely furnished. They had the best of biscuits. And that was the way they showed hospitality and they opened their lives and talked intimately to me about people they missed and children they had and all of that. And when the last of the big gates raised behind me on those nights . . . there were 13 doors you had to go through to get out or in, and the last one slammed behind you and I knew I had met Jesus in there.

Timothy's story highlights how meaningful relationships with the traditional enemy, not just Catholics but IRA prisoners, made his religious beliefs more inclusive and led to what he sees as a moderation of his faith. This journey started with a small connection, sharing lunch and talking about football with a Catholic workmate. Later Timothy connected with Catholics on a spiritual level, describing his meetings with republican prisoners as akin to meeting Jesus. The hospitality shown by IRA inmates also challenged stereotypes of a hostile enemy. This echoes life-cycle research which finds that cumulative life experiences, such as Timothy's, can lead to faith becoming more contemplative in later years. When the complex reality of people's experiences does not match initial, inflexible beliefs, those beliefs are often revised and softened (Fowler 1981, Tornstam 2005, Dillon and Wink 2007).

But what might have prompted Timothy to develop deeper relationships with Catholics, where many of his evangelical counterparts would never have considered sitting down to lunch with a Catholic workmate, never mind talking to IRA prisoners? Part of the answer is found in Timothy's family background. Although Timothy became converted into a fairly traditional form of evangelicalism at 21, one of his grandparents was in a mixed marriage – 'there were 11 brothers and sisters in her family and all the boys were brought up Catholic and all the girls Protestant'. Timothy therefore always had Catholic as well as Protestant cousins, and attended Catholic as well as Protestant weddings and funerals.[3] Although there were religious tensions in the family, especially with the outbreak of the Troubles, Timothy says that from an early age he was 'very comfortable mixing'. Timothy's story echoes Yeakley's (1979) research, which shows that people with a mixed religious background are more likely to change their religious ideas than people with a homogeneous religious family background. Rambo (1993: 63) says we can look at this finding in two ways. One, that mixed families may be more tolerant of new opinions, and may allow members to more freely explore new ideas. And two, that mixed families simply have less power over their members than homogeneous religious families – they may offer less resistance to change.

It could be argued that Timothy never held extreme views, and whilst his religious ideas have become more inclusive, he did not undergo a radical change. The same cannot be said of Jacob. Jacob is in his fifties, lives in Belfast and works for an NGO. He grew up in a working-class Protestant home in Belfast, attending the Church of Ireland and various evangelical Mission Halls. He was converted in his later teens at an Orange Lodge, after a revivalist meeting. Jacob says he joined the Orange Order as it was 'the biblical thing to do'. He also joined a local flute band and, in his words, 'inherited all the tribal bigotry and bitterness – as much as one could take on board as a young person'. He says he was 'a fundamentalist, Calvinistic evangelical . . . an ardent loyalist and supporter of the Free Presbyterian Church'. Today, however, Jacob holds radically different views. He remains a devout believer but he has problems with the term evangelical because of its exclusive overtones. He says that he has a personal relationship with God and that he wants only to do God's will. Jacob now also sees himself as Irish – a far cry from the staunch loyalism he embraced when he was younger.

Like Timothy, Jacob feels that his religious journey is connected to the development of relationships with Catholics in Northern Ireland. He says this represented 'radical change in relation to one big issue'. All the other issues for him were easier to resolve, whereas he initially 'had the greatest difficulty in accepting my Catholic friends as fellow pilgrims'. One of the stepping stones to change came through relationships at work. A Catholic man with a 'neutral' sounding name came to work in Jacob's organisation, and after a few months it occurred to Jacob that he did not know what religion the man had. This was a turning point for Jacob, who suddenly realised that his world was increasingly not defined by the narrow stereotypes of his youth. Jacob was to push this idea much further some ten to fifteen years later, when he 'made a determined effort' to join a prayer group with charismatic Catholic members. Jacob says, 'they came to our house for a prayer meeting and then we went over to their home for a meeting'. This shows again how hospitality and friendship profoundly challenge people's assumptions about each other. Now Jacob says that this 'joint worship coming together with Catholic friends' is the most exciting aspect of his religious journey. Jacob sums up his process of change saying, 'I think that where I am spiritually is a world that would have remained closed had I not been able to move forward and embrace right across the divide.'

Once again, though, it is important to ask *why* Jacob built relationships with Catholics that ultimately reshaped his faith. In fact, Jacob actively *chose* to do this, saying he made a 'determined effort' to join the Catholic prayer group. Again, the importance of family comes to the fore. Jacob was raised in an ultra-Protestant family, so he did not, like Timothy, have relationships with Catholics as a child. But Jacob was adopted, and when he began to trace, and ultimately meet, his birth mother, he uncovered an Irish and Catholic ancestry. He found relatives in various Irish towns, and even traced his grandfather's plot of land in the west of Ireland. Jacob says he began to appreciate the richness of Irish culture, and his political attitudes began to shift. He started to favour the idea of a united Ireland and came to see himself as an Irish person. Indeed the very first sentence he spoke in our interview was: 'For me my faith journey is all mixed up with who I am as an Irish person.' These events took place about 15 years prior to our interview, and happened around the same time Jacob was beginning to build relationships with Catholics in work. We do not know what direction Jacob would have taken if he had not uncovered his Irish Catholic birth family – perhaps his new relationships at work would have propelled him in the same direction. However, it is certainly clear that Jacob's working through his feelings about adoption were highly significant. Discovering that Catholicism was actually part of his own story provoked a profound change of religious and political identity.

The charismatic movement featured in many stories of those who were on a moderating religious journey.[4] Like Jacob, most people saw it as a catalyst for inter-Christian relationships, which had, in turn, opened up their religious beliefs. Cameron, a full-time Christian worker in his fifties, experienced charismatic Christianity for the first time in his late teens, within his local Anglican church. He credits this as a decisive turning point in his religious journey, and that of his whole family. In his words,

> We met Catholics for the first time within the whole charismatic thing. Although we never had any personal animosity to Catholics, we would have thought that they were at best mistaken. But within the charismatic movement we saw that Catholics, at least within their spiritual experience, were not any different from us.

Clive, a professional in his fifties, goes even further. He says that the fact 'that evangelicals are comfortable and happy to worship with and pray with Catholics who would have an orthodox and personal faith is a terrific and positive development. And I think it's perhaps the major theological development in Northern Ireland in the past 50 years.' He goes on to say that the charismatic movement made this inclusiveness possible 'by simply plunging people experientially into this huge pool of people who had a common spiritual experience and they weren't able to rationalise it theologically but they realised that they were experiencing something that was common to both groups'. Adam, whose religious conversion inside jail we talked about in chapter 4, was also 'greatly influenced by the whole charismatic renewal theology'. A former UVF prisoner, Adam went on to marry a Catholic woman whom he met though the charismatic movement. In fact they got married in a Catholic Church. This helps us understand the extent to which charismatic Christianity has been important in drawing evangelicals into meaningful relationships with Catholics, which in turn impacts deeply on their religious journeys.

But we should not assume that these changes of religious identity are easy. When evangelicals build relationships with Catholics in Northern Ireland, this always takes place within the context of ongoing divisions. This was particularly the case during the Troubles, when many people felt torn between wanting to be tolerant of difference, and being hurt and angry at the violence inflicted on their own community. As a result, journeys towards moderation can be halting and uncertain.[6] For example, Albert is a Baptist minister in his forties from a provincial town. His family belonged to a small, separatist Congregationalist church and many were involved with the DUP or the Orange Order. Albert grew up in a working-class area of Belfast and did not meet any Catholics until he went to university at Queen's. He speaks about his interaction with Catholics as having a life-changing effect on him. Meeting with Catholic Christians at a university group called 'Christians Together at Queen's', Albert says 'all of a sudden I began to have some sort of exposure to people from very, very different backgrounds to me that would seem to have a very living faith – all of that challenged me greatly'.

Albert is acutely aware of the changes in himself, but at the same time admits that he still struggles 'tooth and nail' with sectarianism. In his words,

> I don't want to give you the impression that this [change in me] was overnight. Actually I'm 40 years of age now and I have been in ministry 20 years but still the sectarianism rises within me way too easily, way too easily. I remember when the bomb, the Shankill bomb was planted which killed 9, 10 people, 1993, October '93. The guy who planted that, Sean Kelly, was released as part of the Belfast Agreement, and the bitterness in my heart at that time, I – I scared myself. So scratch beneath the surface of me and there's still some pretty ugly stuff in there, and that maybe I'll never get rid of. So I suppose the journey still goes on and over many years now, maybe 24 years since I've been a very definite Christian there's been a constant shaping [of my beliefs].

So Albert's relationships with Catholic Christians challenged his spirituality, exposing his faith as too narrow. But at the same time, Albert recognises that the change has been gradual and that he still struggles with the beliefs he used to hold about Catholics. This reminds us that personal change is a slow process and is often difficult. Religious journeys rarely represent a once-and-for-all change from one position to another. Rather they unfold gently, with various experiences confirming or challenging new ideas.

Overall the stories of people on moderating journeys lend some qualified support to the popular academic notion of the 'contact hypothesis' – the idea that when people meet and get to know their traditional enemy they become more open-minded (Niens and Cairns 2005, Varshney 2005, Pettigrew and Tropp 2000). Certainly this is the case for many people we talked with who were on moderating journeys. But research also shows that people who are not open to the idea of contact in the first place can become aggravated by it – it can be too much too soon (Amir 1998, Connolly 2000, Hewstone et al. 2005). The stories of people on moderating journeys show that many had some social cues in early life that allowed them to contemplate friendship with Catholics, the traditional 'enemy', as adults. For Timothy this was experience of a mixed marriage; for Rick it was growing up for some time in Ireland where his father was a travelling preacher; for Sammy it was having a Catholic best friend as a child – despite all the odds in a town that was around 90 per cent Protestant. Others spoke of building relationships with Catholics through their discovery of the charismatic movement. These types of experiences provoked a radical change of ideas about the desirability of social contact with Catholics, which in turn impacted on their religious beliefs.

Internal evangelical dialogue: 'God might not be a white, loyalist Protestant'

We suggested in the second chapter how aspects of Northern Ireland's evangelical subculture actually encouraged an active interrogation of one's faith and how that related to the self, to society and to politics. Indeed, many evangelicals on moderating journeys told us about how reading and dialogue *within* evangelical circles had helped change their ideas (see Mitchel 2003, Ganiel 2008a). Practically all evangelicals on moderating journeys emphasised the importance of intra-Christian relationships. Sometimes people sought out these moderating influences, reading books or getting in touch with more liberal Christian organisations, in Northern Ireland and internationally. Sometimes the liberal evangelicals came to them – demonstrating how advocacy is not just the preserve of conservative evangelicals. In some cases, the charismatic movement provided an arena in which new relationships, including relationships with Catholics, were formed and certain traditional evangelical ideas were challenged. These evangelicals felt that they had a stronger, more realistic faith because of the questions they had asked.

Some, especially those who went on to become ministers, mentioned Bible College as one of the first places where they were introduced to new theological ideas and required to think through their faith. Jacob, above, began to 'jettison' his 'fundamentalist' ideas at Bible College. He highlights his relationship with a Baptist minister who helped him work through the idea that a person's politics did not matter 'at the foot of the cross'. This was the first step in a long journey towards religious and political moderation. Similarly Phillip came into contact with different interpretations of evangelicalism for the first time at Bible College through debates with liberal students and tutors. Some people on moderating journeys talked about university as a time where they had scrutinised their faith. But unlike those whose faith is transforming (see chapter 8), who engage with the secular and post-modern ideas taught in university classrooms, people on moderating journeys tended to stress the importance of engagement with *theological* learning. Often university was important because these evangelicals came into contact with more liberal evangelicals and other Christians there, rather than because of their interactions with secular classmates and culture.

People on moderating journeys also did their religious questioning outside the formal structures of university and Bible College. Timothy describes a re-thinking of his evangelical ideas in his discovery of the Mennonite tradition. In his twenties, he was introduced to an American Mennonite who was studying history in Ireland, and who had read some of the writings of Mennonite theologian John Howard Yoder. He said 'I was really intrigued that this Jesus was on the side of the poor and really identified with them. I always thought somehow Jesus was on the side of the – not the rich but the good – people. But he was saying, no, Jesus was on the side of the poor.' Timothy soon came to embrace 'this peace theology which also had justice in it'. He compared this favourably to traditional evangelicalism, which he came to see as judgemental.

Study of the Bible was itself a catalyst for religious change in some cases. Rick, a Presbyterian minister in his forties from Belfast, describes an ongoing educational process that involved his training for the ministry in North America and his own reflections on the Bible. Rick's upbringing was firmly situated within conservative evangelicalism. His father was an itinerant missionary who travelled throughout the south of Ireland and distributed Bibles there. Films, television and the other corrupting influences of modern life were frowned upon. As an adult, his study of Scripture led him to a 'more liberal form of evangelicalism, including embracing Catholics as fellow Christians. He says that the work and publications of the political action group Evangelical Contribution on Northern Ireland (ECONI), and the influence of some moderate Presbyterian ministers helped him to interpret biblical teaching in a different way. These ministers questioned the ways in which unionist identity had been linked with Protestantism, leading Rick to believe that the Bible stresses spiritual unity and not national borders. In fact he now views using religion to support political unionism as an 'utter abuse of the gospel'.

Indeed, many people on moderating journeys talked about the influence of liberal evangelical advocates such as ECONI in their own journeys. Albert was brought up in East Belfast in 'a fairly hardline loyalist family'. He says the God of his childhood was 'probably white, probably loyalist and definitely a

Protestant'. Albert says his views on this began to change when he became involved with organisations such as the Evangelical Alliance (EA) and ECONI. For Albert, EA 'opened his eyes' to, 'a much more biblical perspective' on Christianity. With his loyalist background, Albert began to think again about 'what it actually means to be a citizen of the kingdom of God and not to be a Christian whose political views are tempered by a particular understanding of Scripture'. As a result, Albert began to shed his sectarian views, he gained 'theological depth', and this eventually broke down barriers between him and 'Christians in other denominations'.

Another example is Grace, a 19-year-old Free Presbyterian and student at Queen's University. Grace talked about how her experience of the Christian Union (CU) at Queen's, a moderate evangelical organisation, had provided space for her to discuss beliefs with others. Earlier in the interview, Grace had described how studying Irish history for A-levels had caused her to question the way in which the Free Presbyterian Church in which she had been raised had at times become too caught up with the DUP. This had already led her to, unlike her parents, become an Ulster Unionist Party (UUP) supporter. She says of her experiences at Queen's,

> I go to CU with other Free Presbyterians, Presbyterians, Church of Ireland, everybody, and everybody is very open to discuss just what they believe and it's not really, 'this is my belief, this is what I believe', but rather 'I'm not 100 per cent sure, what do you think?' Which I think is a very healthy way to be [. . .] Coming to Queen's has sort of lifted away some of the cynicism that I have. There's very, very few people that I've met that sort of have in any way bigoted views, but having said that, that's only a small part of the population and it's only my generation. . . . It's going to take a lot of time for people to gain not even a tolerance but just an understanding of what everybody believes.

Here we see how people on moderating journeys use resources from their own religious subculture to critique and adapt their faith. Their journeys are often sustained by study of the Bible and dialogue with other Christians. These factors, rather than external cultural or social influences, prompt them to rethink previously held beliefs. Sometimes people may seek out this alternative evangelical debate, to help them explore and clarify their own questions. For others, the debate comes directly to them. Indeed it is noteworthy that some people on moderating journeys identify Bible College as one of the first places where they came into contact with alternative interpretations of evangelicalism.

This shows the extent to which evangelical ideas are contested and debated in Northern Ireland, and how evangelical individuals often advocate their own interpretations to be accepted.

Evangelicalism as reformable: 'Church as a haven is not a bad idea'

Most people on moderating journeys are disappointed by their churches. Frustration with church features very strongly for people who are transforming and leaving, as well as moderating. But for those who are moderating, this frustration is markedly different in tone and in its consequences. People who leave are disillusioned with *all* churches. People who are transforming cannot find a church to accommodate their views. On the other hand, nearly all who are moderating were able to leave the conservative evangelical churches they had outgrown, and find another church that they could be happy in. Most who are moderating are not *angry* at the churches in the way that people who are transforming are. And even where they express frustration with evangelicalism as a whole, people who are moderating by and large feel that it can be reformed, and indeed, believe that they can play an active role in its improvement.

Although Rick now views religiously fuelled unionism as an 'utter abuse of the gospel', he does not feel resentful of his conservative evangelical upbringing. In fact, he views it in a benign way. In his words, 'I certainly don't want to underestimate the value that had maybe in protecting me at an impressionable age, and giving me a knowledge of Scripture through memorisation that has stuck with me.' Rick says his family's life and their circle of influences and friends were 'quite narrow', but rather than rebel against them Rick simply says 'I needed to develop and become a little bit more aware of the world in which I lived.' This softness stands in stark contrast to the way that many transformers and leavers talk about their religious upbringings.

Another example is Kara, a physicist in her forties who now lives in Belfast and worships in a Presbyterian church. Kara grew up in a rural area and was raised in a strict Baptist home. She describes her father as a nominal member of the Orange Order and says that she spent much of her early adult life attempting to distance herself from the Order and its culture. She believed that the Order, whilst claiming to be a Christian organisation, gave Christianity a bad name. But her participation at a 'Moving Beyond Sectarianism' weekend sponsored by the Irish School of Ecumenics encouraged her to rethink her attitudes. Kara says she reconnected with her background, and began to think that rather than simply denouncing the Orange Order, she should think about how God might want to transform it. Timothy also expresses frustration with the conservatism of evangelical subculture, in particular evangelicals' reluctance to work with marginalised groups. But, like Kara, rather than abandon evangelicalism, he hopes for change, saying 'I would love to see the church taking more risks and being much more creative on how they work across the divide and climb into society.' So rather than discarding the religious traditions with which they are raised, evangelicals on moderating journeys are interested in using religious resources to change their evangelical subculture.

Part of their optimism comes from their recognition of the value of the sense of community provided by churches, as well as the strong influence of para-church organisations. Kara puts this well when she says,

> I don't want to be critical of the church. I think because church is an extension of family life and most people live in more or less comfortable families . . . church is a comfortable place for them and they don't want to be uncomfortable. I suppose I see a point in that, especially in a world which changes rapidly and in a world where there's a lot of hurt happening at a society level and also at an individual level. So to have church as a kind of haven is not a bad idea. But I would like to see the church shaken up a bit and I do see para-church organisations because of their flexibility to change and grow [as able to instigate change]. . . . If you can accept that the church is meant to be more or less stable and doesn't change as much and that the changing bit of the kingdom comes through the para-church organisations, maybe that's quite legitimate.

Kara, who is single, also said that it is common for evangelical churches to exclude single women from some of the family-orientated aspects of church life. This also can include patronising comments and attempts to 'marry off' the single women. Despite these frustrations, Kara talks about congregational life as akin to 'family', a 'comfortable place', and a 'haven'. Like Kara, most evangelicals on moderating journeys have found outlets that allow them to express discontent with aspects of the evangelical subculture, while at the same time maintaining their faith and working to reform it. For many, this outlet consisted of involvement in evangelical organisations such as ECONI, EA or the CU at Queen's. Others were able to find a congregation where their views were accepted. One man, for example, described the congregation he attended and the area in which he lived as an 'island of moderation in a sea of extremism'. The support networks provided by organisations and congregations allowed these people to draw on and develop religious resources that nurtured more open and moderate beliefs and identities.

Books and music: Creative questioning and space to think

We saw in previous chapters how some evangelicals prefer to close themselves off from potentially corrupting influences. In some strict evangelical circles, contemporary popular culture – from television to books and music – is deeply suspect. Many evangelicals on moderating journeys grew up with these ideas. However, as adults they did not attempt to protect themselves from the effects of popular culture. Rather, they engaged with new ideas, and experienced significant changes. But they continued to interpret those changes through an evangelical lens.

Keith says that real changes started to happen in his religious journey when he moved 'outside of the evangelical Christian way of reading'. This contrasts with many people on a religiously stable journey, who prefer to limit their reading to evangelical thinkers and commentators. People who were moderating cited all sorts of books as marking out significant moments of religious change. For Keith, reading Thomas Merton, a Catholic Trappist Monk and anti-nuclear war campaigner, was significant in his early journey. Films too have been important 'stimuli' for Keith. Gillian talked about the books of Douglas Copeland – contemporary American fiction that is full of existential questioning and ideas of redemption – as helping her think differently about her search for meaning in a modern world (See Dark 2002).

Sammy, a youth worker, was born into a Presbyterian home in Antrim, the rural evangelical heartland of Northern Ireland. As a child he experimented with atheism, but by the age of 17 had become converted into conservative evangelicalism. Sammy describes his early evangelicalism as 'orthodox' and 'fundamentalist'. He says he used to be called the 'machine gun', because when speaking at evangelical events he would come in 'hard and heavy', with a fire and brimstone message. Now in his forties, Sammy describes himself as a 'follower of Jesus', and although he retains core evangelical beliefs about the centrality of the Cross, and the Bible as the inspired word of God, he says his faith is now much more 'open', focusing on God's love and grace.

But Sammy did not necessarily fit the conservative evangelical mould, as his childhood flirtation with atheism might indicate. Reflecting on his religious journey, Sammy now says 'there was always a radical in these ould bones', and that whilst he feels he was culturally conditioned to be a conservative evangelical, a more liberal spiritual self lay inside. In his late twenties, Sammy's lifelong love of rock music brought him to Greenbelt, a large Christian music festival in England, where his liberalism began to take shape. He says 'Green Belt was a major enlightenment experience to me.' Here he met a musician from one of his favourite bands who challenged his ideas about faith. Talking to other Christians with different ideas and lifestyles away from Northern Ireland gave him 'space to think'. So, as with many others, Sammy's questioning process began internally within Christian circles. Sammy goes on to say that music and the arts are what 'saved [him]'. He was deeply influenced by bands like U2, who were grappling with spiritual questions, but not expecting 'perfect and precise' answers.[6] He also says bands like the Horslips made him interested in Irish culture. He says the arts allow creative, experiential and imaginative questioning, concluding that 'it was the music that definitely was the salvation programme'.

Music has played a crucial role in Duncan's religious journey as well. Duncan is a musician in his thirties, who comes from a working-class family in Belfast. Duncan talks about being sent to Sunday school by a nominal Protestant father, and an extended family steeped in loyalism and the Orange Order, although he says that his parents taught him to be non-sectarian. Now Duncan says that he is a 'Christian' and that he has come a long way from the 'right-wing fundamentalism' he tried to embrace early in his religious journey. Duncan has maintained his Christian beliefs, although he has become increasingly detached from organised religion. This detachment from church is not typical for evangelicals on moderating journeys, although it is a good example of what Grace Davie (1994) found was a common trend in Britain – 'believing without belonging'.

Two themes dominate Duncan's story of his journey towards a more liberal faith and his increasing detachment from church. One is his view of himself as a 'trouble-maker', a free spirit who did not fit into conservative church structures. He felt that his church was very materialistic, which jarred with his childhood experiences of growing up in poverty. Secondly, Duncan focuses on music as marking out important religious turning points. For example, when an American musician came to visit his church in the 1990s, Duncan began to realise that 'music could have a spiritual dimension beyond anything I'd ever known'. Duncan says this prompted him to express his spirituality through his own music. Writing songs allowed him to explore brokenness and redemption on a deeper level. He now tours America regularly and has built up strong religious networks there, where he feels his views are accepted.

Engaging with popular culture has helped many evangelicals who are moderating find new ways of being religious. Listening to and making music has allowed people to express creativity, to ask searching questions, to have space to think, and to explore alternative Christian ideas and lifestyles. It provides an outlet to interrogate faith and to express difference whilst holding on to core Christian beliefs. Music and popular culture are also important in the journeys of those who are transforming and leaving evangelicalism. But evangelicals who are moderating have a slightly different take on the issue. They tend to ask what culture can offer to their faith, rather than challenging or replacing it. For example, Sammy says, 'when I'm listening to music I'm listening to music for spiritual twists and spiritual issues and so even when I'm relaxing I'm watching a movie and thinking, spiritually thinking how does this apply to my faith?' Thus the books and music highlighted by evangelicals who are moderating are often on the spiritual side of popular culture – U2 and Douglas Copeland are notable for their emphasis on existential questioning and redemption. Moreover, Sammy and Duncan talk about alternative *Christian* networks, such as Greenbelt and the American Christian music scene, as helping them grow in their religious journeys. Again this points to an internal Christian dialogue, a seeking out of alternative spiritual ideas, rather than a random trawl through secular popular culture.

Leaving Northern Ireland: 'I wanted to live in a different place and to see the world from a different perspective'

Evangelicals who were moderating, transforming and leaving all talked about the impact that living outside Northern Ireland had on their religious journeys. Unlike those who were leaving, evangelicals who were moderating found that their experience of other types of *religious community* helped shape and redefine their religious views. Those who had left evangelicalism were more interested in non-religious experiences and communities outside Northern Ireland.

Julie, a community worker in her forties from Belfast, saw her perspectives changed when she lived in Cork for a summer after graduating from university. Raised a Presbyterian, faith for her had always been experienced as something that was strict and required sticking to the rules. But in Cork she met Catholics who were Christians, who had what she describes as a much more relaxed attitude about their faith. She came to see this attitude as healthy and enabling, in that it took her focus away from the rules – which were not so important –

and allowed her to focus on peace issues, which she deemed as infinitely more important. She said,

> Living in Cork threw up a lot of things that I never questioned before. Because I'd been brought up in the Presbyterian Church and you kind of just assume that the things you've been taught are right. Then you meet all these other people who believe very different things. That was the beginning I suppose of a whole process about my own identity and how I wanted to be defined.

For example, Julie was impressed that the people she met in Cork – Catholics and Protestants – seemed 'so much more relaxed about their faith'. She saw a strong sense of community, which she had not experienced before. After prayer meetings, for example, people would go out to a club, something that would never have happened in the north. When Julie returned to live in Northern Ireland, she became involved in an inter-church community based in County Down. In that community, there were 'groups coming there from all different churches, and there was a lot of sharing of faith, and people's experiences'. Julie says through this she realised that 'God was working in all these different groups all over Ireland and that not one of us could claim that we had everything – there's so much to learn from each other.'

Julie's story is typical of evangelicals who are moderating, many of whom have lived, worked or made extended visits to the Republic of Ireland (See also Jordan 2001: 107–8). Working in Presbyterian churches in the Republic gave both Sammy and Rick time to develop their faith away from the pressures of sectarian politics in Northern Ireland. Sammy worked in the Republic of Ireland for three years, and says it 'was a place those things didn't really matter. I was with a group of people who accepted me for who I was and I didn't have to battle those things.' Like Julie, Sammy felt that there was much more 'freedom and openness' in the Republic of Ireland, which gave him space to question previously taken for granted beliefs. Along with his experiences of Greenbelt and music, Sammy says his time away from Northern Ireland enabled him to return home feeling strengthened in his faith, having refined his ideas of who he was and what he believed.

Not all the experiences outside Northern Ireland were religious. As we shall see with Gavin and Wendy in chapter 9, for Rick, living in England for a time made him feel more Irish. Rick felt that English people saw him simply as a 'Paddy', and did not understand the nuances of his Northern Irish and unionist identity. He says 'it suddenly came to me [. . .] yes, I am Irish. There are parts of me that have much more in common with people in Dublin and Cork than people in the south of England.' This is one of the turning points that, along with his dialogue with EA and ECONI, led Rick towards a more inclusive faith that moved away from the evangelicalism and the unionism of his youth.

Kara was influenced by her time in England in a different way. For Kara, living in England allowed her space and detachment to reconsider her views about faith and politics. When the time came for her to go to university, she says she wanted to get as far away from Northern Ireland as possible. Kara calls this her 'act of rebellion'. She says this was a 'break for my freedom', and that she 'wanted to live in a different place and to see the world from a different perspective' from the one in which she had been brought up. She also wanted to get away from the Troubles, and escape what she saw as the stodgy and limiting trappings of rural unionist culture, including the Orange Order and its parades. Kara presents herself as *choosing* to get away – actively seeking out different experiences. But while in England at university, she began to take an interest in Northern Ireland politics. She began to link this interest with her questions about her own faith, and soon became convinced that it was the duty of Christians in Northern Ireland to work for peace. Kara says she never considered how her faith related to the conflict in Northern Ireland until she moved away from home. She retained the faith of her youth through involvement in Christian organisations and a local congregation while at university. So for her it was natural to relate her new-found interest in Northern Ireland to her already well-established faith.

It was not only differing experiences of Ireland and Britain that prompted re-evaluations of faith, but also coming into contact with more secular ideologies whilst abroad. Joan is a Baptist in her twenties from a rural part of Northern Ireland, who says she was led to reconsider her faith after time she spent studying abroad at a university in the United States. She describes the ethos of the university as 'feminist- feminist- feminist- feminist' and very much into grassroots political action. When she returned to Northern Ireland, like Kara she found herself integrating these new insights into her already established evangelical faith. Rather than focusing on feminist critiques of faith, Joan started to think about how feminist ideas could improve her church for the better. She says she finds that 'Christian girls' are more willing to become involved in grassroots community activism, as opposed to the 'guys' who like 'the hierarchical structure' and think 'get me into the pulpit'. Whilst this is of course a stereotype of gender roles within the church, what is interesting is how Joan incorporates her new experiences and secular ideas into an already existing evangelical framework.

In these ways, time outside Northern Ireland was important for evangelicals on moderating journeys, giving them space to think and opportunities to develop relationships with people that challenged their previous assumptions. Time outside Northern Ireland often overlapped with periods of study at university, and included sustained, quality interaction with Catholics. It is important to note the difference between those who are moderating and those who have left evangelicalism, because those who have left also stress their time away from Northern Ireland as catalysing changes in their religious identity. Most of those who are moderating continued to be involved in church life when they left Northern Ireland, and indeed it is primarily their experience of different types of religious community, and different ways of being religious, that prompted them to open up their religious identities. In contrast, those who had left evangelicalism tended to emphasise new experiences and relationships *outside* church. When evangelicals on moderating journeys had experiences outside of Northern Ireland with secular ideas and organisations, they tended to use these ideas to improve rather than disprove their evangelical faith.

Spiritual experiences: God working in our everyday lives

Keith, whom we briefly introduced earlier in the chapter, is a writer in his late thirties. He was raised in the Exclusive Brethren, a separatist branch of the Plymouth Brethren, until he left in his mid-twenties. He describes the Exclusive Brethren as 'very mind-controlling and life-controlling', saying 'we weren't allowed to watch TV, listen to radio, music, or read novels. It was like being brought up in a very repressed system.' Keith says that 'Christianity has screwed a lot of people's lives up', and he now rejects much of the teaching of his youth. However, he still sees himself as a Christian, saying 'I still believe that the life and the teachings of Jesus Christ are fundamentally the right way to live.' He says that inside Northern Ireland he definitely does not see himself as an evangelical, but outside Northern Ireland he identifies with more positive forms of evangelicalism.

Closeted away from the outside world and popular culture, Keith says that a series of 'mystical experiences' in his mid-twenties started his journey towards religious moderation. These were quiet experiences that took place when he was on his own. On one occasion he felt a 'very clear experience of enlightenment'. In his words,

> For me it was a kind of transcendent experience where I saw totally that this was not what it was about. This is totally wrong. It was an epiphany whereby I realised I no longer had to be a certain kind of Christian to please God.

On another occasion, Keith recalls 'lying in bed and feeling an amazing amount of peace and excitement', which was 'an experience of release'. Another time he cried for the first time since his childhood, and says 'the psychological well-being I felt was unbelievable'.

At the time, Keith was still living in the family home. He had just begun to meet some other Christians, charismatics and Anglicans who, he was 'gob-smacked' to discover, had a genuine faith – contrary to what he had been taught. But Keith says that meeting other people played only a minor role at the beginning of his religious journey, and emphasises the importance of his spiritual experiences. He says that 'these experiences were almost an escape from the stress I was under at the time', but also argues that this does not diminish their significance. In fact Keith makes parallels between psychology and faith, arguing that he has an experiential personality, which makes him open to spiritual experiences, as well as recognising the relationship between his own stress and spiritual experience of release. God's intervention is not therefore experienced as a thunderbolt, but rather God is seen to use people's individual situations and predispositions to work changes in their lives. Keith also highlights the role of spiritual experience for people who are culturally isolated, saying 'at that time in my life there was very little to stimulate me [. . .] Now I find that there are more stimuli in ordinary life, I don't need those anymore.'

Others who were involved in the charismatic movement also talked about the importance of spiritual experiences in their journeys towards moderation. Cameron said that feeling the presence of the Holy Spirit, and sharing this experience with Catholic charismatics, helped shift his thinking towards a theology of inclusion. Phillip talks about God using everyday situations to challenge him. When his wife sought ordination, Phillip says that 'God pulled the rug out from under my feet', and he had to revise his assumptions about women in the church. Again we see how evangelicals who are moderating feel God uses human relationships and experiences to work changes in their lives. It is important to underline the role of spiritual experiences for moderating evangelicals, who very much continue to operate within the framework of an interventionist God. Their journey towards moderation is not simply cerebral or based on relationships alone. Rather, their journey is guided and shaped by their experiences of God.

Conclusions

Evangelicals on moderating journeys highlighted many of the themes – reading and education, time outside Northern Ireland, explorations of popular culture – that are also important for people who are transforming and who have left evangelicalism. But there is a very distinct emphasis on *internal Christian* seeking and dialogue amongst those who are moderating. Their experiences outside Northern Ireland were often shaped within the religious sphere – working or worshipping in other congregations in Ireland, Britain and abroad. Dialogue with other Christians and para-church organisations were deeply influential in changing their views. Where popular culture played a role in their journeys, it often took the form of alternative Christian networks, and spiritually seeking music and literature.

Like those who are transforming and leaving evangelicalism, people on moderating journeys often expressed frustration with evangelical churches in Northern Ireland. But unlike the others, they believe strongly that religion can be reformed. Their frustration with churches does not spill over into helpless anger. Instead they work to change the evangelical subculture that they are part of. They emphasise activism and advocacy. After all, the activism and advocacy of others is what changed many of their own religious views. Para-church organisations also provide an important valve for the release of their frustrations. Even where evangelical churches are criticised, para-church organisations have emerged to accommodate and promote their perspectives.

The fact that moderating evangelicals seek out religious answers to their questions does not mean that they are shut off from the outside world. Unlike those whose faith is deepening in a conservative direction, and some of those on a steady religious journey, they do not attempt to closet off their faith from the outside world. They do not restrict their friendship groups to other evangelicals only – although of course because of the closeness they experience in their churches many of their most intimate friendships may be with other Christians. Nor do they avoid contact with ideas that may threaten their faith. Many have gone to university, even if they cite new religious networks at university rather than the secular classroom as influencing their religious journey. And they do not cut themselves off from popular culture. In fact rather than derailing faith, popular culture has allowed these evangelicals room for self-expression and difference. It has given them space to explore grey areas of belief and doubt, to ask creative questions, and in so doing has helped them hold on to their core Christian beliefs.

One of the single most important patterns that arose in practically all the stories of moderating evangelicals was their development of meaningful relationships with Catholics. Building social relationships with Catholics soon spilled over into people's religious ideas, and most came to see Catholics as 'fellow pilgrims'. This profoundly altered their views about religion and politics in Northern Ireland. But it is important to ask what prompted this openness to friendship with Catholics in the first place, where many other evangelicals would have preferred not to mix. In fact we usually find that evangelicals on moderating journeys have had social experiences in early life that allowed openness to come more easily later on. Examples include the mixed marriage in Timothy's family, or Rick's father's missionary activity in the Republic of Ireland. These early relationships may have caused moderating evangelicals to be less guarded about the boundaries of their own faith from the outset, and un-policed religious changes slowly unfurled via the relationships they developed with Catholics as adults. In other cases, dramatic turning points are experienced as adults – for example Jacob's discovery of his Catholic birth family or others' introduction to the charismatic movement – that cause people to think about faith in new ways. This, in turn, prompts some people to push even further, deliberately seeking out ever more meaningful relationships with their traditional 'enemy'. It is also important to note just how difficult a transition this has been for some evangelicals, who have essentially had to dismantle the foundations of their early faith. For some, this change is a slow and halting process, rather than a swift and total change.

Like people on other journeys, moderating evangelicals demonstrate a remarkable capacity for self-critique and change. In fact it seems that they deliberately sought out religious challenges – doing controversial cross-community work or beginning to question Protestant unionist norms – that led them deeper into their journey of religious openness. Perhaps they sought out these challenges because of a pre-existing disposition to build peaceful relationships. In some cases this disposition seems to come from cues in early family life. But others seem to have started their questioning process as a result of relationships built as adults. Others again seem to have a questioning nature, and a desire to engage with, rather than simply shelve, difficult questions. Moreover, as we suggested in chapter 2, elements within Northern Ireland's evangelical subculture can actually encourage existential questioning about a variety of issues.

But rather than draw randomly on outside resources to critique their faith, people on a moderating journey sought out religious solutions. This should not lead us to conclude that their choice of religious path was not as open as for people on other journeys. In large part moderating evangelicals deliberately *chose* to seek out religious critiques and answers to their questions because they were happy with the core tenets of their faith. They were not angry with evangelicalism as a whole, like those who are transforming or who have left evangelicalism, and many even appreciated the strictness of their upbringings as protecting them. As Kara points out, church is like 'family' for people, it is 'comfortable' and feels like home. Thus they carved out new roles for themselves within evangelicalism, and found ways to express dissent, that did not threaten the core of their faith. This allowed them to hold on to the aspects of faith and church that made them happy, whilst adapting and improving the things that they did not like. Again, this demonstrates creative adaptation, and shows how people manage their dispositions and thought processes, their social experiences as children and as adults, to come up with a package of faith that works for them.

Finally, evangelicals on moderating journeys believe deeply in an interventionist God, and are quick to attribute events, experiences, and changes in themselves to his providential care. Whilst we are highlighting the significance of social relationships and internal Christian dialogue, moderating evangelicals themselves understand these processes also to be spiritual. Although they use a language of choice to explain the religious changes they have experienced, they see this as a choice catalysed by God putting them in certain situations and opening up certain ideas to them.

CHAPTER EIGHT

Transforming Evangelicalism

This chapter considers the stories of people who at one time considered themselves evangelicals, but now think about and practise their faith in a radically different way. Although most continue to see their lives as part of a Christian story, they now interrogate and critique their former evangelical subculture. They have varying degrees of attachment to evangelical institutions, networks and friends. The people who were interviewed for this chapter form a unique group in that they have created for themselves a new religious network or community, often centred on Belfast-based 'post-evangelical' or 'emerging church' groups such as Ikon. Their continuing engagement with faith, combined with continuing practice of community, is what distinguishes them from those in the next chapter, who have left evangelicalism and religion altogether. People who are transforming evangelicalism still care about what happens to evangelicalism – or at least to Christianity. Some of the people we talked to for this chapter called themselves post-evangelicals. Others felt that this term was too bound up with their evangelical past and preferred to identify themselves as part of the emerging church movement (Tickle 2008, Gibbs and Bolger 2005). A few said simply that they were Christians on a journey. A significant number resisted attempts to categorise their new identity, as their faith was now more about fluidity and openness than labels and specific beliefs. To put it differently, for these people the journey of exploration is more important than any fixed position. We have chosen to describe these people as transforming their faith, because we think transformation captures the radical change people have experienced, whilst alluding to the fact that faith itself has not been abandoned.

We should say at the outset that people who are transforming their faith are very unrepresentative of the wider population. All of those we spoke to were highly educated, holding an ordinary if not a higher university degree. Although some come from working-class backgrounds, nearly all could now be described as middle class. One of our interviewees described them as 'a sort of liberal, intelligentsia, middle ground'. Another calls it a group of 'disillusioned intellectual Christians'. They are also a very small group in Northern Ireland. There were 11 in our sample. It is difficult to estimate overall numbers, but we do know that the groups that we focused on, Ikon, Zero28 and a less formal book group, have a few hundred members between them. Having said that, these groups overlap with a wider range of churches, they connect with moderating evangelicals and those who have left evangelicalism, and are linked in with a global network of 'emergence' Christianity. So it is probably fair to say that their influence is more than the sum of their members.

Whilst their numbers in Northern Ireland are small, some scholars of religion highlight the central importance of the post-evangelical/emerging church movements on wider evangelical and Christian cultures. Phyllis Tickle's (2008) influential book *The Great Emergence: How Christianity is Changing and Why*, argues that Christianity is being changed into something new and dynamic, and responding to the probing questions of the present age.[1] For her, Christian ideas about the location of authority are moving steadily from the Bible (the 'answer' to that question during the Reformation) to *experience* (2008: 45). While this may sound relativistic, people usually interpret their experiences in the context of a community of friends, rather than simply deciding for themselves what is right. In the process, people are questioning the way the Bible has been read and interpreted throughout the modern period, and whether evangelicalism has the resources to cope with post-modernity. Another leading 'post-evangelical', Dave Tomlinson[2] argues that evangelicals would be better off without damaging and inhumane beliefs about how the Bible should be read, particularly interpretations of the meaning of the atonement, whether or not the resurrection actually happened (and if it matters), interpretations of the uniqueness of Christ, the efficacy of prayer, and the existence of hell (Tomlinson 1995, 2008).[3] Brian McLaren, a prolific American writer associated with the emerging church, raises similar issues in his wider body of work (McLaren 2005, 2008, 2010). In a 2005 foreword to the second edition of McLaren's book, *A Generous Orthodoxy*, Tickle likens McLaren to Martin Luther nailing his 95 theses to the door of Wittenberg church, inviting readers to 'join thousands and thousands of others who have already read these words and subsequently assumed them as the theses of a new kind of Christianity and the foundational principles for a new Beloved Community' (2005: 12).[4]

In Northern Ireland, the most prominent expressions of the emerging church have been the Belfast-based communities associated with Ikon and Zero28 (Ganiel 2006b, 2008a, 2010c). Peter Rollins, a then-doctoral student in philosophy at Queen's University Belfast, helped to found Ikon in December 2001.[5] Ikon's main event is a monthly meeting in a pub or bar. These meetings were described to us as 'performance art' or 'transformance art'.[6] Zero28 began out of an informal discussion group among Queen's students in January 1999, led by a doctoral candidate in sociology, Gareth Higgins. Its main and original remit focused on peace and reconciliation. Zero28 disbanded in 2007, and Higgins has since emigrated to the United States. During our research, we found that most of the people we interviewed were involved in both of the groups. Some others were part of informal 'book groups' that meet in each other's homes to discuss their faith journeys.

People who are transforming their faith gave many reasons for leaving evangelicalism, with some people echoing the wider concerns of the international emerging church movement, and others disappointed with the way evangelical churches have responded to politics in Northern Ireland. They also critiqued what they perceived as shortcomings in the more distinctly religious aspects of the evangelical subculture, ranging from evangelical attitudes towards money and sexual morality. A few talked about a rather high-level intellectual process that included reading post-modern philosophers, and becoming convinced that evangelicalism does not have the resources to address post-modernity. Others reflected these concerns on a more everyday level, describing how they had come to embrace grey areas and doubt in their faith. Relationships with parents and partners, as well as like-minded friends trying to build a sense of community, were also significant.

Faith and doubt: Removing your head from the sand

The tagline for Peter Rollins's blog is 'To believe is human; to doubt divine.'[7] This encapsulates the attitude about doubt that is held by many who are transforming their faith. In previous chapters, we saw how those whose faith was deepening in a conservative direction usually attributed doubt to attacks from the devil, whereas some on a steady religious journey tended to interpret doubt as a sign that they were not measuring up to God's standards. But for people who are transforming, doubt is generally embraced as positive rather than threatening. They also allow themselves to engage much more radically with different kinds of doubt. They not only have doubts about the teachings of the churches, but also about the nature and even the very existence of God. But this intense questioning exists in conjunction with spiritual seeking.[8] In

Sophie's words, '[we] are definitely questioning the prescriptiveness of what [we] felt for a long, long time, but are not necessarily throwing the baby out with the bathwater'. Some articulated high-level philosophical arguments about relativism and deconstruction. Others focused on how, at a more down-to-earth level, we simply will never be able to have all the right answers, but that it is important to ask the questions. Having said that, practically all people who are transforming their faith are widely read and take a keen interest in contemporary theological and philosophical debates. Nearly all are intellectually critiquing evangelicalism and reflecting deeply on their journey towards transformation. For them, engaging with the grey areas is what makes their faith relevant.

Peter Rollins was one of our interviewees, and his story resonates with others on a transforming journey. After being raised as nominally Church of Ireland, Peter converted to a charismatic form of evangelicalism at the age of 18. After working for a few years with church youth and as a church planter, he decided to go to university and study religion. At Queen's in Belfast, he was introduced to post-modern philosophy, as well as ancient Christian mystics. He cites an extensive list of philosophers and mystics as influences, including Meister Eckhart, Pascal, Kierkegaard, Nietzsche, Freud, and Hebrew mythology. Peter talks often about deconstruction, post-metaphysical ideas and the uncertainty of post-modernity. He is keen to point out that 'none of us know the answer', that Christians must embrace intellectual humility and celebrate difference, saying that there is something 'that you try to reach but never get there'. He says that our own language and discourse limit the ways we think about God, limiting faith to specific cultural forms. He couples this with a critique of how evangelicals have read the Bible literally, rather than understanding it as myth and allegory. He says that Ikon is not about 'telling people what to believe, but actually creating a place for people to think for themselves'.

In contrast, Peter sees evangelicalism as a product of modernity. For him, evangelicalism reflects modern assumptions about being able to ascertain 'truth' and to verify facts. For evangelicals this means constructing an overarching religious narrative that explains everything, from the formation of the universe to the most intimate details of people's lives. People like Peter disagree with over-arching narratives and want to construct alternative, diverse, open-ended narratives that they feel are more helpful for having a meaningful spiritual life and authentic relationships with other people. This opposition to modern under-standings of truth, and black and white thinking, was shared by all of those we spoke with who are transforming their faith. But this openness to uncertainty and doubt by no means precludes religious seeking. Peter says 'for some people religion is the very shutting down of your mind, you stop thinking. But for me it was really the opening up of all those kind of questions about life.' Peter characterises his involvement in Ikon as being part of a friendly critique of the church, and especially the evangelical tradition. Peter talks about religious heretics in the Bible, who 'were inside the religious tradition, they loved the tradition but they read it differently'. He says that Ikon too tries to 'read the tradition differently from the dominant Northern Ireland paradigm'.

Jake is a Christian worker in his forties, originally from America but now living in Belfast. He also sees doubt as integral to Christianity. Jake echoes Peter's language of heresy, as critique from within. He also speaks about his identi-fication with 'the mystics and the doubters' in the Christian tradition. He says that the Christian tradition of heresy,

> Goes all the way back to St Thomas – you know – the doubt. He was not reprimanded by Christ for doubting. That was the thing, Christ met Thomas where he was. Put your hands in my side, put your hands in my hands, don't doubt – believe. And he met him where he was. And you know Paul, he was willing to say, wretched man that I am you know, the things I want to do I don't do, the things I do I don't want to do, you know, I'm a mess. I'm a mess. That's the tradition we want to fit into.

Sophie, a teacher in her fifties from Belfast, also talks about how embracing the grey areas has changed and improved her faith. Sophie converted to evan-gelicalism in her teens and soon joined a charismatic church, where she remained for 20 years. Because of in-fighting in the church, Sophie left and joined a Presbyterian congregation which was 'much less intense'. After another five years at this church, Sophie did not attend anywhere for quite some time. Looking back, Sophie says her disengagement with evangelicalism was a very slow process. Although she describes her faith as fervent for many years, she now says she can see a trail of questions and doubts. She felt let down by Christians and churches at various junctures, and experienced more existential questions such as 'why does prayer not always work?' For example, for years she was worried about her son, who had been getting into trouble at school. And the more she prayed – she says for hours at a time – the worse he became. She says this sowed seeds of doubt in her mind, which paved the way for her departure from church later on.

Sophie says that while she was actively involved in church, she tried not to focus on her questions and doubts. She says she tried to gloss over incidents where the church had failed her, and thought 'maybe it's just me'. When she finally left the Presbyterian Church, disillusioned with religion, Sophie continued not to engage with her doubt. She describes this as 'ostriching', long periods of time where she would bury her head in the sand, trying not to think about her doubt, because it was just too frightening and difficult. Sophie was interviewed with her friend, Melanie, also in her fifties from Belfast, who says she considered herself to be an evangelical until four years ago. Melanie agreed that 'ostriching' had been an important strategy for her over the years – a sense that all was not well with her faith, but a reluctance to ask the difficult questions because it was too painful.

For the last two years, Sophie and Melanie have attended a weekly book group, in the home of a friend. For the first time, Sophie says she 'allowed [herself] to be honest', and to engage with her questions and doubts. She says she is much happier because of this; she feels a connection with people who are 'journeying', and who ask spiritual questions. Exploring the grey areas of faith has, in fact, deepened Sophie's engagement with her faith. But this is an open-ended, open-minded belief, encompassing more questions than answers. She says that now science fiction, such as Dr Who, helps her appreciate the mysteries of the universe and deepens her faith in God. For Sophie, this embracing of mystery and ambiguity, alongside a search for God, is a radically different way of approaching her religious journey.

Melanie says she too has started to be able to articulate and engage with her doubts. For a long time she had been quite good at glossing over her doubts, but after she was diagnosed with cancer, her questions became too big to ignore and she began to actively explore them. Now she says it is quite 'scary' not to have certainty of belief, but she also feels relieved. She feels that she has reached an age where she can let herself be herself. Again this echoes research about the increasingly contemplative nature of faith in mid-life, where varied life experiences lead people to embrace the contradictory nature of life rather than seeing things in black and white (see Fowler 1981). And indeed, exploring contradictions and doubts has enabled Melanie to engage with faith in a way that she might not otherwise have been able to.

Not all people who are transforming their faith are high-level philosophers or are interested in exploring the minutiae of post-modern theology, like Peter Rollins. But transformation is, for most people, at least in part, an intellectual process. Practically all of those whose faith was transforming read widely and consistently on theological and philosophical topics. Their bookshelves are stocked with popular authors such as Tickle, Tomlinson, McLaren, Rob Bell

(2005), Donald Miller (2003), Samir Selmanovic (2009), Kester Brewin (2010) and others identified with the emerging church movement, who are asking similar questions. They log on to the blogs where the philosophies and practices of Tickle's 'Great Emergence' are being debated. Even someone like Melanie, whose primary focus for transformation is perhaps more experiential than intellectual, allows herself to experience doubt and actively engage with the grey areas of faith. In such a way, their faith becomes open to constant questioning, and the journey of exploration is valued just as much, if not more, than the final destination. In Gary's words, 'the journey is the important thing and we don't necessarily know where it's going to go, but [we] just try and enjoy the journey that we're on'.

Disappointment, confinement and frustration: 'Church can seriously damage your health'

For people who are transforming their faith, their now open-ended approach is a far cry from their previous experiences with evangelicalism. Their stories were full of examples of how they had felt hemmed in by church teachings and norms, and had ultimately felt disappointed by the church. This is similar to the stories of people in the next chapter, who have left evangelicalism, and is an unsurprising precursor to radical religious change.

So when we asked Sophie and Melanie what they enjoyed about their new religious ideas, they did not have to think long to come up with answers:

MELANIE: You don't have to get your neighbours saved – what a relief.

SOPHIE: We don't have to go and do street meetings any more – isn't it great?

MELANIE: And you don't have to be nice to earn brownie points.

SOPHIE: You can just make friends with people and be friends, you don't have to think 'oh this person's really nice, I want to be friends, oh, I wonder are they saved?'

Indeed there was a widespread feeling amongst people we spoke to that evangelicalism forced them into a zealous public persona that they were not comfortable with. The heavy emphasis on evangelism, sharing the good news with friends and strangers, was a source of discomfort. As Geoff, a 37-year-old artist, says, 'I used to try and talk to people about God all the time and felt guilty when I didn't.' He says this made him deeply uncomfortable, and he has now come to a point where he thinks 'it's not my job to convert people anymore. God can convert people whenever God wants to convert people.' This unease echoes the stories in the next chapter of people who have left religion. But whereas those who have left often described their feelings in strong terms, saying they were humiliated and deeply embarrassed by their former proselytism, people on a transforming journey are more likely to talk about discomfort and a sense of relief that they can now conduct their religious journey in private.

People spoke about a number of other reasons for their disappointment with their former evangelical churches. Some were alienated by the church's positions on money. Melanie says she disliked her former church's attitudes to money and felt that those, like her, who had little money were looked down upon as second-class Christians. Melanie says, however, that she did not dwell on this. In her words, 'if there was a square peg and a round hole, [I] made it fit'. She was happy with her faith and glossed over any problems. Then, four years ago, things changed. Melanie says this was catalysed by a number of simultaneous events, but it is only looking back that she can see how the doubts mounted up and the changes took place. Her diagnosis of cancer was the main turning point. This caused Melanie to question, and ultimately doubt, her faith. She does not say she was angry at God for her illness, but instead she focuses on how the church let her down. She says people in the church were not there for her, or able to support her in the way she needed. Before her diagnosis, Melanie had been attending a home group, which coincidentally wound down around this time, so she lost her connection with other people in the church. This loss of relationships, combined with her frustration at the lack of understanding from the wider church, soon led her to withdraw from the church. Melanie's financial situation was also made worse with her illness, and not being able to work. She thinks that the church did not really recognise this or help her through – and asks 'isn't that what church is for?'

Frustration with the churches' attitudes to social-economic issues also catalysed Allison's journey towards religious transformation. Allison is a youth-worker in her late twenties. She grew up in a non-evangelical household but became involved in what she describes as an 'aggressive' form of born-again Christianity in her teens. We explore below how Allison's early life and family background influenced her later religious journey. But for Allison, the first time she began to question her new found evangelicalism was when she went to

America, as a Christian worker in a large Pentecostal church. This church was heavily into, in Allison's words, 'the prosperity gospel – positivity – ask God and it will happen'. When Allison compared this to the lives of the congregation – economically poor, African American, without much access to opportunities to improve their situation, she found a jarring mismatch.

This unease came to a head one night as Allison was driving home from the church with a friend who was visibly upset. But her friend would not say why she was upset, as the pastor of her church had said that articulating negative thoughts gave the devil a hold. Allison found this difficult to accept, in the light of what she knew about the woman's circumstances. Another woman in the church had a picture of a luxury car taped up in the small one-bedroom house she shared with her family. She was praying for the car. Allison knew that there was no way, living where and how she did, that she would ever own the car. Again this made her question the teachings of the church. These experiences sparked a whole chain of questioning and soul-searching that Allison would never look back from. She began then to reflect on evangelicalism in Northern Ireland. In her words,

> I would have grown up with having a very dogmatic view on homosexuality, on abortion, you know, without ever questioning, it was like, well my minister told me it's wrong so it must be wrong. I didn't even know where in the Bible it says it's wrong but, you know, you just swallowed all that stuff and thought that it was right, it was not until I began to question those things that I realised that maybe we were being lied to.

Allison says she began to think through the issues for herself, and slowly, over the next few years, readjusted her beliefs in a more open, liberal direction. The Eureka moment came when two years after leaving America, Allison went back to visit and she could not believe how far her views had changed. She describes this process as very gradual, with a final moment of realisation. She says 'it was like I had new eyes'. Now, Allison believes that that there 'probably is a God', that life has some spiritual meaning and that religion is 'more than just psychology'. However, she has journeyed very far away from her evangelical teenage experience and from traditional evangelical churches.

Allison was certainly not alone in highlighting the evangelical churches' positions on moral and lifestyle issues. Ross is in his thirties, from Belfast and a civil servant. He grew up in the evangelical subculture, but began, like so many others who are transforming their faith, to rethink his beliefs at university. Ross feels that conservative evangelicalism has 'had a disastrous effect on this society and it's had a disastrous psychological effect on many people growing up in the church'. In its worst forms, Ross says evangelicalism 'can be reduced to agreeing with the penal substitutionary theory of the atonement, not doing conspicuously conservative moral things like smoking or being drunk or having the wrong kinds of sex, won't let women drive cars, forms that won't let people who have been divorced and remarried pray in church.' He goes on to say that 'it breaks my heart that Jesus has just become this formula for restricting people'. Further, he says,

> Everybody in Northern Ireland has had a conversion experience as a teenager, and clearly for most of those people it didn't work out. I'm not saying that they don't bear a degree of responsibility for what they do after having a conversion experience but when you're 14 and you go forward at a meeting and you cry and you feel like you are going to go to hell if you don't do this, and when someone tells you afterwards – not using these words – even though you're 14, and you like to stay up late, and you don't get up early for school, and you have difficulty at home, what you have to do to maintain this faith commitment is to read the Bible every morning, with Bible reading notes. And if you're an adolescent male, to not masturbate. And the reason I use those examples are adolescent males don't get up early, they don't read, and they're adolescent males, and they're going through normal human development. And there seems to be a culture within conversionist, conservative evangelical movements that have dominated in Northern Ireland that actually impede normal human development.

Peter agrees with Ross's analysis of the damage that churches can do to individuals. He says, 'I think churches should have like cigarettes, you know, a health warning: church can seriously damage your health.'

Kate echoes Ross's frustrations. Kate, who is self-employed and in her thirties, is originally from England and was not raised in an evangelical sub-culture. She converted in her late teens. She says she was introduced for a time to evangelicalism, and did not like what she saw. Kate believes that people become disillusioned with evangelicalism when they have experiences that do not fit into the frameworks that it provides. She thinks this can happen to people at any age, and that the experience is usually a negative one that causes a great deal of hurt and anger. She says she has tried to pinpoint what triggers this process, and has settled on calling it the 'X factor':

The X factor has something to do with the fact that at some point that [evangelical explanation] no longer makes sense in terms of people's experience in reality. For me the question within that then is what is it that causes the fundamental trigger? Is there some common thing that spurs that change? To me it seems to be frequently a point of hurt, pain, or anger. When their life doesn't fit into that box and when questions are posed, be it through relationships or be it through lifestyle choices, where their general experience of the world doesn't fit. Exposure to things which don't fit neatly into that evangelical box.

A key disjuncture emerged in the stories of those who are transforming between their own experiences, and the churches' views on sexuality and sexual activity. Ross hints at this when he mentions masturbation. Other interviewees talked about sexual relationships outside marriage and homosexuality as areas where their own desires, relationships and views increasingly did not fit into norms prescribed by other evangelicals.

Only one of those we spoke to, Christopher, was gay, and he talked only in the most general terms about his coming out, his subsequent problems with family and the church. Now a gay activist in his forties, he preferred to focus on the work of his organisation rather than his personal life. He says his organisation works with young gay, lesbian and transgendered people, 'to empower them, so that they're not hiding behind corners, not hiding behind a false life, not telling lies about their lives and so forth'. Christopher continues to see himself as a Christian – of which he says, 'I strive to be, day by day, but it's bloody difficult.' Christopher is adamant, however, that he has not left Christianity, and that he is keen on dialogue with the churches 'if they will talk to us'. In such a way Christopher has had to rethink the contours of his relationship with the church, and his own faith, in the light of his own sexuality.

But it was not only people who were themselves gay that talked about frustration with the churches' attitudes to sexuality. In fact most of those who are transforming highlighted this as a key issue for them. Paul, a church youth worker in his twenties, originally from England, describes the issue of sexuality as a 'time bomb' for the church. He highlights the fact that there are plenty of gay people in the church who have to keep their sexuality a secret, and that the church refuses to talk about it. Gary criticises the church for being obsessed with issues like sex before marriage and homosexuality 'yet they have no problem with the church having shares in arms companies, and companies that are exploiting people in the third world'. Kate describes the experiences of friends who have found that their sexual orientation has clashed with the 'very clearly defined rules' of the evangelical subculture, which has led not only to their, but also to her own, rethinking of faith.

These narratives emphasise how distinctive aspects of the evangelical subculture are perceived as stifling, including the imperative to convert others, unrealistic ideas about money, and narrow views on sex and sexuality. When people's experience did not fit with the norms of the churches, they sought new ways to understand and live out their faith.

Disillusionment with churches' response to politics: 'Churches are full of war memorials, which deeply offends me'

People who are transforming their faith are disillusioned with the churches' responses to Northern Ireland and global politics. It is perhaps unsurprising that politics was such an important concern, given that many of those we interviewed were involved in social and political activism. Indeed there is a chicken and egg relationship between religious change and political activism for these people. It is difficult to say whether frustration with Northern Irish politics is the cause or the product of their religious rethinking.

A few of our interviewees were born outside Northern Ireland. Paul, a church youth worker in his twenties originally from England, finds the churches he encounters in Northern Ireland to be very restricted and compromised by the conflict. He was frustrated with how he felt politics had corrupted the term 'evangelical' in Northern Ireland. Whereas he says he would be happy to describe himself as an evangelical in England, in Northern Ireland it has a 'political connotation' and 'when people describe themselves as evangelical they often mean that they're very right wing conservative Christians'. Allison agrees that evangelicalism in Northern Ireland has a lot more 'baggage' than in other places. She feels that, because of the conflict, evangelicalism has become bound up with divisive politics and a victim mentality – it has revolved around defending Protestantism rather than focusing simply on faith. She says that this baggage has caused her, and many of her friends, to leave the church. Ross grew up within the evangelical subculture but increasingly found it unable to respond to the political problems in Northern Ireland. Ross felt that at best traditional evangelical churches were silent on the topic of the conflict, and at worst they were vitriolic.

Jake, an American in his forties, had Irish Catholic forebears but was raised in a Protestant evangelical environment, including being sent to Christian school as a child and attending a Christian university. He now works for a Christian organisation based in Belfast. He first became interested in the churches in Northern Ireland as a child listening to U2's album 'War' and watching a TV programme in school about the Reformation that included pictures of the Troubles in Northern Ireland. This made a deep impression on him, ultimately culminating in his moving to Northern Ireland in his twenties to do reconciliation work. Jake was horrified to find just how strongly churches in Northern Ireland threw their weight behind particular political traditions. He says that theologically,

> I would pretty much throw my hat in the ring with the Anglicans in Ireland, but the Anglican churches are full of war memorials, and things like that, which deeply offends me. Churches have union jacks flying on them. And so that's an enormous stumbling block for me in the Church of Ireland.

It was reflection on the Northern Ireland context that led him to reject use of the term 'evangelical'. To him it has now become 'such a loaded word', to the point that he now no longer identifies himself as such.

Gary is a writer in his thirties who grew up in a large town outside Belfast. Forming relationships with Catholics at university made him question the politics of the evangelical church he had grown up in. He says he was 'born again a few times' as a child, was taken to church several times on Sunday, and had a traditional evangelical upbringing. As a child and teenager, sermons on the evils of the Catholic Church were commonplace, complete with expositions of the book of Revelation where the antichrist is the Catholic Church, the 'whore of Babylon'. For Gary, going to university was a catalyst for starting to 'think for myself' about how the churches in Northern Ireland had demonised Catholics and contributed to the Troubles. Gary says university was the first time he had met a substantial amount of people from 'the other side' and remembers thinking 'well actually, they're not as bad as I thought'. He goes on to say 'I met Catholics who perhaps have a more real faith than [I had]. You think there must be something wrong. Maybe I should go and check this out.'

So Gary was prompted to think again about the traditional evangelicalism he was raised with, by meeting Catholics who had real and vibrant faiths. He came to feel that the version of evangelicalism he grew up with 'ignored huge parts of the Bible', and that it was compromised by its links with unionist politics. This is similar to the experiences of many of those on a moderating journey, discussed in the previous chapter. Like them, Gary did not decide to reject evangelicalism outright. Rather he says he realised he needed 'a much bigger faith, a much bigger God'. It was just that Gary went further in his critique and rethinking than most who were moderating.

As a response to this political disillusionment, people who are transforming their faith have set up radical initiatives. Some of Zero28's activities included meeting with Sinn Féin politicians in pubs, and organising a film club in a monastery. Ikon's 'Evangelism Project' has involved inviting other religious groups to 'evangelise' them, which has meant visits to Muslim, Quaker, Atheist, Jewish, Hindu, Russian Orthodox, Free Presbyterian and Scientologist groups in Belfast. All of these activities represent a very self-conscious crossing of political and religious boundaries, driven by the conviction that participants can really learn something worthwhile from the 'other'.

People on a transforming journey also expressed a deep frustration with the churches' response to global social issues. They said that evangelicals had become too caught up in narrow Northern Irish concerns and failed to see the bigger picture. Ross, Jake, Geoff, Gary, Allison and Kate all perceived evangelicals to lack concern for social justice, in contrast to their obsession with sex. Many interviewees talked about the war in Iraq as galvanising their dissatisfaction with the church. They also frequently talked about third world debt and fair trade. Likewise, concern for the environment mattered deeply to some we talked to, and they were aggrieved that the evangelical churches did not seem interested. In Geoff's words, 'I got involved in politics through the environmental [movement]. That was seen by some of my old friends as not being a very Christian kind of thing to be involved in. There were no Christians there because they were more worried about heaven.'

However, despite this deep-seated frustration with the churches, people on a transforming religious journey continue to see themselves as motivated by religious concerns. They do not want to abandon faith, or even the churches altogether; rather, they seek to radically transform them. For example, Kate says,

> Our interest in a lot of those issues actually comes out of our understanding of the gospel. We believe that the gospel is a social inspiration and that we should be doing something with our lives. It's not so much about issues of personal morality. Instead it's much more about social responsibility. The difficulty is that when people discover that message, however they might discover it, the difficulty is that their churches typically aren't thinking about that.

She goes on to say,

I think it's quite amusing in a sick kind of way that those on the fringes of the church are those who seem to give a crap more than anybody else. The problem is that they give a crap but the church doesn't change, you know it sits there. We worry about this stuff, it really matters. [But] this dominant [church] culture, it just carries on.

These narratives, like the previous ones, are laced with frustration, in particular with the Northern Irish as well as the global political context. People on a transforming journey have come to see evangelicalism as a political and a loaded term, one that hinders their participation in the public sphere. They believe evangelicalism had become bound up in perpetuating division and conflict, and feel if they are to lead authentically Christian lives they can no longer fully identify with it. Yet transformers still have a desire to engage traditional evangelicalism in conversation, most still think that the churches can be influenced by their ideas, and much of their critique comes from a biblical, social justice-based, perspective. This very much distinguishes them from people we meet in the next chapter, who have left their faith.

Significant others: 'My dad was devastated when I became an evangelical'

As we have seen in other chapters, it is often the case that parental beliefs, and the religious socialisation they provide, heavily influence individuals' beliefs as children and throughout their adult lives (Baston, Shroenrade and Ventis 1993). Strikingly, many of those on a transforming journey do not have conventionally evangelical upbringings. Some do of course. However, at least amongst the people we talked to, most had some alternative religious influences in their family life. Sometimes people found in later life that they were drawn away from evangelicalism towards their parents' positions, and in some cases not. But it does appear that there is a relationship between having a template of diverse beliefs in one's family, and the tendency to experiment with faith later in life.

Allison was the most explicit about the influence of her father on her own religious journey. We met Allison earlier in this chapter, railing against what she felt was the fallacy of the prosperity gospel. Indeed, Allison's story is very much characterised by an emphasis on social justice. Even during her years in 'aggressive' evangelicalism, Allison was doing volunteer work for a community project for Catholic working-class children in Belfast. This would not have been at all typical amongst her evangelical peers, and was one of the things that started her thinking about social justice and wondering about how the church fitted into this in Northern Ireland. Allison reflects that this interest in social justice, and the impetus for becoming involved in community work, probably came from her father. Although Allison's father is not a Christian, she describes him as having a firm moral code, passionate about justice and keen to stand up for the underdog. Allison believes this made a deep impression on her growing up, and says she is increasingly aware of her father's influence in her life and now appreciates how much she has been shaped by him.

In fact, Allison's father was extremely upset when she became involved with evangelicalism. She remembers him crying on a number of occasions, because he was devastated that she had chosen this path. Allison says she was always trying to convert her father. In fact Allison's mother did become converted, thanks to her influence, but this was to a milder form of Church of Ireland Christianity rather than fervent evangelicalism. But Allison's father remained opposed to her evangelicalism, and although she says she did not realise it at the time, she thinks that this has been an important factor in her gradual journey away from born-again Christianity and towards a more open-ended faith.

Although Allison is explicit about her father's influence on her convictions, other interviewees rejected the idea that their parents' faith, or lack thereof, played a role in their own religious journeys. Neither Sophie's nor Melanie's parents were evangelicals. Sophie's had no faith at all and in fact religion represented a means of escape from her parents. She did not see her parents as role models and wanted to be as different from them as possible. Converting into evangelicalism gave her freedom to create a new life. Melanie also says that her parents' faith did not influence her. Whilst they professed some belief, and sent her to Sunday school, they did not live an evangelical life. Even though Melanie's faith is becoming more deconstructed in the present, she said her mother is actually becoming increasingly religious.

Sophie and Melanie dispute the fact that their parents' beliefs mattered to their own religious journeys; however, the lack of uniformly evangelical parents does seem to be a common feature in the lives of many who are transforming their faith. Peter's and Kate's parents were also non-religious. Geoff says that although his wider family are evangelical and have difficulties with his current theological ideas, his father has 'come a long way' from his own religious background and no longer identifies as an evangelical. Ross too is keen to point out the religious diversity in his background. He says,

My father is Belfast born, his mother was a Limerick Catholic, his father was a Donegal Protestant, my mom's Scottish and her parents were Welsh and she was bereaved by republicans, dad was bereaved by loyalists, and I've Welsh, Scottish, Northern Irish, southern Irish, Protestant, Catholic blood in my parents and my grandparents' generation, so where does that leave me?

It is possible that these early reference points of non-uniform religious families somehow act as markers for journeys later on (Rambo 1993). Perhaps they do give people more templates for how to do religious life, if at all. This reminds us that many of those who are on moderating journeys also had diversity in their family upbringing – in this case often mixed Catholic–Protestant marriages. Even if people do not turn out like their parents, or in some cases explicitly reject their parents' values, they seem to operate with a degree of freedom that many whose families continue to be staunchly evangelical do not have.

Of course some who are transforming have traditional evangelical families too. But although their ideas are seen as subversive by many mainstream evangelicals (and heretical by some conservative evangelicals) the fact that transformers are still able to talk in an evangelical language, and are keen to engage rather than walk away from faith, means that relationships are not as strained as they might otherwise be. People who are transforming may need to use some delicate strategies when talking to traditional evangelical family members so as not to offend or shock too deeply, whilst still putting forward their alternative ideas. Given that one of their goals is to change evangelicalism from within, they seem to be willing and able to engage in this way. This contrasts with the people in the next chapter who have left their faith; many of these found that their exit strained relationships with evangelical families, sometimes to an unbearable degree. Although we did not interview them, we know a number of people who have come from extremely conservative evangelical backgrounds, who had walked away completely from religion, but were actually able to reconnect with their faith through the open-ended version of religious journey offered by Ikon. And this helped improve their relationships with family members.

Alongside parents, partners sometimes had profound influences on the direction of people's religious journey (Dillon and Wink 2007: 102–3, Hout and Fischer 2002). Allison, for example, is engaged to be married to an atheist. We have seen in other chapters the extreme pressure that some people experience when their partner's religious beliefs are different from theirs. However, since a lack of prescriptiveness is at the heart of what it means to be on a transforming journey, it is perhaps unsurprising that we saw more romantic relationships intersecting across beliefs in this than in any other group. When we asked Allison how she felt about marrying an atheist, she said that her years in Ikon had opened up her ideas to the point where she no longer felt that people had to share the same ideas to be compatible. Initially she thought her partner's lack of interest in spirituality was going to be a problem. She found that adapting to his very different way of looking at the world, and his logical reasoning, was 'traumatic' at the start. However, she says that she now appreciates his outlook. She has had to make a conscious decision to open up and not to judge his views, to appreciate that someone from a very different background to hers has come to very different conclusions. This has represented another 'profound step in [her] religious journey'. Allison says she has now come to a place where she has just stopped worrying and stopped agonising over people's differences.

Desire for community: A support group for misfits

Many people who are transforming their faith had experimented with time outside religion, and had missed the feeling of community that they enjoyed in their previous churches. Geoff reflects that one of the advantages of church is that,

> It does provide everything you need – somewhere to go, spend the weekend, probably somebody to marry, it's a whole comfortable social set up there that everybody looks after each other so it's very appealing to a lot of people, while feeling that God loves you in the middle of that. I mean, why wouldn't you?

People who are transforming continually emphasised this desire to reconnect with like-minded individuals, and to share each other's lives. All of them were actively exploring alternative ways of creating community. This very much distinguishes them from people in the next chapter, who had left their faith.

The desire for community becomes clear through the language that people use to describe the post-evangelical groups they have set up. At one point, Gary refers to Zero28 as a 'support group', and Allison to Ikon as 'group therapy'. Geoff talks in terms of the 'survivors' of evangelicalism. Kate says that 'it's a lot of people who are coming from very negative places or trying somehow to actually build up community together and to have friendships ... and try to find the common paths that we're on'. It is as if they see themselves as connected through the trauma of their evangelical past, and they need fellow survivors to dissect what went wrong and forge new paths ahead. Gary puts it this way,

> I think Zero28 is a community of people who are on a journey, most of them are on the journey of faith, most of them have probably struggled with the traditional evangelical Protestant church background that they've come from, and Zero28 gives them an outlet to look at other aspects of their faith. So it's important for people who are on that journey to meet together and maybe not feel like complete misfits because they don't fit into the standard church, and encourage each other.

Kate says that whereas traditional churches are 'not a safe place' for people who think like her, the sense of community she feels with Ikon 'gives [her] strength'. Allison echoes this idea, saying that they are essentially 'disillusioned evangelicals who don't really know where they're looking for God anymore' and that meeting together might 'save some people's sanity when it comes to trying to figure out how to be Christ-like in this society'.

So being involved with other people who continue to see religion and/or spirituality as important has been a key to the transformation, rather than the abandonment, of faith. This has been the case for Gary, who says a crucial part of maintaining his transformed faith has been his interaction in a community of like-minded friends. He sees the events organised by people involved with Ikon and Zero28 as providing a safe space for people who are questioning their faith. Again here we can see how friendships with 'advocates' on a particular journey can influence individuals. Gary says,

> Each time we have an event, people bring along their friends. Other people who are on that journey from the confines of evangelical Protestantism. So it's a good way for them to meet other people who have been through that journey. To see that actually it's not as dangerous or scary outside as probably they think it is. If you imagine the evangelical church to be like a big house, a nice big house that everyone's in, we're the people who are standing outside in the garden saying, it's okay to come out. It's not as bad out here as it's been made out to be. And I think that's an important role to have, and it allows people to come out and look. And maybe they'll go back in the house and that's fine, it's just a way of saying there is a whole other world out there, maybe you want to try it.

The kind of community they seek is in many ways a loose and democratic model. As Ross speaks about his vision of community, he says,

> If you can transcribe my hand movement on the tape I'm drawing a circle in the air indicating a group of people sitting in a circle having kind of equal backwards and forwards sharing rather than someone standing up here and looking down and doing that [shaking his finger menacingly].

Indeed Ikon is run by a loose syndicate of people, which changes in membership over time, and there is a deliberate attempt to avoid top-down leadership. Zero28 employed a similar model. The weekly book group we encountered is also rather unstructured, with people taking turns to suggest readings and lead discussions. Sophie describes the book group as a number of friends who meet at one level, to discuss their ideas about faith journeys. At another level, she says they share their lives together in a way that they felt they missed since they left church. They do read books on post-evangelical topics, but she says she goes just as much to deepen relationships with friends, to eat and drink together and to talk about their lives. Indeed, as Murray points out, the emerging church is seldom institutional in the sense of being centrally planned or organised. It instead relies on 'loose networking, shared stories, "blogging" on websites and developing friendships' (Murray 2004: 69).

For some, participation in Ikon and Zero28 offers them breathing space which in turn enables them to continue their links with the wider Christian community. Gary, for example, has maintained attendance in a Church of Ireland congregation as well as participating in the post-evangelical scene. He says that 'if you believe in community, community is also about sticking with your community even when you don't quite agree with everything they do, or when you are not enjoying it'. It is interesting to see how the emerging church sometimes overlaps with traditional churches. Gary says that amongst his peers in Ikon and Zero28 about half go to a traditional church, and the other half do not. Amongst the people we interviewed for this chapter, three out of eleven also attend a traditional church as well as Ikon, Zero28 or the book group.

The former evangelicals who are transforming their faith sought and found others who are on similar journeys. They are aware of the importance of relationships for their private faith journeys, and highlight how finding like-minded people has sustained them, and in the words of some, kept them sane. They tended to use language such as 'safety, strength, sanity, support' to describe their relationships with one another and the groups they have set up.

This contrasted starkly with, on one hand their discomfort in traditional churches, and on the other, the lonely wilderness of journeying alone. While all of them sought a sense of community, it is a loose, non-hierarchical and quite unstructured form of association, less about specific beliefs and practices and more about sharing each other's lives and exploring their questions together.

Conclusions

The individuals in this chapter have experienced radical changes in their religious identities and outlooks. They represent a very small group within Northern Ireland. But their stories tell us a lot about what is important to people who experience a transformation of their evangelical faith. Some people, like those whose stories will be explored in the next chapter, experienced doubts and frustration with evangelicalism and chose to leave religion behind altogether. But the people in this chapter did not. This seems to be related to the *religious* tools that they chose to interpret their new experiences. For them, faith remains crucial for their own identities. In fact they see faith as a motivating factor behind their critique of evangelicalism, and think that faith is able to make a constructive contribution to their personal lives and in the public sphere. But their ideas about what that contribution could and should look like are very different from those put forward by the evangelicals whose ideas we explored in earlier chapters.

People who are transforming their faith are on an extremely intellectual religious journey. Although people on all types of journeys read widely and think deeply about their faith, they take this to a different level. Most are highly educated and have a keen interest in secular philosophy as well as left-wing theology. They create opportunities to explore these ideas together, for example by setting up reading groups, taking classes or blogging. They are keen to push the intellectual boundaries of their faith. They have come to a point, whether through academic study or experiencing the complexities of everyday life, where they want to question the central tenets of evangelicalism. They are not only willing to live with the ambiguous answers they often arrive at, but actually feel that their faith is improved by a non-prescriptive, open-ended approach. They think that doubt is an important part of faith, rather than a stumbling block, and prefer to emphasise the mystery and the journey of faith rather than any specific positions.

Often, they have been led to this as a result of their frustration with traditional evangelical churches. Their experiences of sexuality and relationships, or money and political aspirations, have clashed with mainstream evangelicalism, and have left them feeling uncomfortable and alienated from most churches. Because they seek to challenge and change mainstream evangelical culture, some have continued to attend church alongside their participation in groups like Ikon. Most, however, operate on the fringes of conventional evangelicalism, attending liberal evangelical churches only sporadically and making the emerging church communities the focus of their faith life.

Indeed, their continuing engagement with faith is very much related to their ability to embed themselves in these alternative religious networks. Unlike those who have left their faith, who often felt cut off from their wider community of origin and sometimes their families, the emerging church groups provided people who are transforming their faith with a support group of others who were going through a similar process. It is difficult to know if these people would have been more likely to abandon their faith altogether had they not discovered these groups. Or perhaps a better way to put this is that they are still engaged with faith to such a degree that they deliberately seek out, and in many cases help organise, alternative religious networks. Like those whose faith is deepening, remaining steady, or moderating, those who are transforming their faith are aware of the importance of relationships with others in their own faith journey. Who we surround ourselves with has a profound impact on our own ideas, and they *choose* to seek out like-minded friends, and put a great deal of effort into creating an alternative community that sustains them.

As well as the relationships that are chosen as adults, early childhood socialisation and family life laid important foundations for a later willingness to experiment with faith. Few focused specifically on the effect of their family on their religious journey, but just less than half had non-evangelical families and more had non-evangelical influences growing up. For those we spoke with, a transforming journey actually takes people a little closer to the more jumbled reality of their early influences. This does not mean that they come to believe the same things as their parents. Rather, there has been a less rigid template for how to do religion early on, and this seems to have given some people a degree of freedom to experiment with radical religious ideas. People on transforming journeys whose families are still traditionally evangelical often found that their continuing engagement with evangelical ideas gave them at least some basis to relate with them. Because of this deliberate effort to engage with evangelicalism, they seemed less cut off from families, and some churches, than those we meet in the next chapter, people who have left their faith.

CHAPTER NINE

Leaving Evangelicalism

We often hear of people 'losing their religion'. This term is misleading. It implies that people have somehow misplaced their beliefs, that faith has slipped away unwittingly. It also implies that there was a specific time and place where faith got lost. But there were very different processes at work among the ten people we talked with who once considered themselves to be evangelicals, but no longer do. Leaving their faith was not an event, but a gradual process, with a variety of experiences acting as turning points along the way. Even when people described a 'Eureka' moment, where something happened and they realised their faith had gone, this was always the culmination of an ongoing process. Moreover, far from passively 'losing' their faith, leaving evangelicalism was always a well-thought-out, agonised-over, decision. People *allowed* themselves to engage with questions and doubts that they knew might ultimately harm their faith.

The kinds of push and pull factors we focus on in this chapter include intellectual processes, such as granting oneself permission to engage with doubts about faith. We also focus on how relationships with other people, especially away from Northern Ireland, made people question their faith, and how family relationships at home have been affected by people moving away from evangelicalism. Another relationship is with the churches, and most leavers underlined that their experiences of church had been largely negative. Unlike people who are transforming or moderating their faith, people who had left their faith found that there was nothing worth saving. In fact, most people's stories about leaving show a layering of these experiences and processes.[1] Finally, we explore how people who have left their faith have journeyed towards unbelief. We examine the ways in which they continue to make meaning in life, as well as the traces of their former religious identities in their reinvented selves.

The interviews in this chapter were sometimes difficult in that some people found their experiences with evangelicalism too painful to speak about in detail. Some interviews contained sections that were off the record. Other people were worried about the consequences of being identified at the hands of their former religious communities. Others described a deep embarrassment, being 'mortified', that they had been involved in evangelicalism. Whilst our interviewees were unfailingly generous in telling us their stories, what follows must be also interpreted in the light of this hesitancy.

Questions and doubts: Passing the 'what if' threshold

In their analysis of autobiographies, McKnight and Ondrey (2008) show how questions about the Bible, including worries about the kind of God presented in the Bible, doubts about hell, and challenges to faith from science, all play a role in people's decisions to leave evangelicalism. Such questions and doubts were important for everybody we talked to. Most people highlighted doubts about the existence of God early on in their transition away from faith.

Michael is a retired teacher in his sixties who now considers himself a humanist and atheist. He was raised Brethren and his family also attended gospel hall services. He looks back to his early teenage years and recalls a series of moments that caused him to question evangelical teachings – doubts that he fleshed out in later life with reference to science and philosophy. As Michael points out 'this is a long time ago, so it's very hard for me to say exactly when these doubts started creeping in'. He is, however, able to recall some specific episodes. When he was nine or ten he opened his eyes during his minister's prayer and was shocked to find that the angels he was expecting to see were absent. Moreover, when he heard about other religions he describes feeling surprised to learn that people had other gods. He wondered what had happened to the Greek and Roman gods, and thought 'if they were wrong, maybe we were wrong'. In Michael's words, 'I just had these doubts, and the doubts were accumulating, and the doubts I suppose were also feeding into this resistance to being sent to Sunday school and church for so many hours on a Sunday, you know. Those things I suppose were working together.'

A series of family deaths cemented these early questions and doubts. When he saw his grandfather in his coffin, aged 11, he simply could not believe 'any story like "he's really gone on somewhere else"'. But it was his father's death, aged 14, that Michael describes as the 'clincher' – the moment when 'I was absolutely certain that I was not a believer, that there was no life after death, and there is no God in charge of things.' The loss of his father 'made [him] cast it all off completely'. This reaction is the opposite of Alan in chapter 5, who responded to the loss of his father by seeking out a father figure in God. In fact, Alan's story echoes the thrust of the literature on this topic, where children who lose fathers often project their feelings on to God the father (Allison 1966). Michael is bucking this trend.

In any case, these early doubts were given weight by Michael's later education. Even in school he was fascinated with science, which he used in religious education classes to argue with the teacher. The scientific view of the world he had been acquiring did not seem to accommodate religious stories very easily.[2] Moreover, he says,

> It looked as though science could actually achieve things, and cleared certain diseases out of our lives. So I had a very positive [attitude] to science in that way. Then when I went on and studied philosophy, well, there were certain philosophers that I preferred, and in a way they reinforced my outlook.

Michael cites Feuerbach, David Hume and Bertrand Russell as informing his thinking, and he was influenced by Feuerbach's idea that 'all this talk about a supernatural entity was just a projection of our own human feelings'. Michael's overall story is one of intellectual enquiry leading to a slow process of abandoning faith.

Eddie, a filmmaker in his late thirties, found his belief in God challenged in his early thirties. Eddie was raised Presbyterian, was then part of the charismatic movement for 12 years, and now considers himself agnostic/atheist. Whilst his story is of a slow disengagement with evangelicalism, he highlights two key turning points in his interview, which he calls his 'anti-Damascus Road moments'. Both of these critical moments involve logical enquiry, and a degree of *allowing* oneself to question faith.

Eddie's first 'anti-Damascus road moment' was watching Derren Brown, the hypnotist and illusionist, on TV. Brown, himself a former born-again Christian, now uses hypnotism, illusion and the power of suggestion in a non-religious context to perform impressive experiments and tricks. Watching Brown's 'Mind Control' TV series, Eddie describes his ideas, 'suddenly', as being challenged. It now seemed possible that the things he could not explain in his own life were not necessarily down to God, but could have resulted from more human phenomena. But Eddie did not immediately cast off his faith in response to this new idea. Rather, he describes allowing himself to ask the 'what if' question. He says, 'it was from that point on that I really started to engage with the fact that "what if it is all bullshit?" And as soon as I started to do that I really started to run with it.' Once he passed the 'what if' threshold, Eddie says there was no going back. This process also emerges in other interviewees' stories – granting oneself permission to question. It speaks to the agency of individuals, who, aware of the possible consequences of such questioning, actively decide to allow themselves to open Pandora's Box.

The second question Eddie was asking of his faith, almost at the same time as he encountered Derren Brown, was about the nature of God and of prophecy. A friend of his had a dream when they were in their late teens, that if Eddie did not stop smoking by the time he was 32, he would die. In a charismatic church that focused heavily on the supernatural, Eddie took this to be a word from God. He describes this as 'a guillotine hanging over me for my whole life'. As he approached 32, however, Eddie began to question why God would want him to die. He started to think 'if I believed in a God of any description, this isn't the sort of shit that he would do'. When his 32nd birthday came and went, and he remained perfectly healthy, Eddie once again talks about allowing himself to engage with the idea of not believing. His wife was worried that his 32nd year was not a good time to be experimenting with non-belief, given the 'curse', but Eddie needed to find a way to deal with it. To regain control over the situation, Eddie said, 'look, the way I am going to deal with this curse over me, is that I don't believe in God, so therefore it doesn't happen'. Eddie's strategy worked for him. In his 32nd year he talks about his life moving forward – no 'thunderbolt struck me down'. Whilst Eddie may still have some unresolved questions about faith, he now says he feels liberated. Again we see Eddie taking control of his religious identity. He responds to the 'curse' by challenging God, allowing himself to test out unbelief and see what happens.

Gavin also describes a period of being 'beset by doubts' and of allowing himself to pursue his questions about faith. A coastguard in his late thirties, Gavin was, like Eddie, raised a Presbyterian and then joined the charismatic movement in his teens. As a teenager Gavin suspected that he was 'not a spiritual person' and attempted to 'strengthen [his] faith' by reading Christian philosophy. Gavin describes this as a 'half-hearted attempt to introduce some kind of objective enquiry', but without allowing himself to ask too many questions as he was still at this stage 'a bit scared that I might not get answers that I wanted and I probably wasn't ready for those answers'. In addition to these questions, by his late teens Gavin was bored with his rural Presbyterian church and felt that there ought to be more to faith than he had experienced so far. This frustration initially led him to join a charismatic house church, which was 'all about affirming and re-affirming and affirming and reaffirming faith the entire time'. He says 'there was something about the confidence of that which is attractive to someone who is doubting'.

But it did not take long before Gavin began to ask questions of his new charismatic evangelical church. He wondered if speaking in tongues was anything more than 'gobbledygook', and says despite the myth that 'some [non-English speaking] African woman stood up [and spoke] in BBC English', he never saw anything like this. He became frustrated with how church members seemed to blame everything on demons, which could be exorcised, and came to see this as a lack of personal responsibility. Like his earlier reading of philosophy, Gavin describes a process of actively testing out his faith. Whilst being prayed for, he describes refusing to become emotional or to fall over. His friend also tested prayer in the same way – Gavin says 'we just stood there and we just looked at them and nothing happened'. One night the church pastor had a 'word' from God for Gavin, delivered in front of the congregation, which was to 'watch his friends', who were becoming a bad influence. Afterwards when the pastor prayed for Gavin, he again found it a 'very empty experience'. These experiences of emptiness, he says, provided an important turning point in the early steps of his journey away from evangelical faith.

For Gavin, these initial questions about the intellectual foundations and experience of charismatic evangelicalism, were reinforced by questions thrown up by new social relationships when he moved away from Northern Ireland. By the time he was 24, Gavin says he finally looked at his faith 'objectively and criticised it and stripped it right back and there was nothing there'. By this stage he had 'decided to open myself up to a line of questioning that meant that ultimately I might have to jack the whole thing in'. Again here we see how people make active choices, to question or not to question, aware of the possible consequences of their decisions.

Some people compared Christianity to other forms of belief, and questioned why only one belief is supposed to be correct. Wendy, for example, has a son who is in the British Army and, at the time of interview, had just been posted to Afghanistan. She thinks about the young men in Afghanistan and the Middle East, similar to her son, and reflects on how where you are born gives you your religion. She says 'everybody says their God's the true God, everyone thinks they're right'. Similarly, it was the cruelty of the idea of hell that began Liz's process of questioning evangelicalism in her teens. She recalls thinking about people she admired, as well as friends at school, and thinking that 'this cannot be their fate'.

Existential questioning – which we have argued is a key component of evangelical subculture – actually played a significant role in many of our respondents leaving faith. People know that allowing themselves to question their faith might open the floodgates of doubt and force a radical change of identity. They actively test their faith in the knowledge that it may be shaken. They seek out ideas that may challenge evangelical Christianity. In the words of Dan Barker, a former evangelical minister and evangelist 'I did not lose my faith, I gave it up purposely' (1992: 53). The comparison with individuals in chapter 5, whose faith was deepening, is striking. Those whose faith was deepening devised strategies to keep questions at bay and interpreted doubts as a challenge from the devil. It seems then that questions and doubts happen to everyone – it is what people choose to do with them that counts.

Experiences of church: Harsh moral codes and 'PhD guilt'

As Eddie told us, 'I lost my faith in religion long before I lost my faith in God.' This feeling of being disappointed by their churches was common among those who had left their faith. Some felt let down in times of personal difficulty, and this, more than any cerebral reflection on the existence of God, is what stimulated their exit from evangelicalism. Others were uneasy with the way their churches were run. Interviewees also highlighted aspects of their lifestyle and circumstances that did not fit with the moral compass of their church. A range of issues – divorce, alcoholism, single motherhood – were described by people who found evangelical churches unable to support them on their own terms.

Wendy is in her fifties and works in an office. She attended a variety of evangelical churches from her early thirties, until she finally left in her mid forties. She describes herself as 'angry at God'. But as her story progresses, it is churches that emerge as the focus of her anger. At first Wendy found church to be extremely welcoming. Although she was interested in evangelicalism from being sent to Sunday school as a child, it was not until Wendy had her first nervous breakdown in her thirties that she began to attend a small Pentecostal church. She was accompanied by her then husband, who had at one point been born-again but who was now a 'backslider'. Wendy says 'he was always welcome and it was always very much a family-type thing'. So initially church was a respite from her illness and a source of close family-like relationships. This echoes the research discussed in chapter 1, which found that faith can help people cope with depression and illness.

But a tragic string of events five years after her religious reawakening kick-started Wendy's journey away from faith. Wendy wryly sums up the events of that year, 'my mother died in the February, I had a hysterectomy in the June, my father died in July, then I had a nervous breakdown at the end of July, and then my husband left me two weeks before Christmas'. Wendy's initial response was to turn to God. At first her Christian friends rallied around and supported her. She read her Bible to find guidance, focusing in particular on the passage 'What God has joined together let no man pull asunder.' She took from this that her husband would come back. She prayed constantly, fasted and gave money to the church. She took in 'all the Scriptures about how God hates divorce and to abstain [from new relationships]'. After many years of this, Wendy realised she had been putting her faith in something that was not going to happen and she became very disillusioned. She felt that her divorce went against the moral norms of the church, and that ultimately the church could not support her on her own terms.[3] She felt judged by church members.

At the same time, Wendy was witnessing plenty of 'bickering and in-fighting' amongst her fellow believers. The first church she attended split over the Toronto blessing (a religious revival begun in Toronto in 1994, focusing on the supernatural), and she left only to have her next two or three churches follow the same pattern.[4] Her sister, who had worked for an elder of her church, had experienced an industrial accident after which her employer turned nasty, trying to wangle out of responsibility. Wendy struggled to comprehend how someone who professes to be a Christian could tell such lies. Now, Wendy says 'every church for me just stands for hypocrisy'. So a series of disappointments where Wendy did not feel that God answered her prayers, combined with souring relationships with people in her church, by whom she felt judged, cul-minated in her exit. This was a slow process of disengagement over ten years, with Wendy concluding, 'it didn't work for me in the end'.

Liz was also left reeling by her experiences with church, and it is these negative experiences that seem to be the primary reason for her disengagement with evangelicalism. Liz is in her forties and works in a pharmaceutical company. She grew up with different religious emphases, ranging from Methodism, which she describes as 'loving' and 'caring', to Brethren, which she sees as 'harsh', 'rigid' and 'punitive'. She now sees herself as agnostic. For Liz, having a child outside marriage incurred harsh disapproval and a lack of understanding from fellow Christians. This delivered a blow from which her faith could not recover. In fact Liz says that this is a 'bit of a shame, because if I hadn't have had that negative experience, I might have been someone who would have quite liked to have gone [to church]'. When she had her son and decided to try church again, she found herself at a Methodist church where they sang a hymn that included a line about 'all the poor single parent children who Santa wasn't coming to visit'. Liz describes how singling out single parents as victims of poverty made her feel 'awful' and 'very small'. She did not go back.

Liz also cites feelings of guilt as part of her bad experiences of church. She poetically describes the Brethren influence growing up as 'a big wet blanket on life', going on to say that,

> No matter what, whenever life or enjoyment or fun sprung up there was something wrong with it. They say that Catholics have A Level guilt, but if you are brought up in something like the Brethren tradition it's more like PhD guilt. No matter what it is, you feel guilty about it. We didn't have a TV for most of the time we were growing up because it was considered such a corrupting influence, and that kind of thing. And so when we did get one, you felt responsible for what was on it, as if it was your fault. Say, if a male and a female had been on the screen together and it was all completely innocent, you were still sitting there terrified in case they might kiss.

Indeed guilt about sex and relationships loomed large in quite a number of stories.[5] People lamented about not being allowed to date outside their evangelical circle as well as being made to feel as though sexual relationships were 'dirty'. Liz explains how this makes the transition to adult life difficult outside the religious context. This echoes Dillon and Wink's (2007: 34) finding that a very strict religious upbringing can suppress rather than foster religious participation in later life. Gavin says he felt guilty 'for not living up to a perceived ideal standard, the ideal standard for Christ' and connects this with not having 'the Catholic mechanism of confession to try to sort that out'. David highlights that in his experience many churches use guilt to hold communities together, encouraging people to come to church because they feel guilty about the 'bad' things they have done. He says this is one of the reasons he left. Eddie says that whilst in church, he always felt 'a bit of inferiority, I could never measure up'. Now that he has left evangelicalism, Eddie speaks about feeling 'a great liberty from guilt', a 'great sense of relief that there's no God'. This echoes the work of McKnight and Ondrey (2008), which is full of people's stories about freedom and relief upon leaving faith behind. On the other hand, Tucker's (2002) work contains stories of heartache upon leaving faith, as well as stories of relief. This pain usually relates to the loss of relationships with friends and former communities, which some of our interviewees also described.

Grace, in her early twenties, was raised Elim Pentecostal but is now agnostic. Her story focuses upon her church's lack of understanding of her father's alcoholism. Although her father was not born-again like the rest of the family, the church tried to reach out to him for a short while, particularly when problems began to take over her parents' marriage. Grace felt that the church did not try very hard to help her family, and when they saw that no religious quick fix was possible for her father, they 'abandoned' their efforts. She describes her frustration with the church who would simply 'cut off' people whose lifestyles did not fit within church frameworks.

Grace identifies aspects of her Elim Pentecostal church as 'cultish'. She talks about the way the church encouraged individuals to 'close themselves off into the church and not really have friends outside the church unless they're going to bring them to church'. This included strict rules about whom people are allowed to date – only other conservative evangelicals were suitable. The moral conservatism of the church ultimately played a role in turning Grace away from evangelicalism. She has a positive view of Christianity in general, but she is very critical of the churches in Northern Ireland. She says, 'to me Christianity is supposed to be about tolerance and open-mindedness, but my experience of Christians in Belfast is like they're very, very closed-minded and there's a lot of hatred'. She refers to evangelical protests against Gay Pride, against plays like Jesus Christ Superstar, and the aggressive way that anti-abortion campaigns are run.

Eddie also compares the charismatic church he attended to a cult, high-lighting a range of practices that he was uncomfortable with. On the surface the church was vibrant and radical, there was no dress code and worship consisted of a rock band playing contemporary Christian songs. However, this stylistic vibrancy was accompanied by conservative evangelical theology and strict top-down leadership. He also found the organisational culture difficult, for example where church elders were appointed on the basis of God speaking to the leadership through prayer. The youth team was at one point disbanded, he reports, for not having tight enough control over the church's young people. Eddie increasingly had problems with church teachings such as, 'you can't go out with a non-Christian', and that 'homosexuality was wrong or abnormal'. Despite these early question marks, Eddie maintains that he kept attending and 'really wanted to make it work for a long time'. Initially he says, he did 'feel a real connection', and that 'it was the first time I'd ever felt I was in a church where people understood me and didn't judge me'. However, in the final analysis, the authoritarianism of the church was too much for Eddie to take. These stories contrast to those told to McKnight and Ondrey (2008), who found that those who had left an orthodox faith did not reflect very much on the controlling nature of their former churches. McKnight and Ondrey argue, nonetheless, that this must have been a source of frustration. Indeed, all of our interviewees talked about the excessive control exerted by their former churches.

Not everyone, though, had negative experiences of evangelicalism. Sarah – an artist in her thirties, raised as a Presbyterian – retains an interest in Christianity. She talks about the positive aspects of religion, even though she does not now see herself as religious in a traditional evangelical sense. At the same time as being frustrated by her church, Grace says that she enjoyed some of her teenage experiences of evangelicalism. Although raised as Elim Pentecostal, she began to attend a Methodist youth group at 13, which 'was so easy-going and we all had fun and stuff'. Grace is now an agnostic who finds meaning in various alternative philosophies and, as we have seen, does not like the conservatism of evangelicalism in Northern Ireland. But she is not bitter about evangelicalism. She occasionally attends church with her grandmother because, 'I love the worship sessions, and the really lively music, and everyone singing together, and people dancing and being really free. It's amazing to watch.'

All of our respondents who had left evangelicalism talked in some way about having negative experiences of church. Some describe feeling judged and ultimately abandoned when facing key personal issues, such as divorce, alcoholism in the family, or having a child outside marriage. Others pointed to evangelical restrictions on lifestyle that they felt hemmed them in and did not allow them to enjoy life. They said they felt guilty that they were not good enough Christians. While new experiences and ideas pulled some people away from evangelicalism, these were usually combined with these more negative feelings and experiences.

Family and friends: Being the odd one out, and breaking your mother's heart

We also identified social relationships as one of the central reasons for people leaving their faith. Prominent in these were stories about friends and travel opening people's eyes to new experiences, which led them to question aspects of their faith that they had taken for granted. Occasionally people described how their family members', most importantly parents', loss of faith coincided with their own journey to unbelief. Much more common, however, were stories of strained relationships with family members who continued to believe.

In a minority of cases, parents' more relaxed attitude seemed to give their children the freedom to explore their religiosity without guilt and pain. Michael, for example, says he had some clashes with his mother when he began to disengage from evangelicalism in his teens. But she would let him and his brother watch TV on Sunday nights, whilst she played cards with her sister. When her other sister would visit on her way home from the gospel hall on Sunday nights, the cards would be swept off the table and hidden, but the TV would remain on.

Grace stopped attending the Elim Pentecostal church when her mother stopped. She says of her mother, 'when she was a Sunday school teacher, she wouldn't smoke or drink and she never went out, she was kind of like the perfect housewife, and now she's out drinking every week and yes, it's like she's a completely different person.' Grace perceives this to be a positive change and says she has a much better relationship with her mother now, as she is much more laid back. Grace's father was never a born-again Christian, so she says, 'I think we're kind of in the same place, now, actually.' This likely informs Grace's untypically easygoing attitude about leaving her faith.

In contrast, when Grace reflects on social relationships in her childhood, her story is one of embarrassment and awkwardness. Grace says that the church encouraged the children to evangelise amongst their friends – they would receive extra sweets if they brought their friends to Sunday school. Grace, now deeply embarrassed about this, describes how this played out in her school life. She recalls a friend who was Catholic, and remembers 'that I would always be on at her that it wasn't proper Christianity and stuff and I suppose in a way I hate to say it but I probably did bully her, like, for not being a proper Christian'. In fact Grace was in serious trouble on one occasion when she sent the girl a note. The note included,

> A little quiz to see if she could figure out this Bible verse. And it was something like, it must have said 'blood' in it, and I sent her like a pair of scissors wrapped inside the note and I said 'if you cut yourself', like, 'this will be the answer'.

Grace was called to the headmaster who presented her with the 'evidence' of the incident, and Grace, now 'mortified' about this, recalls thinking 'why would that make anyone want to become a Christian if they think that I am the type of person that they think is a Christian?' She identifies this as a turning point in her religious journey. She says 'that's when I really like switched on, and it just made me re-evaluate everything'. It also made a deep impact on her mother, Grace recounts, who started to think she should leave the church on account of how 'brainwashed' she saw her children becoming.

This sense of embarrassment at being the odd one out, particularly amongst one's peers, was a common theme in the interviews. And, as Gordon says, this was often accompanied by feelings of guilt, 'because I knew that as a believer I shouldn't be embarrassed'. The imperative to convert others, particularly as children and teenagers, led to much anxiety for our interviewees. Sarah says she found religious campaigns in university 'invasive' and hated doing them. Gavin remembers the exuberant worship at his charismatic church as deeply uncomfortable for him, although he did try to go along with it – 'it just seemed to be the thing to do, sacrifice all dignity and act like a buck eejit'. But it was evangelism that Gavin found most difficult. He says 'I was extremely uncomfortable with the notion that I had to spread the gospel', and says when he thinks back about the times he did try to say something 'they are amongst some of my most embarrassing memories', and 'desperately inappropriate'.

Four people highlighted the negative effect that their leaving the church had on their parents. Gordon, a retired writer in his seventies, grew up in the Brethren tradition and now describes himself as agnostic/atheist. He feels that 'essentially life is meaningless', but that human beings 'import a little bit of meaning and some sense into our life for a while' – centred around career, family and children. This is in stark contrast to Gordon's childhood religious beliefs, where he lived in constant fear of being left behind in the Rapture – an event which some evangelicals believe will happen at the end of the world, when God will remove all Christians from the planet before subjecting the rest of the inhabitants of the earth to a great tribulation. He says he was 'terrified of hell' and believed that when the Lord came back, which could happen at any moment, he would fly up through the roof. For Gordon, the central turning points away from religion were rather 'worldly'. He says he was learning about difference from his non-evangelical school friends, that he became 'hooked' by the 'sinful cinema after seeing Orson Welles's *The Third Man*', and 'then there was sex, of course'.

Gordon was an only child, and when his father died in the Second World War, it was just Gordon and his mother. When Gordon was nine, his mother lost her leg and was in hospital for years. He describes feeling under immense pressure about his mother's welfare, and went to great lengths to protect her.

For example, Gordon explained that although he ceased to believe in the church teachings at the age of 17, he had so dreaded upsetting his mother with his decision to leave that he had let himself be carried along by the machinery of church life until he was 25.[6] In his words,

> When I started not to believe, I knew this would be the worst thing in the world that I could have told her [. . .] So I went on and on and got more and more involved with the Brethren, even preaching, but I didn't believe a word [. . .] I had to go on for years, until I was 24 or 25, when I eventually broke my mother's heart by leaving.

Gordon acknowledged a sense of sadness at now being 'cut off' from the friends and family that had constituted his world for all of those years. Barbour (1994) and Tucker (2002) recount similar stories.

Owen, a designer in his forties, who was brought up Free Presbyterian, now describes himself as a nihilist. Owen also knows that his lack of belief upsets his family. Growing up, Owen found the strictures of Free Presbyterian life suffocating. In fact Owen is the only person we talked to who says he never, ever had a faith. He found church 'boring' and recalls never taking anything from it. However, Owen's father enforced a strict policy of church attendance – 'if you didn't go, right, you'd be out on your ear'. As a result Owen says that,

> At the very first opportunity, I moved away. And even now if I ever go up to visit for a prolonged period, I don't go [to church] because they can't sling me out on my ear, I don't live there any more. . . That power has gone.

Owen says that he has never discussed his views with his father, as 'there's no point' and there is no need to upset him. As a result, Owen says, 'we live pretty much separate lives'. Owen appears nonchalant about this, but the fact that he talks about his father's 'power' over him being broken suggests that this has not always been an easy compromise.

Moving away from home: 'I had to come to London to experience this'

Our interviewees also talked about making new friends, travelling and having new experiences as turning points away from faith. For example, Gavin initially says his simultaneous move away from Northern Ireland and his loss of evangelical faith are a 'coincidence'. But it soon emerges that moving away from home was a crucial part of his process of change. Having moved to Glasgow, Gavin continued to explore faith, attending an 'avant-garde', late night service – resembling a nightclub more than a traditional church. He says 'the move away from Belfast was healthy. To get perspective of what people do in other places was healthy and to also get out of a certain type of Northern Irish thinking.' Unable to find work in Glasgow, Gavin moved to London where he began to work in a charity for homeless people. He remembers talking to his mother who 'has never lived any more than a 20 mile radius from where she was born' and thinking how different his daily experiences were now from those of his family back in Northern Ireland. Although the homelessness charity was Christian in ethos, Gavin found his earlier religious beliefs challenged. He says that 'London [was] one of the main places then where I started to change across a range of issues.'

In fact, Gavin says one of the most important turning points for him was attending a Church of England 'healing service' in London. As part of the service, there was a liturgy that involved apologising for painful events in England's past, such as colonialism. Gavin says that this was 'light years away' from his experiences of church at home. He was initially annoyed because he felt as if he had to apologise for himself and where he came from, as part of a line of Protestant settlers in Ireland. But at the same time as causing him discomfort, Gavin says the liturgy was 'interesting and challenging'. He says 'I'd never seen anything like that and it just hit me like a ton of bricks.' In his words,

> I think at that moment it hit me that 'oh my God we are so blind to it. We don't even think about it', and I thought, there is never anything like this at home. There is not even talking about the other side, there's no kind of healing process at all goes on from the clergy. It just struck me how much the church had let us down and utterly and abysmally failed us. . ... There has been the odd figure that has tried to do this and some of them have been run out of town for it. . ... 25 years sitting in a Presbyterian Church I never heard anyone say, love your neighbour and that means the Catholic family down the road too. And yet they have this organisation [the Orange Order] which is a bigoted organisation into their Church . . . for a nice service. . ... I think in terms of what Northern Irish Christianity is or how it manifests itself, the lights went out there and then. . ... Sectarianism is the main cancer in our society, and we've never made a real effort to address it. . . ... I couldn't believe I had to come to London to experience this.

We know that Gavin was already having doubts about religion, and had been testing his faith before he left Northern Ireland. But this epiphany finally came in London. Not only was his new job challenging his taken-for-granted beliefs about the world, but he came to see that the form of evangelicalism with which he had been raised was quite culturally specific to Northern Ireland, and, to his mind, was deeply flawed in its failure to address the issue of sectarianism, as well as in its cosy relationship with the Orange Order. Gavin returned to Northern Ireland a few years later, saying 'I still carried some remnant of faith in Christianity home with me, but by this stage had realised that I needed to face my doubts honestly and with real objectivity. Going back to university and intellectual enquiry finally set the stage for my leaving faith.' Gavin now sees himself not only as religiously agnostic, but also as Irish and as a nationalist. Gavin is the only leaver to mention political stimulus in his religious journey. Themes related to politics and conflict were much more muted for people who had left their faith than for those on other types of journeys. Where politics did come up, people generally talked about not fitting in, having no political voice, and realising that religion in Northern Ireland was not 'normal' and could be done differently.

As with Gavin, David describes how the 'big break' with religion came when he moved away from Northern Ireland. A civil servant in his thirties who had joined the charismatic movement in his teens and left in his twenties, David also moved to London and 'cut ties completely' with his church and his 'home group' (a group of friends from his church who met weekly in each other's homes) in Northern Ireland. So he describes a slow process of social disengagement with evangelical friends. Initially this took the form of reduced contact when he went to university, followed by the 'big break' when he moved to London. He adds that the close friend with whom he started going to the church drifted away from it all over the same period as he did.

Liz moved to England to attend university. She says at this stage she was making a 'conscious decision to get away from home as soon as possible'. Aside from the religious environment that she felt was stifling her, she says Northern Ireland in general at the time was a 'grim place' with few prospects for young people. Liz describes the 'culture shock' of university. Whereas she had 'never ever been in a bar or had a drink in my life', she suddenly found herself tied to drunken students in a three-legged pub-crawl. After a while, though, Liz says that she 'did get into the way of it'. University was the beginning of a process of opening herself up to new experiences and finding out finally who and where she wanted to be in life. But it is her time in Greece that Liz highlights as really exposing the cultural specificity, as opposed to the universal truth, of religion. She talks about being attracted to the Orthodox Church, with its much more 'relaxed' form of religious practice, and realising that what she was brought up with was 'local culture and it's not necessarily the gospel truth at all'. She remembers realising, 'no, God didn't change the water into Ribena, he changed it into wine, because there was no alcohol or anything in the Baptist church'. In other words, Liz saw religion being done differently by other people, and this made her question the ideas of her upbringing.

Liz travelled for many years, 'drifting' she says 'subconsciously I was just trying to move further and further and further away [from my upbringing]'. She says the further away she went, the more secure she felt. Liz describes how her geographical and faith journeys impacted upon her relationship with her parents. Both of Liz's parents continue to attend their local Baptist church and she says that their lives revolve around it. Concerned about what she was doing on her travels, her mother wrote her letters filled with scriptural verses. Like many others, Liz describes how she learned to 'hide what your real life is'. Even now she tends to make small talk about 'safe' subjects, and says that they 'don't really know who I am'. She calls this a 'survival technique'. Because of this Liz says she could never go to her parents for emotional support and that she is just 'used to it'.

Liz's story highlights the double-edged role of social relationships for the majority of people whose families remain religiously devout. On the one hand there is a freedom brought about through moving away from the beliefs of one's parents, but this also brings with it a certain isolation. Liz's story underlines a tendency amongst people who have left their faith to consciously travel away from the place where one's parents live, as if to try to win back freedom through anonymity. Again we see how individuals make conscious choices about their lives that they know will impact upon their religious journeys.

Leaving and the life-cycle

So far we have paid attention to a variety of factors that prompted people to move away from evangelicalism. Having heard these stories, we are now able to ask *when* these changes happened in people's lives. Could there be wider patterns in play, to do with their stage in the life-cycle, as described in chapter 1?

All of our leavers were socialised into evangelicalism at an early age. All went to Sunday school as children. In a number of cases where parents were not regular churchgoers, grandparents would take children to church on Sundays or the children would simply be sent by themselves. But more commonly, as children they would have to attend church multiple times a week, as well as live by religious moral codes at home. The life-cycle literature tells us that most people who have had a religious socialisation are at their most religious in their teens and early twenties. This certainly resonates with the people we talked to – seven out of ten peaked religiously at this time. However, this was not true for everyone, and three people (Michael, Owen and Grace) abandoned their faith early, in their late teens/early twenties. Another, Gordon, had stopped believing in his teens, although he did not leave until he was 25.

If people's teenage years and early twenties are a high point of religious involvement, the research shows that people's mid-life, from their thirties onwards, is a low point. Certainly, the social roles that people were playing by their late twenties/early thirties – with new friendships, romantic and sexual relationships, demanding jobs and international travel – have been highlighted by our interviewees as playing a role in edging them away from faith. But of course in other chapters we have met people whose faith has continued to be as strong as ever in their late twenties, early thirties and beyond. So it is obvious that age alone is not a decisive factor in why people make more dramatic religious changes. The difference is that people in this chapter describe how they *allowed* themselves to contemplate change. Perhaps it is that this process of allowing oneself to ask questions is something that people mature into around this stage of life.

We also know that there is a relationship between ageing and rediscovery of faith, but our sample does not allow us to expand on this. Our two eldest respondents were two of our most convinced atheists. But then again, they were also the two people who had spent 30 years living through a conflict in Northern Ireland, which was in part defined by religion. Michael in particular wanted to disassociate himself from the conflict and carve out an alternative identity. What we cannot tell from our interviews is whether the people who are now in their thirties and forties will ever turn again to religion in later life, to help cope with illness or loneliness, or to answer existential questions about life and death. As we see in the next section, some of our interviewees do not rule this possibility out.

Convinced atheists now? 'I can feel myself burning as I'm saying that'

So far this chapter has focused on experiences and processes that have led individuals to abandon an evangelical faith. But Brewer (2002: 22–38) points out that at least some of the 'no religion' group in Northern Ireland share many religious beliefs with Christians, for example in life after death. In fact, 40 per cent say they believe in God and a further 26 per cent believe in some higher power (Mitchell 2005: 28). This section explores how complete the abandonment of faith actually is, and to what extent our respondents might continue to be influenced by their former religious identity.

Only three of our ex-evangelicals say they have absolutely no religious belief whatsoever – Owen, Michael and Gordon. Owen provides the strongest example of atheism. He says 'I don't believe in God, I don't believe in the devil; don't believe in anything religious whatsoever, no, none, nothing, not at all.' When we asked if life had any meaning, Owen said no, it was all 'random chance', 'it's like asking a dog why it's alive, it just is'. He goes on to say that he is 'not looking for meaning at all'. Instead Owen says that he lives to 'enjoy life', that his goal is to be content and do the best he can for other people as well as himself. In fact Owen is a keen environmentalist, highly motivated by 'saving the planet'. Owen plays this down, joking 'save the planet – that's where I keep my stuff', but at the same time it is clear that whilst believing life is meaningless, Owen has developed a personal framework by which he lives his life. This is, however, within an entirely non-religious context.

In contrast, two interviewees suggested that they would still like to find a church that they could 'feel at home' in. Sarah is the most religiously open of those we interviewed for this chapter. She no longer sees herself as an evangelical, but continues to identify as Christian. Looking at the things happening in the world she says she now finds 'it a lot harder to trust in the idea of a loving God'. She says she wakes up each morning asking questions about the nature of God, although she is unable to condense such complex ideas into a neat statement of position. She is attracted to the idea of being part of a community, although she does not currently attend church because she cannot find one she feels at home in. She sometimes spends time in quiet reflection, praying and reading the Bible. For Sarah, 'the main difference is that my idea of God has got bigger and I definitely feel less sure about things'. So by no means can all our ex-evangelicals be described as atheists or anti-religion.

Liz was 'totally put off' by her experiences of church, but says that she still has 'a small amount of faith left'. For her this currently lies in 'a sense of wonder in nature and a belief in a God-given conscience'. She calls this a 'basic spirituality' but not religion. She goes on to say 'I suppose I feel that there certainly is someone there who did create the whole world and that kind of thing, but further than that I don't – I don't sort of put any other constructs on it really, it's just an instinct and a feeling.' Liz also says she is attracted to the idea of community that accompanies church. As she gets older, she says she can feel herself thinking about 'going back to that if I can find a way of doing it'. She also says though that she will take her time – she will explore the idea over 'many years'. Moreover, seeing her sister, who Liz believes is developing inflexible religious ideas, makes her step back from faith. She says her sister is 'very, very conditioned, now, and in some ways is not herself anymore'. As a result Liz now feels attracted to and repelled by faith at the same time.

The rest of our respondents are more or less agnostic. As Gavin says,

> I'd say that I probably do not generally believe in God. Most of the time I don't, but I refuse to embrace science the way I once embraced religion. . . . So that's why I would go for agnostic but I don't have any kind of working faith.

Wendy too identifies as agnostic. She says, 'I think there's something there but I don't know what it is.' Living with depression, Wendy has had to confront the reality of death as she made two attempts to take her own life. Now she says death holds no fear for her, and would in fact be a relief compared to living with her illness. Rather than God, Wendy says her partner and her children are now her reason for living. Wendy's brand of evangelicalism was charismatic/ Pentecostal, so she had embraced the supernatural side of life as a born-again Christian. Although she says she is angry at the churches, she retains this spiritual awareness. She watches 'psychic programmes' on TV, and feels that she has experienced things that she cannot explain – for example feeling the presence of her mother and father after they had died.

Grace is typical of a 'mix and match' type of believer. Like two of the others we interviewed for this chapter, she still considers herself a Christian. However, she does not see herself as part of any Christian denomination – especially not an evangelical one. Grace has also incorporated other beliefs into her framework for understanding life. She says she is attracted to paganism and a kind of spirituality that sees that 'everything comes from the earth and goes back to the earth, like the natural cycle of life'. She says,

> I think I've just adopted and picked my own beliefs that I like from there and I have them for myself, kind of intertwining with Christianity as well. So it's just like I've kind of made up a religion for myself.

In his interview Eddie wore a bright red t-shirt with the word 'Anti' written in bold letters across his chest. He identifies himself as atheist, but seems to have shades of grey in this belief. He is simultaneously resolute about the fact that he feels (for now) that 'this is it' and also somewhat nervous that, for all of the freedom and enjoyment he derives from deciding *not* to believe in God, he might end up finding out that he is wrong. His interview is peppered with statements that point to his embracing of atheism and the concomitant insecurity of his new position. For example he says of evangelicalism, 'Even if there's some truth in some of it, it is just a big fucking lie.' Reflecting on his atheism, he maintains, 'I'm a fiery person: if I go for something I really go for it, I can't be fucked with half-arsedness. That kind of reflects itself in my atheism now, kind of, in a way, I guess.' The language of uncertainty that follows the definitive statement of unbelief is revealing. Eddie uses humour to defuse this insecurity. When he talks about no longer attending church he jokes 'I can feel myself burning as I'm saying that', and laughs nervously. Perhaps baldly stating one's beliefs in an interview situation, however, brings these uncertainties to the surface in a way that can be more easily ignored in everyday life. At a number of junctures, Eddie indicates that he feels he is nailing his colours to the mast by consenting to be interviewed. He says, 'regardless of what you believe about God, words are powerful – that's something I learnt in church, that when you say something out loud, it has a power [. . .] That's why I'm nervous even about saying this stuff today, you know?'

Several of our interviewees described having, in Michael's words, a 'relapse', or a time where they temporarily came back to religion. For Michael it was a college romance, ironically with a Catholic girl. He says that 'somehow just the emotion of it all swept me off down a religious – a funny religious track [. . .] for some funny reason, for a while when I was with this girl, I latched on to this idea that "God is love . . .". It was a kind of 60s thing.' This, however, co-existed with his doubt about the existence of God and faded as soon as the romance came to an end.

Although Grace left evangelicalism in her mid teens, she describes her first 'really hard religious experience' (as opposed to, in her words, 'faking' under social pressure) in her late teens. It was at Summer Madness, a large festival for young Christians in Northern Ireland. Grace describes the powerful atmosphere in a large praise tent, and the 'amazing feeling' that hit her. She was crying for hours and could not control it, and she describes feeling free from everyday pressures, as though she could escape from the stresses of modern life. But for Grace, this religious experience, within an evangelical context, was a limited moment of 'relapse'. She says in retrospect, 'it was a constant high, you were always buzzing on adrenaline – just because there's so many people there for the same thing and just the intensity of being in a crowd'. When she returned to everyday life, she says it was 'so hard to keep it going whenever you're not getting that buzz all the time'. She says the practicalities of faith – prayer and Bible study – were difficult to maintain. Given her wider narrative of disillusionment with the conservatism of the church, it is perhaps unsurprising that Grace's religious 'high' is compartmentalised in such a way. The many influences pushing and pulling her away from evangelicalism are ultimately more powerful than a temporary religious experience.

The people we spoke with who had left evangelicalism have taken rather different paths. Some continue to see themselves as Christian in some sense. Others are less sure but do not want to definitely rule anything out, and so plump for agnosticism. Others again are sure that God does not exist and so have opted for atheism (Gordon), humanism (Michael) or even nihilism (Owen). In some cases atheism, like religious faith, can be tinged with doubt. And interestingly, leaving your religion is not a one-way street – sometimes people 'relapse' back into earlier forms of belief. Amongst the people we spoke to, these relapses were temporary. But this is not to say that atheism or agnosticism always represent the end of a religious journey.[7] These positions too may be adapted over time.

Conclusions

The stories in this chapter show how far people are able to change the religious identities they were born into. Individuals exercise a significant degree of choice over their own religious journeys – choosing to embrace questions and doubts, or choosing to move away from home and to find out how other people live.

The people who have told their stories in this chapter often have siblings who continue to be religious. Michael says 'I have a younger brother, he's just a year younger than me, he's very religious now, so we're quite different. But he's led a very different life to mine.' Liz's sister, as we have seen, has a conservative faith. Wendy's sister is very religious. Owen has eight brothers and sisters. He says that 'almost everyone else, all of my siblings, has a religious belief, but I don't'. So whilst experiencing religious socialisation is very important in shaping individuals' lives, it does not dictate what positions we take as adults. Instead, the religious ideas of our upbringing combine with all the experiences we have and roles we take on as we move through life.

The experiences that push and pull people out of evangelicalism seem to centre on a few main axes. Firstly, people had negative experiences of church, where they felt their lifestyles and circumstances harshly judged. Or they felt that their individuality was being suppressed by conservative churches. Unlike people who are transforming their faith, they felt that nothing could be salvaged from their religion. Secondly, people who had left evangelicalism were much more likely than the people in other chapters to have moved away from Northern Ireland and had a wide range of social interactions outside their comfort zones. Thirdly, evangelicalism had made most people who eventually left their faith feel uncomfortable in their peer groups. They report feeling like the odd one out, and becoming acutely aware of how different their ideas were to those of their friends. These experiences combined with intellectual processes of reflection and questioning. They began to doubt their faith and, instead of suppressing these doubts, they allowed themselves to entertain them. These push and pull factors layer over each other, unfurling over time.

Many people also said that leaving their faith was a bittersweet process. Whilst the choice to leave was on the whole a positive and liberating experience for all of the interviewees, many acknowledged a range of feelings of vulnerability and isolation early on in the process. For some the decision to leave evangelicalism had serious personal consequences, particularly insofar as it put a strain on relationships with parents, other family members and old friends. However, they eventually devised strategies to sustain these relationships at some level – sometimes by living separate lives or not allowing their parents to know their real thoughts and feelings. This underlines the fact that leaving a faith involves, if not breaking away from, then at least changing, valued relationships with the family unit or close friends. This contrasts to the people on moderating and transforming journeys, who had sometimes radically changed their faith, but who still operate to some extent within a wider evangelical family. They are also critical of the churches, but from *within*. And the fact that their dialogue with evangelicalism is ongoing seems to have enabled some to maintain less fraught relationships with families and people from their past.

CHAPTER TEN

Conclusions: Explaining Religious Journeys

How do evangelicals in Northern Ireland come to journey in different religious directions? We can often trace the evolution of a religious journey back to a person's childhood socialisation, their family relationships and formative experiences of church. But sometimes we find that people on very different religious journeys have shared relatively similar experiences early on in life. What differs is how people process these experiences, and how they choose to organise their lives. People develop different ways of dealing with the same kinds of problems. Some turn their back on God when things go wrong in their lives, whilst personal hardship makes the faith of other people even stronger. Coming into contact with new ideas and critiques of religion has caused some people to radically redefine their faith, whilst others' faith held firm in the wake of such questioning. Some people see Derren Brown on TV, decide he is a Satanist and switch over the channel, whereas others become profoundly challenged by the new insights on offer.

Although it is never the case that one factor causes someone to become more religiously moderate or conservative, there do, however, seem to be some patterns at work. For each different journey we found *patterns of experiences* that operated in tandem with one another to push and pull people in a certain direction. Rather, it is these *combinations of factors*, chains of thoughts, relationships, experiences and events, that help to explain why people respond so differently to ostensibly similar types of experiences.

We are not claiming that these patterns of experiences and combinations of factors should be understood as immutable laws. They do not constitute another theory about religious change. They do not provide foolproof predictions of the types of religious journeys that people will undertake. But we think that these patterns and combinations can function as *indicators* of the religious directions that evangelicals are *likely* (though not guaranteed) to take when confronted by their socio-political context and by packages of experiences. These patterns and combinations have been explored in-depth in the previous chapters, for each variety of journey. Below, we compare which factors and experiences are most likely to point to various directions of religious journey, thus offering a brief synthesis of the insights from previous chapters.

Patterns in social relationships: family, friends, advocates and the 'other'

The social psychology literature reviewed in chapter 1 argued that early experiences in life lay down markers for later in life, and this is very much the case for people's religious journeys. For example, all of those who experienced religious conversion as adults had early religious reference points. In cases where parents were not religious, sending their children to Sunday school and evangelical churches laid a foundation for later religious re-awakening. But we found people on *all six* religious journeys who had conservative evangelical upbringings, and who then made very different religious choices in later life. Clearly early religious socialisation alone cannot account for religious identity choices.

Rather, it matters what type of relationships evangelicals have with their families. Those whose faith was deepening in a conservative direction tended to have family networks that were tightly religious, and relationships with non-evangelical family members were a source of tension. This encouraged them to shore up their faith, particularly in times of trouble. On the other hand, variation within family composition, in particular mixed marriages with Catholics in an extended family, seemed to lay foundations for some evangelicals who changed in a moderate direction. This provided contact with a different culture from an early age. Eventually, relationships with Catholics later in life challenged their previous evangelical lifestyles and world-views.

Many of those on a transforming journey had families who never liked evangelicalism in the first place, and this seemed to allow them a degree of comfort in radically changing their beliefs. Many of those who left evangelicalism, but whose families remained evangelical, found continuing relationships with their family painful. For others, parents' leaving evangelicalism happened in tandem with children's leaving and this was a source of camaraderie. In these ways, family relationships are absolutely central to practically everyone's religious journey. However, being born into one type of family does not neatly predict one's later religious choices. Rather, it lays down markers that may incline people to take one path or another, or predict the ease or difficulty with which a person can make significant religious changes.

We do not choose our families. But we are usually able to choose our friends. For example, people whose faith was deepening tended to cut out non-evangelical influences, restricting social circles to like-minded individuals. And this had the desired effect of bolstering their existing beliefs. Those on steady journeys did not cut themselves off from all non-evangelicals, but were careful to prioritise a close evangelical circle. They did this quite deliberately to avoid external challenges to their faith.

In contrast, those whose faith was moderating were happy to engage in ecumenical dialogue and often counted non-evangelicals in their close social circle. People moving towards religious transformation enjoyed wide and diverse social circles, although they were also keen to surround themselves with like-minded people for support and to explore their religious journeys together. People who had left evangelicalism behind now tended to have social circles that include few evangelicals. Whether someone has a religiously diverse circle of friendships really depends, it seems, on how receptive they are to allowing external influences to shape their ideas. And people usually achieve the outcome they expect. Restricting social networks to religious people only is a very effective way of buffering one's faith, whereas seeking out diverse social relationships usually pushes people further down a path of religious openness. In all of these cases, the deliberate nature of friendship selection is striking.

As with friends, those on a steady journey tend to select partners that share the same beliefs as themselves. Evangelicals whose faith was deepening by and large also sought like-minded partners, but some who had converted as adults found themselves married to non-believers. This often created tension within the family – generally where a non-believer would see their partner as 'nutty' and the evangelical partner, worried for their spouse's soul, would try to engage them in conversations about faith, meeting with varying degrees of annoyance. We do not know how these will be resolved in the future, whether differences can be shelved, whether one partner will become persuaded by the other's views or whether this may ultimately lead to marital problems. No doubt all of these are options, depending on the other factors at play in an individual's life. Some people who were transforming their faith were open to having partners with different religious views to themselves, and we saw how they could influence one another. For example, an atheist partner would prompt a post-evangelical to question their faith even more critically; and a post-evangelical partner could soften the views of an atheist.

Further, nearly all converts described the influence of advocates – people who initiate conversations with others about faith – at some point before they became saved. Advocates often come from within the family circle, but also include colleagues, religious workers and sometimes strangers, who take the potential convert under their wing. We also discovered that there are liberal advocates – people who had moderated themselves and who sought to bring other evangelicals down this path with them. Indeed this kind of internal evangelical dialogue was one of the major stimuli for religious moderation. Why someone is prepared to listen to what an advocate has to say, rather than brushing them off, is of course linked to all of the other factors we are discussing here – for example whether someone is familiar with evangelical ideas from childhood, or whether they are in the midst of a personal crisis and looking for comfort or explanation. In these ways, evangelicals' religious journeys are not just informed by the families they were born into, and the friends and partners they select, but are also shaped by people in society – strangers and proselytisers – who actively seek to influence their faith.

Finally, we found that where evangelicals developed meaningful relationships with Catholics – the primary 'Other', or out-group, for many Protestants in Northern Ireland – this often prompted them to make moderating, transforming or leaving religious journeys. Northern Ireland remains a highly segregated society, so mixing with Catholics cannot be taken for granted. The opportunities for relationships with Catholics are not spread evenly across social classes and geographical location (Shirlow and Murtagh 2006). But for our interviewees, sometimes relationships with Catholics started at home – for example having a mixed marriage in an otherwise evangelical extended family. In other cases relationships developed when people spent time outside Northern Ireland, often in the Republic of Ireland, where developing genuine friendships with Catholics made it difficult for them to maintain anti-Catholic views. Many people's contact with Catholics began within the religious sphere – through the charismatic movement or through liberal evangelical advocacy organisations – and when people encountered Catholics as genuine believers, they were compelled to revise their own beliefs in a moderating or transforming direction. Very often *all* of these points of contact with Catholics were at play for individuals, reinforcing one another.

On the other hand, those who wanted to maintain, or deepen, a conservative form of evangelicalism had very minimal contact with Catholics. For these latter groups, contact with Catholics was based around evangelism, and did not involve an equal sharing of views. This is because these evangelicals believe that Catholicism is heretical and that Catholics' souls must be saved. And to date in their religious journeys, there had been no events or experiences that had caused them to question this interpretation, and they did not seek these opportunities out. Although this does not mean that no conversations occur between these evangelicals and Catholics, occasions of *meaningful* or *mutual* social interaction, outside proselytism, are extremely limited.

Life-course patterns: religious change is just a matter of time?

Life-course research indicates that a high point for religiosity is the teens and twenties, the low point is mid-life (from people's thirties to fifties), and that there is increased interest in religion again in old age. Among our interviewees, people were most likely to change their religious beliefs in their late twenties and thirties. This was particularly the case for people who were moderating and transforming their faith. Of those who left evangelicalism, most did so in their teens and twenties. None of the older leavers we spoke to had been tempted back to faith as they aged. Of those who experienced religious conversion as adults, we found a spread of ages over the teens, twenties, thirties and forties – so mid-life was actually a time of quite radical change for many.

Some of these processes are not quite in line with general life-course findings, although our sample is too small to make definitive alternative arguments. Further, the focused nature of our sample – for example, when we deliberately sought out evangelicals whose faith was moving in a moderating direction – also creates a bias towards experiencing change at any age. Where our study did fall into step with life-course researchers is the deepening of faith in later life, where faith has helped people cope with problems that arise at this time such ill-health, divorce or loss. We found that there is indeed some relationship between the life-course and religious journeys, but only in a loose way. Being at a certain age or stage in life often correlates with other experiences, such as periods of study, or declining health, but it did not predict, at least for our interviewees, what decisions they made on the basis of these experiences. Once again, it was the *combination* of other relational and cultural factors with people's age and stage of life that came to shape religious choices.

Political factors: can politics prompt personal religious change?

Many people's stories in this book have a distinctly Northern Irish flavour. Some converts initially became interested in religion, and started attending church, for political reasons. Once they had started to use religion for political purposes, they ended up becoming sincerely interested in faith. A similar process was at work for those whose faith was deepening in a conservative direction. Their concern at what they perceived to be unionist loss had caused them to strengthen their faith. They gave up hope that politics could meet their needs and focused instead on religious goals.

The political climate was also important in shaping religious journeys towards moderation and transformation. For those who were moderating, relationships with Catholic colleagues, friends and family members challenged the conservative evangelical ideas with which they were raised. These relationships forced them to think again about the political situation in Northern Ireland, which in turn led them further down a path exploring reconciliation. People moving toward religious transformation were also unhappy with the divide in Northern Ireland. Their anger at evangelical churches' maintenance of the segregated status quo was a factor in their radical redefinition of religious identities. Also, their focus on global political issues, social justice and peace-building led them to further deconstruct their faith.

People on steady religious journeys and people who had left evangelicalism did not talk about politics very much. For those maintaining a steady journey, this is largely related to the form of pietistic evangelicalism that most of them espoused (Jordan 2001, Ganiel 2008a). Those who had left evangelicalism tended not to cite politics as a reason for their personal religious changes. But nearly all said that they felt politically irrelevant in Northern Ireland, and that this was frustrating. So some people are more engaged with politics than others, and politics shapes some religious journeys more than others. Again, we did not find that politics alone could explain individuals' religious choices, but, in combination with other factors, it was often a potent catalyst for religious identity change.

Popular culture: Patterns in engaging with the world outside evangelicalism

Evangelicals in Northern Ireland and elsewhere have had ambivalent relationships with popular culture, at times shunning it and at other times engaging with it and using its tools, such as television and the internet, to advance their goals. It was no surprise, then, that our interviewees talked about their involvement with popular culture. Some actively resisted what they perceived to be inevitable challenge from the world outside evangelicalism, whilst others deliberately wanted to test their faith to see if it would hold up to scrutiny. Again these predispositions are linked to other factors, for example having encountered diversity in early family life, or having had negative experiences with church in the past. Although we do not explore personality in this book, it is also no doubt related to people's level of curiosity and attitudes to risk.

And of course these predispositions to dealing with outside influences impact deeply on people's religious journeys. Those who try to hold the world at bay – not studying 'threatening' subjects at university, or reading only evangelical literature that confirms their faith – unsurprisingly found that their faith did not change much or became stronger. In a few cases people accidentally became exposed to new ideas – for example through study at school – and tried to compartmentalise questions they could not answer to protect their faith. In contrast, those who actively sought out new ideas from secular culture, television, music, travel, reading history, psychology and philosophy, often found they were compelled to reassess their existing religious ideas. They experienced quite different religious journeys with more dramatic changes.

Subcultural factors: dealing with existential questions and doubts

Most of the evangelicals we spoke with had thought deeply about their faith. At times their reflection was prompted by the evangelical subculture's emphasis on questioning, at other times it was sparked by their experiences in secular education. Most of the people whose faith was moderating and transforming, as well as those who had left evangelicalism, held university degrees; most people whose faith was deepening in a conservative direction did not. On the other hand, some of the most conservative evangelicals we spoke to actually became more conservative at university, whilst others who were leaving or moderating left school at an early age. Clearly, there is not an absolute correlation between the types of education evangelicals receive and their subsequent religious journeys.

But there is an important relationship between study, intellectual engagement with faith, and religious journeys. People whose faith was deepening in a conservative direction were well versed in the Scriptures, and had rehearsed evangelical arguments in detail. However, they tended to provide experiential rather than intellectual explanations for their faith and their journeys – much like Jordan's (2001) oppositional evangelicals. A handful were more like Jordan's confessional evangelicals, for whom detailed doctrinal study had pulled them in a conservative direction.

In contrast, those who are transforming their faith are intellectually driven in a different way, seeking outside secular ideas and philosophies to interrogate their faith. Many have postgraduate degrees, and are interested in post-modern philosophy and the creative arts. Most evangelicals on moderating journeys are keen consumers of theological literature and biblical criticism and like to explore their faith at an intellectual level. Most people on a steady journey also like to engage intellectually with faith, but this is usually through engagement with *evangelical* literature and exegesis. We found one person on a steady journey who studied an academic subject that critiqued religion, but most others on a steady path avoid intellectual critique, or at least try to compartmentalise critiques of their faith. This is a key characteristic of pietistic evangelicals, described by Jordan (2001), which emerged as the dominant mode of faith amongst those on a steady journey. Some of those who have left evangelicalism have been motivated by secular critiques of evangelicalism, from science, philosophy and history. But by no means all those who left were motivated by intellectual concerns, as might have been expected given the prominence of 'new atheist' discourses in the contemporary public sphere (Dawkins 2006).

Finally, evangelicals dealt with doubts about their faith in different ways. For those whose faith was deepening, doubts, like personal crises, were interpreted as tests of faith and attacks from the devil, and therefore were to be actively resisted. People maintaining a steady journey expressed no doubts about the existence of God, nor about the truth of evangelical teachings; instead, they described doubts about their ability to live up to evangelical ideals. Again this was seen as a test of their faith. Those whose faith was moderating, on the other hand, expressed a range of doubts about conservative aspects of evangelicalism and worried about its connection with exclusive unionist politics. Seeing other people's ways of doing things helped individuals reflect on their own beliefs, and many did some editing. It did not, however, make them question the essential validity of their belief system. Those who were transforming their faith spoke of a wide range of doubts about the nature and existence of God. But eventually, they embraced doubt as a natural and healthy aspect of faith. Finally, many of those who left evangelicalism expressed persistent doubts about the existence of God, often beginning at an early age. Again, what people choose to do with doubts is linked to a variety of other factors – how their family deals with doubt, how intellectually risk-averse they are, or whether they have developed deep friendships with non-believers that compel them to question their own ideas.

Subcultural factors: the role of the churches

Evangelicals had different experiences of their congregations and wider networks of evangelical churches, which prompted them to change in particular directions. For example, people who had left evangelicalism, and those who are transforming their faith, were frustrated and sometimes angry with evangelical churches. When facing personal issues with sexuality, alcohol, divorce and mental health, many people felt that the church would not or could not engage with them realistically or without judgement. They felt that the churches simply ignored or even attacked them when a quick, spiritual, solution to their problem could not be found. Again, disappointment or anger at the churches was never the only reason for people disengaging with evangelicalism, but it often initiated a new openness to questioning beliefs that were previously taken for granted. This worked in combination with their disillusionment to take them on a journey towards change.

In contrast, those on religious journeys of deepening, steady maintenance, and to some extent moderation, were comfortable in their churches – or, in the case of moderating inclusivists, willing to overlook or forgive the churches' shortcomings. Church offered close relationships and, for some, acted as a kind of replacement family where relationships with the biological family were difficult. Those on steady and deepening journeys talked about the warmth, comfort and structure that church provided in their lives. Even when people on moderating journeys were dissatisfied with churches, most were able to find a denomination or congregation where they felt at home. Indeed, positive relationships with church and feeling part of a wider religious family were an important factor in keeping people in the evangelical fold. People who were transforming and had left traditional evangelical churches behind rued the loss of relationships, and set up alternative community structures, for some the 'support group' of what might be called pub Christianity or the emerging church. Even some of those who had left evangelicalism identified aspects of church that they enjoyed – the music, the sense of togetherness – and felt sad that their negative experiences outweighed the positive. In short, people whose journeys continue to take place within evangelical churches do so for a reason. These people find support, warmth and structure in churches, so they do not journey too far away from them.

Moments of crisis

Personal crisis, such as a loved one's death or a trauma, is often the immediate catalyst for religious conversion or change. But it is never the only factor in what are always long, multilayered journeys. For those whose faith was deepening in a conservative direction, personal crises are often interpreted as tests of faith or attacks from demonic forces. In fact a focus on the afterlife, where earthly troubles will melt away, provides great comfort to many people and helps explain why they would not turn against God in a crisis. Moreover, many feel that whilst they cannot cope with the hardships of life by themselves, God provides them with the strength they need. These include people on steady, moderating, and in some cases transforming journeys.

On the other hand, some people we met who had left evangelicalism said they were angry with God for not helping them in times of crisis, for not answering their prayers. Anger at God is often layered on top of negative experiences of church, where people felt judged or abandoned. It is rarely the case that a personal crisis knocks an otherwise completely stable religious journey off course. More usually a personal crisis emerges as the straw that breaks the proverbial camel's back, after a much longer period of questioning and dissatisfaction.

The stories we have shared in this book demonstrate that religious change is dynamic and multi-faceted. We have found that there is not any overarching theory of religious change. But, rather, elements of previous theories on the life course, on social relationships, on political catalysts, work in tandem with one another to shape people's religious identities. We have found that religious journeys are gradual processes that are shaped by the cumulative effects of influences, events and experiences over the course of a lifetime. It appears to be the *combinations of factors*, or the *patterns of experiences*, that shape religious identity choice and change. This helps us understand, for example why two people might have very different religious responses to an experience of a personal trauma, or being sent to Sunday school at an early age. These are links in a much wider chain of experiences that an individual goes through, and it is this wider chain that must be understood in order to really grasp how personal religious change works.

Choosing their religion?

Religious identities should be viewed as works in progress, as journeys over a lifetime, rather than as ultimate identity positions. This is something that is obvious to religious people themselves, whose everyday lives are marked by a gentle ebb and flow of religious belief and practice, as well as by dramatic religious turning points. But this is not always obvious to people on the outside looking in at religious subcultures, particularly if those subcultures have been caricatured or stereotyped – as is the case with strong forms of religion such as Northern Irish evangelicalism.

In this book, we have emphasised that evangelicals' religious beliefs, practices, identities and positions can and indeed do change over the course of their lives. As we have shared the stories of evangelicals, we have demonstrated how that change happens. Most of the theories of religious change that we discussed in chapter 1 emphasise the importance of macro-level or structural factors in stimulating religious change. Informed by these theoretical approaches, we felt it was also important to reach underneath the broad patterns which they identify and demonstrate how change works for real people in their everyday lives. And the stories we share have, we hope, provided an insight into the complexity of personal religious change that would not otherwise be accessible.

We argue that individual choice plays a central role as people live out their everyday religious lives. Evangelicals are able to live with contradictions and grey areas in their religious beliefs and practices, and often they deliberately choose to do so. Most endure spiritual lows in which their faith is tested, and times of spiritual peacefulness when they feel secure and happy. They revise and adapt their religious ideas as they age, or in response to personal and political experiences. The people we talked to had put a great deal of thought, and intentional work, into constructing their religious identity. Evangelicals in Northern Ireland are extremely active agents in their own religious journeys. Rarely was an evangelical identity held in a passive, unthinking way. Nobody told us they were an evangelical because they were born into it. Indeed, the degree of creative management people exercise over their religious journeys is striking. Even where people do not experience great change in their religious journey over time, this does not mean that they are unthinking products of their religious upbringing. To a large extent, they *choose* the status quo. Their strategies for maintaining faith are self-conscious and often just as creative as those who totally transform or abandon their religious identities. People limit their friendship networks, or choose not to read books that challenge their beliefs, in a very intentional way when they want to protect their faith. They make extremely rational cost-benefit analyses when deciding whether or not to become converted into evangelicalism in the first place.

Those who choose to make radical changes to their identity, by leaving their faith altogether, for example, often face considerable opposition from family and former friends. But whilst this may make leaving uncomfortable and upsetting, this does not ultimately stop people from responding to new social influences over their primary religious socialisation. Again, we were interested to discover how deliberate people were when they made radical changes in their religious identities. Individuals often experienced a gradual chipping away at certainty, and reached a point where they felt they had to *choose* to entertain their doubts further, rather than continue to ignore them. When they finally allowed themselves permission to question their beliefs, they knew very well that this might lead them away from faith. Often they were nervous about making this choice, and were forced to make personal sacrifices such as family relationships. But they also enjoyed the sense of freedom that such questioning brought with it and forged ahead regardless.

Northern Irish evangelicals are indeed choosing their religion. But these changes and choices are not random. Evangelicals are responding to experiences within their subculture, popular culture, political structures within Northern Ireland, and wider social influences, and are making changes accordingly. This brings us back to Ammerman's (2003: 212) argument that agency is located 'not in freedom from patterned constraint but in our ability to invoke those patterns in non-prescribed ways'. So, in the end our religious journeys are products of our own intentions, deliberations and decisions. However, the outcomes we come to pursue, and the way we make decisions, whilst they are not dictated, are profoundly shaped by earlier social influences and pre-existing political circumstances. It is in this context that we call sociologists of religion to pay more attention to the role of individual choice, by highlighting the complex ways in which people interact with religious, social and political structures, and the different outcomes this might have for personal identity.

Concluding thoughts

Northern Ireland remains a deeply divided society, and the legacy of the conflict continues to shape people's everyday lives. As we have argued, the everyday lived religion of Northern Irish evangelicals is embedded in an overarching subculture in which political issues are not the only, nor even the main, concern. In this post-conflict era, we think that it has been important to focus on the everyday lives of evangelicals, demonstrating the range of issues they are interested in beyond the political sphere. Undoubtedly, experiences of the Troubles are important to many people's religious journeys. But people spend just as much time talking about the more mundane, everyday aspects of their lives: marriages and families, friends and colleagues, health and illness, books and music. Our focus on everyday life reflects what is actually on evangelicals' minds now in Northern Ireland. This is a first and essential step in broadening the debate about religion in Northern Ireland beyond the parameters of a predominantly Troubles-focused literature.

Further, there is also a new fluidity and openness in Northern Ireland – a window in which identities might be experimented with and religious practices might be adjusted. The absence of daily violence and the increasing 'bread and butter' focus of local politics have introduced a new context for evangelicals, who are adapting in different ways. Some are horrified that unionists now sit in government with republicans and choose to focus instead on religious goals, whilst others are seizing the opportunity to explore their relationships with their Catholic neighbours more deeply. Some are picking through popular culture to find things that strengthen their faith, whilst others are allowing their faith to be fundamentally challenged by contemporary cultural ideas. Some use Belfast city centre to protest against civil partnerships, whilst others meet in pubs to explore their faith with friends over a pint of Guinness. These differing voices and perspectives on change co-exist within the subculture, often in tension, but also frequently in dialogue, with one another.

Just as the evangelical movement is adapting to change in a of variety ways, there is also complexity within the lives of individual evangelicals. They are ordinary people who are engaged in a process of exploring, critiquing, doubting, confirming, enjoying, and struggling with their faith. Even when it might seem on the surface that some evangelicals do not change their beliefs much over time, probing more deeply we find that everybody is on some form of religious *journey*, where beliefs are not static but need continual support or review – in Ammerman's words (2003: 208), 'active identity work'.

Indeed the very act of writing about these evangelicals' stories in a book endows their religious journeys with a permanence that is not quite real. A book allows readers to receive only an incomplete snapshot of evangelicals' lives, and a partial understanding of the direction in which they were journeying when we had our conversations with them. We close with a reminder that these evangelicals are still working out their faith in innovative and unexpected ways. They are constantly adapting to, as well as shaping, society in Northern Ireland after the Troubles.

Notes

Chapter One: Perspectives on Personal Religious Change

1   This particularly applied to those who had rather stable religious trajectories over time, whether this was always being religious or always being non-religious.

2   Erving Goffman in *The Presentation of Everyday Life* (1959) argued that we are all like actors on a stage, delivering the lines of a play – the script – that has already been written by society.

3   For more on social identity theory see Abrams and Hogg, eds (1990).

Chapter Two: Evangelical Subculture in Northern Ireland

1   Northern Ireland Life and Times Survey, 2008, 1998. In 2008, 7 per cent of Protestants attended church several times a week, 20 per cent attended once a week, 9 per cent attended nearly every week and 8 per cent attended two to three times a month. In 1998 the answer options were slightly different, and 36 per cent said they attended once a week or more, whilst a further 7 per cent said they attended at least once in two weeks.

2   Mitchell and Tilley (2008: 745) found that 64 per cent of Protestants who identified as evangelical, 80 per cent who identified as born-again and evangelical, and 88 per cent as born-again, evangelical and fundamentalist, attended church at least weekly. If we examine denominations which are known to contain evangelicals, we find a similar pattern, with up to 87 per cent of members of the Elim Pentecostal Church, and 60 per cent of Brethrens and Free Presbyterians attending church at least weekly (Mitchell 2005: 24). But of course not all Protestant church attenders are evangelical. Mitchell and Tilley (2008: 743) found that over a third (35 per cent) of weekly church attendees simply identified as Christians and as Protestants.

3   Reports on the surveys can be accessed here: http://www.ecumenics.ie/research/visioning-21st-century-ecumenism, Ganiel (2009a, 2009b).

4   Brewer also talks about a secular form of anti-Catholicism, but this appeals to secular unionists and political loyalists, rather than to evangelicals.

5   For a comparative analysis of the role of religion in peacemaking, see Brewer (2010: 56–67).

6   This is also the case for evangelicalism in other parts of the world, though this point can often be underplayed in analyses of evangelicalism that focus on its political effects.

7   Weber (1958 [1915]) talked about salvation anxiety, and argued that Protestants constantly sought proof that they were going to heaven. For Weber, this helped to explain the 'Protestant ethic' – the emphasis on hard work, living a frugal life and building successful businesses that many Protestants took as evidence of God's blessing and which eased the burden of anxiety.

Chapter Three: Methods

1   The appointment of Rev. Cheryl Meban, a Presbyterian minister, as the chair of the Centre for Contemporary Christianity is an exception to this rule. Despite Meban's considerable ability, it is worth pointing out that she has not attained the high public profile of Porter, who has since moved on to become the Director of the Centre for Reconciliation at Coventry Cathedral. It is also the case that ECONI/CCCI is now a much smaller organisation and no longer has a paid director. As chair, Meban could be considered to have the highest current 'rank' within the organisation. Previously, ECONI/CCCI had an unpaid chair that performed duties similar to Meban. This post has also been held by a woman in the past, Ethel White, a research scientist.

2   Respondents are assessed on their views on the importance of each of the seven types of reconciliation, and also on their overall attitude. A 'high view' is here defined in regard to an individual question as a respondent giving a rating of 4 or 5, or in regard to overall attitude, achieving an aggregate score of 28 or more on summing the ratings given to each of the seven questions. This data appears in Ganiel (2010b). Initial reports on the surveys can be accessed at http://www.ecumenics.ie/research/visioning-21st-century-ecumenism/ (Ganiel 2009a, 2009b). We are indebted to Chris Morris for assisting with this analysis

3   Data on educational attainment is taken from the Northern Ireland Life and Times Survey 2008. Data on urban/rural population is based on the 2001 Census. Northern Ireland Statistics and Research Agency, 'Northern Ireland Census 2001 Population Report'.

4   Ikon is a post-evangelical group in Northern Ireland and is discussed in more depth in chapter 8.

Chapter Four: Converting to Evangelicalism

1   Rambo's (1993) book is by far the best overview of conversion that we have read. He pulls together a century's worth of research in psychology, sociology, cultural anthropology and missiology, and draws on numerous interviews with converts, to shed light on the process. He argues that all converts go through a similar cycle – emerging from a cultural *context*, potential converts experience a *crisis* that stimulates a *quest* to find answers, they *encounter* other believers, and this leads them to make a *commitment*. In this way, Rambo identifies four central dimensions of conversion – cultural, personal, social and religious. We address all of these here – we deal with culture when we talk about the political context of conversion in Northern Ireland, the personal dimension when we talk about active deliberation and emotions, we address the social dimension when we discuss socialisation, family and the 'advocate', and we address the religious dimension of conversion when we talk about existential questions and religious experiences.

2   For a full discussion of the advocate, the advocate's strategy, and typical encounters between advocates and converts, see Rambo (1993: 66–86).

3   On loyalist prison conversions see Mitchell (2010); Dillon (1997). For another perspective, see the autobiography of former loyalist paramilitary Alistair Little, who discusses his own experience of conversion in prison and the factors that led him to move away from evangelicalism to a more generic spirituality (Little with Scott 2009).

4   Ex-UVF reconciliation worker, and former prisoner, Billy Mitchell also talked about the influence of a Methodist minister in his journey from violent loyalism to religious conversion. See Fearon (2002) and Orr (2008).

5   This echoes Allison's (1966) study of male converts in a Protestant seminary, all of whom had absent or dysfunctional fathers.

Chapter Five: Deepening Evangelicalism

1   This term is borrowed from Dillon and Wink (2007: 63).

2   In fact, this change in religious identity often had the corresponding effect of loosening once strongly held ethnic and national identifications. See also Mitchell and Todd (2007).

Chapter Six: Maintaining a Steady Faith

1   This number is lower than in other studies – for example Dillon and Wink (2007: 105–6) found that the vast majority of their study participants remained fairly religiously stable across adulthood. In their sample, three per cent showed a marked increase in religiousness and three per cent decreased in religiousness after midlife, largely prompted by personal adversity. But Dillon and Wink define stability as the absence of radical change, such as moving from Catholic to atheist, from Protestant to Muslim. They were not looking for subtler changes, for example someone who had always been an evangelical, but who had redefined what evangelicalism meant to them. Even Dillon and Wink (2007: 98) emphasise the 'gentle ebb and flow' of personal religiosity over time. Nearly all of the participants they introduce to us have undergone personal religious change at this lower level.

Chapter Seven: Moderating Evangelicalism

1   We do not try to include analysis of all 34 people in this chapter, instead selecting the stories of a smaller number of individuals who exemplify wider themes, so that we can replicate the depth of analysis of other chapters.

2   The truism also works the other way: 'Some of my best friends are Protestants …'.

3   For more information, see the Northern Ireland Mixed Marriage Association (NIMMA) (http://www.nimma.org.uk/). According to a recent NIMMA Report, about 12 per cent of people in Northern Ireland are in mixed marriages. See 'Celebrating the Work – Evaluating the Impact, 1974–2007', Belfast: Northern Ireland Mixed Marriage Association, 2008. In previous generations, one partner would usually convert to the religion of their spouse, which often had the result of loosening their ties with their own family. Since the 1990s, NIMMA reports that more couples are attempting to form 'dual tradition' homes. We are indebted to Jayme Reaves, who conducted this research for NIMMA, for supplying us with this information. See also INCORE's guide to internet sources on mixed marriages, (http://www.incore.ulst.ac.uk/services/cds/themes/marriages.html).

4   Using data from the 2001 census, Liam Murphy estimates the number of charismatics in Northern Ireland at 13,476. Murphy, however, concludes that the census figures are 'highly misleading', noting that they are based largely on the numbers of people involved in recognisably charismatic denominations (overlooking charismatics within traditional Protestant churches and the Catholic Church). The data also may underestimate the numbers who attend mega churches such as the Whitewell Tabernacle in Belfast. See chapter 1 in Murphy (2010).

5   See Todd (2005); Todd, O'Keefe, Rougier and Canas Bottos (2008, 2009).

6   For more on U2 and spiritual seeking see Stockman (2005) and Scharen (2006).

Chapter Eight: Transforming Evangelicalism

1   Tickle notes a tendency for change to happen in grand, 500-year cycles, placing 'emergence' at one of those 'hinge' points of Christian history.

2   Dave Tomlinson, house-church leader turned Anglican vicar, wrote one of the early seminal works of the movement, *The Post Evangelical*, in 1995.

3   See also http://www.davetomlinson.co.uk/.

4   This may seem like grand claims for a numerically small movement that is prominent largely in North America and the UK, and which seems virtually unheard of in the majority world, where Christianity is thriving. But, as Tickle points out, the charismatic and Pentecostal expressions of Christianity that are so popular in the majority world are overwhelmingly answering the key question about 'authority' in the same way as post-evangelicals/emergents: authority lies in *experience*.

5   Increasingly, the work of Rollins (2006, 2008, 2009, also http://peterrollins.net) and Ikon has been recognised as significant internationally, or at least in North America, Australia and the UK. For example, Rollins was featured in a cover story in *The Christian Century* magazine in 2009, and was identified as a leading figure in the emerging church in a 2007 story in the magazine *Christianity Today*. American philosopher John Caputo (2007), in his book *What Would Jesus Deconstruct?*, chose Ikon as a paradigmatic example of how Christianity might function in post-modernity. See 'Seeds of doubt: Ikon's Peter Rollins', *The Christian Century* 2 June 2009, available at: http://www.christiancentury.org/article.lasso?id=7087, accessed 15 March 2010; see also McKnight (2007).

6   For a description of an event, see Ganiel (2006b), and Rollins (2006).

7   www.peterrollins.net. Accessed 12 March 2010.

8   Ruth Tucker (2002) further explores the question of doubt in her book *Walking Away From Faith*, explaining that although her faith is often challenged by doubt, she chooses to believe. She says that 'unbelief is part of faith'.

Chapter Nine: Leaving Evangelicalism

1   These themes echo John Barbour's (1994) study of autobiographies of people who had left their faith. Barbour found four common patterns: people doubted the truth of their previous beliefs; they questioned the morality of their former life; leaving their faith caused them emotional upheaval; and they felt rejected by their former community. All of these are found, to a greater or lesser extent, in our own research.

2   For more on science and loss of faith see Babinski (2003) and Rosen (2005).

3   For similar stories see Tucker (2002).

4   Loftus (2007) describes the in-fighting in his church as the final blow to his faith.

5   See Wicker (1999).

6   Winston (2005) describes similar feelings amongst Hassidic Jews who struggle deeply with the prospect of leaving their faith, feeling guilty because they know their decision is likely cause their families pain, and even shame.

7   For examples of people who have gone back to faith, see Tucker (2002).

Bibliography

Abrams, D. and M. A. Hogg (eds) (1990) *Social Identity Theory: Constructive and Critical Advances*. New York: Harvester Wheatsheaf.

Akenson, D. H. (1992) *God's Peoples: Covenant and Land in South Africa, Israel, and Ulster*. New York: Ithaca Press.

Allison, J. (1966) 'Recent empirical studies in religious conversion experiences', *Pastoral Psychology* 17, 21–34.

Amir, Y. (1998) 'Contact hypothesis in ethnic relations', in E. Weiner (ed.), *The Handbook of Interethnic Coexistence*. New York: Continuum, 162–81.

Ammerman, N. (1987) *Bible Believers: Fundamentalists in the Modern World*. New Brunswick: Rutgers University Press.

Ammerman, N. T. (2003) 'Religious identities and religious institutions', in M. Dillon (ed.), *The Handbook of The Sociology of Religion*. Cambridge: Cambridge University Press, 207–24.

Anderson, A. (2004) *An Introduction to Pentecostalism: Global Charismatic Christianity*. Cambridge: Cambridge University Press.

Argyle, M. and P. Delin (1965) 'Non-universal laws of socialisation', *Human Relations* 18, 77–86.

Arweck, E. and M. Stringer (eds) (2002) *Theorising Faith: The Insider/Outsider Problem in the Study of Ritual*. Birmingham: Birmingham University Press.

Asch, S. E. (1956) 'Studies of independence and conformity: a minority of one against a unanimous majority', *Psychological Monographs* 70 (9), 1–70.

Atchley, R. (1999) *Continuity and Adaptation in Aging: Creating Positive Experiences*. Baltimore MD: Johns Hopkins University Press.

Atkinson, P. (2005) 'Qualitative research – unity and diversity'. *Forum Qualitative Sozialforschung / Forum: Qualitative Social Research* 6 (3), Art. 26, available at http://nbn-resolving.de/urn:nbn:de:0114-fqs0503261

Atkinson, P. and D. Silverman (1997) 'Kundera's immortality: The interview society and the invention of the self', *Qualitative Inquiry* 3, 304–25.

Babinski, E. T. (2003) *Leaving the Fold: Testimonies of Former Fundamentalists*. New York: Prometheus.

Back, C. W. and L. B. Bourque (1970) 'Can feelings be enumerated?', *Behavioural Science* 15, 487–96.

Baillie, S. (2001) *Evangelical Women in Belfast: Imprisoned or Empowered?* London: Palgrave Macmillan.

Barbour, J. (1994) *Versions of Deconversion: Autobiography and the Loss of Faith.* Charlottesville: University of Virginia Press.

Barker, D. (1992) *Losing Faith in Faith: From Preacher to Atheist.* Madison Wisconsin: Freedom from Religion Foundation.

Baston, C. D., P. Shroenrade and W. L. Ventis (1993) *Religion and the Individual: A Social-Psychological Perspective.* New York, Oxford: Oxford University Press.

Bauer, M. (1996) *The Narrative Interview.* London: London School of Economics and Political Science, Methodology Institute.

Bauman, Z. (1998) *Globalization: The Human Consequences.* Columbia: Columbia University Press

Bebbington, D. (1989) *Evangelicalism in Modern Britain: A History from the 1730s to the 1980s.* London: Unwin Hyman.

Bell, R. (2005) *Velvet Elvis: Repainting the Christian Faith.* Grand Rapids, MI: Zondervan.

Berger, P. (1967) *The Sacred Canopy.* New York: Anchor.

Berger, P. (1995) *Modernity, Pluralism and the Crisis of Meaning: The Orientation of Modern Man.* Gutersloh: Bertelsmann Foundation.

Beyerlein, K. (2004) 'Specifying the impact of conservative Protestantism on educational attainment', *Journal for the Scientific Study of Religion* 43, 505–18.

Blee, K. (2002) *Inside Organised Racism: Women in the Hate Movement.* California: University of California Press.

Boal, F. W., M. C. Keane and D. N. Livingstone (1997) *Them and Us? Attitudinal Variation Among Churchgoers in Belfast.* Belfast: Institute of Irish Studies.

Brewer, J. D. (2002) 'Are there any Christians in Northern Ireland?' in A. M. Gray, K. Lloyd, P. Devine, G. Robinson and D. Heenan (eds), *Social Attitudes in Northern Ireland: The Eighth Report.* London: Pluto, 22–38.

Brewer, J. D. (2010) *Peace Processes: A Sociological Approach.* Cambridge: Polity.

Brewer, J. D. with G. Higgins (1998) *Anti-Catholicism in Northern Ireland 1600–1998: The Mote and the Beam.* Palgrave Macmillan.

Brewin, K. (2010) *Other: Loving Self, God and Neighbour in a World of Fractures.* London: Hodder & Stoughton.

Bruce, S. (1986) *God Save Ulster! Religion and Politics of Paisleyism.* Oxford: Oxford University Press.

Bruce, S. (2002) *God is Dead: Secularisation in the West.* Oxford: Wiley Blackwell.

Bruce, S. (2007) *Paisley: Religion and Politics in Northern Ireland.* Oxford: Oxford University Press.

Bruner, J. (1987) 'Life as narrative', *Social Research* 54, 11–32.

Caputo, J. (2007) *What Would Jesus De-Construct? The Good News of Post-modernism for the Church.* Grand Rapids, Michigan: Baker Academic.

Chase, S. (2005) 'Narrative inquiry: Multiple lenses, approaches, voices', in N. Denzin and Y. Lincoln (eds), *The Sage Handbook of Qualitative Research*, 3rd edn. Thousand Oaks CA: Sage, 651–78.

Chaves, M. (1991) 'Family structure and Protestant church attendance: the sociological basis of cohort and age effects', *Journal for the Scientific Study of Religion* 30, 501–14.

Chong, K. H. (1998) 'What it means to be Christian: the role of religion in the construction of ethnic identity and boundary among second-generation Korean Americans', *Sociology of Religion* 59 (3): 259–86.

Christensen, H. T. and K. L. Cannon (1978) 'The fundamentalist emphasis at Brigham Young University', *Journal for the Scientific Study of Religion* 17, 53–7.

Connolly, P. (2000) 'What now for the contact hypothesis? Towards a new research agenda', *Race, Ethnicity and Education* 3 (2), 169–93.

Dark, D. (2002) *Everyday Apocalypse: The Sacred Revealed in Radiohead, The Simpsons, and Other Pop Culture Icons.* Michigan: Brazos Press.

Davie, G. (1994) *Religion in Britain Since 1945: Believing without Belonging.* Oxford: Blackwell.

Dawkins, R. (2006) *The God Delusion.* London: Bantam.

Dillon, Martin (1997) *God and the Gun: The Church and Irish Terrorism.* London: Orion.

Dillon, Michelle and P. Wink (2007) *In the Course of a Lifetime: Tracing Religious Belief, Practice and Change.* Berkeley: University of California Press.

Dougherty, K. D., B. R. Johnson and E. C. Polson (2007) 'Recovering the lost: remeasuring US religious affiliation', *Journal for the Scientific Study of Religion* 46, 483–99.

Durkheim, E. (1915) *The Elementary Forms of Religious Life.* London: Free Press.

Ebaugh, H. R. (2003) 'Religion and the new immigrants', in M. Dillon (ed.), *The Handbook of the Sociology of Religion.* Cambridge: Cambridge University Press, 225–39.

ECONI (1995) *A Future with Hope: Biblical Frameworks for Peace and Reconciliation in Northern Ireland.* Belfast: Evangelical Contribution on Northern Ireland.

Edgell, P. (2006) *Religion and Family in a Changing Society.* Princeton: Princeton University Press.

Elliott, M. (2009) *When God Took Sides: Religion and Identity in Ireland.* Oxford: Oxford University Press.

Ellison, C. G. and J. Levin (1998) 'The religion-health connection', *Health Education and Behaviour* 25, 200–20.

Ellison, C. G. and L. K. George (1994) 'Religious involvement, social ties, and social support in a Southeastern community', *Journal for the Scientific Study of Religion* 33, 46–61.

Fearon, K. (2002) 'The conflict's fifth business: a brief biography of Billy Mitchell', *Conflict Transformation Papers*, Belfast: LINC Resource Centre.

Feldman, K. A. (1969) 'Change and stability of religious orientations during college', *Review of Religious Research* 11, 40–60 and 103–28.

Ferraro, K. and J. Kelley-Moore (2000) 'Religious consolation among men and women: do health problems spur seeking?' *Journal for the Scientific Study of Religion* 39, 220–34.

Festinger, L., H. W. Riecken and S. Schachter (1956) *When Prophecy Fails: A Social and Psychological Study of a Modern Group that Predicted the End of the World.* Minnesota: University of Minnesota Press.

Flick, U. (1998). *An Introduction to Qualitative Research.* London/Newbury/Delhi: Sage.

Fowler, J. (1981) *Stages of Faith.* New York: Harper & Row.

Galanter, M. (1980) 'Psychological induction into the large group: findings from a modern religious sect', *American Journal of Psychiatry* 127, 1574–79.

Galanter, M. (1989) *Cults, Faith, Healing and Coercion.* New York: Oxford University Press.

Ganiel, G. (2006a) 'Ulster says maybe: The restructuring of evangelical politics in Northern Ireland', *Irish Political Studies* 21 (2), 137–55.

Ganiel, G. (2006b) 'Emerging from the evangelical subculture in Northern Ireland: A case study of the Zero28 and Ikon community', *International Journal for the Study of the Christian Church* 6 (1), 38–48.

Ganiel, G. (2008a) *Evangelicalism and Conflict in Northern Ireland.* New York: Palgrave.

Ganiel, G. (2008b) 'Explaining new forms of evangelical activism in Northern Ireland: Comparative perspectives from the USA and Canada', *Journal of Church and State* 50, 475–93.

Ganiel, G. (2009a) '21st century faith: results of the survey of clergy, pastors, ministers and faith leaders.' Dublin and Belfast: The Irish School of Ecumenics, Trinity College Dublin, available at http://www.ecumenics.ie/wp-content/uploads/Clergy-Survey-Report.pdf, accessed 12 August, 2010.

Ganiel, G. (2009b) '21st century faith: results of the survey of laypeople in the Republic of Ireland and Northern Ireland.' Dublin and Belfast: The Irish School of Ecumenics, Trinity College Dublin, available at http://www.ecumenics.ie/wp-content/uploads/Lay-Survey-Report.pdf, accessed 12 August 2010.

Ganiel, G. (2009c) 'Battling in Brussels: The DUP in the EU, 1979–2009', *Irish Political Studies* 24 (4), 575–88.

Ganiel, G. (2010a) 'Pentecostal and charismatic Christianity in South Africa and Zimbabwe: a review', *Religion Compass* 5, 130–43

Ganiel, G. (2010b) 'Visioning 21st century ecumenism: the view from the pulpit, the view from the pews', *Doctrine and Life* 6 (5), 31–46.

Ganiel, G. (2010c) 'Ethno-religious change in Northern Ireland and Zimbabwe: a comparative study of how religious havens can have ethnic significance', *Ethnopolitics* 9 (1), 103–20.

Ganiel G. and P. Dixon (2008) 'Religion in Northern Ireland: rethinking fundamentalism and the possibilities for conflict transformation', *Journal of Peace Research* 45 (3), 421–38.

Ganiel, G. and C. Mitchell (2006) 'Turning the categories inside-out: complex identifications and multiple interactions in religious ethnography', *Sociology of Religion* 67(1), 3–21.

Gibbs, E. and R. K. Bolger (2005) *Emerging Churches: Creating Christian Community in Postmodern Cultures.* Grand Rapids, MI: Baker Academic.

Goffman, E. (1959) *The Presentation of Everyday Life.* New York: Anchor.

Goffman, E. (1961) *Asylums: Essays on the Social Situation of Mental Patients and Other Inmates.* New York: Doubleday Anchor.

Gorski, P. (2003) 'Historicizing the secularization debate: an agenda for research', in M. Dillon (ed.), *The Handbook of the Sociology of Religion.* Cambridge: Cambridge University Press, 110–22.

Greeley, A. (1985) *American Catholics since the Council: An Unauthorized Report.* Chicago: Thomas More.

Greeley, A. and M. Hout (2006) *The Truth about Conservative Christians: What They Think and What They Believe.* Chicago: University of Chicago Press.

Hammond, P. E. and J. D. Hunter (1984) 'On maintaining plausibility: the worldview of evangelical college students', *Journal for the Social Scientific Study of Religion* 23, 221–38.

Handy, R. (1982) 'Protestant patterns in Canada and the United States: similarities and differences', in Joseph D. Ban and Paul R. Dekar (eds), *In the Great Tradition: In Honor of Winthrop S. Hudson, Essays on Pluralism, Voluntarism, and Revivalism*. Valley Forge, PA: Judson Press, 33–51.

Harris, E. (2006) 'The word of Buddha and Jesus: conversions from Christianity to Buddhism and from Buddhism to Christianity', in C. Partridge and H. Reid (eds), *Finding and Losing Faith: Studies in Conversion*. Milton Keynes: Paternoster Press, 39–55.

Hayes, B. C. and I. McAllister (1999) 'Ethnonationalism, public opinion and the Good Friday Agreement', in J. Ruane and J. Todd (eds), *After the Good Friday Agreement: Analysing Political Change in Northern Ireland*. Dublin: University College Dublin Press, 30–48.

Hayes, B. C. and I. McAllister (2004) 'The political impact of secularisation in Northern Ireland', *IBIS working paper* no. 36. Dublin: Institute for British-Irish Studies.

Heise, D. R. (1967) 'Prefatory findings in the sociology of missions', *Journal for the Scientific Study of Religion* 6, 49–58.

Hewstone, M., E. Cairns, A. Voci, S. Paolini, F. McLernon, R. Crisp, and U. Niens (2005) 'Intergroup contact in a divided society: challenging segregation in Northern Ireland', in D. Abrams, J. M. Marques, and M. A. Hogg (eds), *The Social Psychology of Inclusion and Exclusion*. Philadelphia, PA: Psychology Press, 265–92.

Hitchens, C. (2008) *God is Not Great: How Religion Poisons Everything*. London: Atlantic Books.

Hoge, D. R. and G. H. Petrillo (1978) 'Church participation amongst high school youth', *Journal for the Scientific Study of Religion* 17, 359–79.

Holstein, J. A. and J. F. Gubrium (1995) *The Active Interview*. Newbury Park, CA: Sage.

Hout, M. and C. Fischer (2002) 'Explaining the rise of Americans with no religious preferences: politics and generations', *American Sociological Review* 52, 325–45.

Hunsburger, B. E. (1976) 'Background religious denomination, parental emphasis and the religious orientation of university students', *Journal for the Scientific Study of Religion* 15, 251–5.

Iannaconne, L. (1990) 'Religious practice: a human capital approach', *Journal for the Scientific Study of Religion* 29 (3), 297–314.

Ingersoll, J. (2003) *Evangelical Christian Women*. New York: New York University Press.

Ingersoll-Dayton, B., N. Krause and D. Morgan (2002) 'Religious trajectories and transitions over the life course' *International Journal of Ageing and Human Development* 55, 51–70.

Inglis, Tom (1998) *Moral Monopoly: The Rise and Fall of the Catholic Church in Modern Ireland*. Dublin: University College Dublin Press.

Jelen, T. G., C. E. Smidt and C. Wilcox (1993) 'The political effects of the born-again phenomenon', in D. C. Leege and L. A. Kellstedt (eds), *Rediscovering the Religious Factor in American Politics*. Armonk: Sharpe, 110–34.

Jenkins, P. (2002) *The Next Christendom: The Coming of Global Christianity*. Oxford: Oxford University Press.

Johnston, R. K. (2000) 'Evangelicalism', in Adrian Hastings, A. Mason and H. Pyper (eds), *The Oxford Companion to Christian Thought*. Oxford: Oxford University Press, 117–220.

Jordan, G. (2001) *Not of this World? Evangelical Protestants in Northern Ireland*. Belfast: Blackstaff.

Kahoe, R. D. and R. F. Dunn (1975) 'The fear of death and religious attitudes and behaviour', *Journal for the Scientific Study of Religion* 14, 379–82.

Kellstedt, L. A. and C. E. Smidt (1991) 'Measuring fundamentalism: an analysis of different operational strategies, *Journal for the Scientific Study of Religion* 30, 259–78.

King, E. F. (2007) 'The Image as an Agent in the Social Construction of Identity: Shifting Images and Evolving Religious Identifications in Contemporary Northern Ireland.' Unpublished PhD manuscript, Queen's University Belfast.

King, E. F. (2009) *Material Religion and Popular Culture*. London: Routledge.

King, T. (2003) *The Truth About Stories: A Native Narrative*. Toronto, Canada: Anansi.

Kirkpatrick, L. A. and P. R. Shaver (1990) 'Attachment theory and religion: childhood attachments, religious beliefs and conversion', *Journal for the Scientific Study of Religion* 29 (3), 315–34.

Koenig, H. (ed.) (1998) *The Handbook of Religion and Mental Health*. San Diego: San Diego Academic Press.

Koenig, H. G., M. McCullagh and D. Larson (2001) *Handbook of Religion and Health*. New York: Oxford University Press.

Kraft, W. A., W. J. Litwin and S. E. Barber (1987) 'Religious orientation and assertiveness: relationship to death anxiety', *Journal of Social Psychology* 127, 93–5.

Lamont, M. and M. Fournier (1993) *Cultivating Differences: Symbolic Boundaries and the Making of Inequality*. Chicago: University of Chicago Press.

Liechty, J. and C. Clegg (2001) *Moving beyond Sectarianism: Religion, Conflict and Reconciliation in Northern Ireland*. Dublin: Columba.

Little, A. with R. Scott (2009) *Give a Boy a Gun: One Man's Journey from Killing to Peace-Making*. London: Darton, Longman & Todd.

Loftus, J. (2007) *Why I Rejected Christianity: A Former Apologist Explains*. Victoria, British Colombia: Trafford.

Lyon, D. (2000) *Jesus in Disneyland: Religion in Postmodern Times*. Cambridge: Polity.

Marsden, G. (1980) *Fundamentalism and American Culture: The Shaping of 20th Century Evangelicalism 1870–1925*. Oxford: Oxford University Press.

Martin, D. (2002) *Pentecostalism: The World Their Parish*. Oxford: Blackwell.

Maruna, S., L. Wilson and K. Curran (2006) 'Why God is often found behind bars: prison conversions and the crisis of self-narrative', *Research in Human Development* 3 (2&3), 161–84.

Marx, K. (1844) *A Contribution to the Critique of Hegel's Philosophy of Right*, Deutsch-Französische Jahrbücher, February.

McCullagh, M. and T. Smith (2003) 'Religion and health: depressive symptoms and mortality as case studies, in M. Dillon (ed.), *The Handbook of the Sociology of Religion*. Cambridge: Cambridge University Press, 190–204.

McFadden, S. (1999) 'Religion, personality and ageing: a life span perspective', *Journal of Personality* 67: 980–91.

McGarry, J. and B. O'Leary (1995) *Explaining Northern Ireland*. Oxford: Blackwell.

McGuire, M. (2008) *Lived Religion: Faith and Practice in Everyday Life*. New York: Oxford University Press USA.

McKay, S. (2000) *Northern Protestants: An Unsettled People*. Belfast: Blackstaff.

McKnight, S. (2007) 'Five streams of the emerging church: key elements of the most controversial and misunderstood movement in the church today', *Christianity Today*, 51 (2), 35–9.

McKnight, S. and H. Ondrey (2008) *Finding Faith, Losing Faith: Stories of Conversion and Apostasy*. Waco TX: Baylor University Press.

McLaren, B. (2005) *A Generous Orthodoxy*, 2nd edn. Grand Rapids, MI: Zondervan.

McLaren, B. (2008) *Everything Must Change: Jesus, Global Crises and a Revolution of Hope*. Nashville: Nelson.

McLaren, B. (2010) *A New Kind of Christianity: The Questions that are Transforming the Faith*. London: Hodder & Stoughton.

Miller, D. (1978) *Queen's Rebels: Ulster Loyalism in Historical Perspective*. Dublin: Gill & Macmillan.

Miller, D. (2003) *Blue Like Jazz: Nonreligious Thoughts on Christian Spirituality*. Nashville: Thomas Nelson.

Min, Pyong Gap (2010) *Preserving Ethnicity Through Religion in America: Korean Protestants and Indian Hindus Across Generations*. New York: NYU Press.

Mitchel, P. (2003) *Evangelicalism and National Identity in Ulster, 1921–1998*. Oxford: Oxford University Press.

Mitchell, C. (2003) 'Protestant identification and political change in Northern Ireland', *Ethnic and Racial Studies* 26 (4), 612–31.

Mitchell, C. (2005) *Religion, Identity and Politics in Northern Ireland: Boundaries of Belonging and Belief*. Aldershot: Ashgate.

Mitchell, C. (2010) 'The push and pull between religion and ethnicity: the case of loyalists in Northern Ireland', *Ethnopolitics* 99(1), 53–69.

Mitchell, C. and J. Tilley (2004) 'The moral minority: evangelical Protestants in Northern Ireland and their political behaviour', *Political Studies* 52 (4), 585–602.

Mitchell, C. and J. Tilley (2008) 'Disaggregating conservative Protestant groups in Northern Ireland: overlapping categories and the importance of a born-again self-identification', *Journal for the Scientific Study of Religion* 8 (4), 738–52.

Mitchell, C. and J. Todd (2007) 'Between the devil and the deep blue sea: nationality, power and symbolic trade-offs among evangelical Protestants in contemporary Northern Ireland', *Nations and Nationalism* 13 (4), 637–55.

Moloney, E. (2008) *Paisley: From Demagogue to Democrat?* Dublin: Poolbeg.

Moloney, E. and A. Pollack (1986) *Paisley*. Dublin: Poolbeg.

Morris, C. (2010) 'Protestants and Dissenters, Past and Present: Historical and Modern Differences of the two main Non-Catholic Groups in Northern Ireland.' MPhil dissertation in Reconciliation Studies, Trinity College Dublin at Belfast (The Irish School of Ecumenics).

Murphy, L. (2010) *Believing in Belfast: Charismatic Christianity After the Troubles*. Durham, NC: Carolina Academic Press.

Murray, S. (2004) *Church After Christendom*. London: Paternoster Press.

Neitz, M. J. (1987) *Charisma and Community*. New Brunswick, NJ: Transaction Press.

Neitz, M. J. (2004) 'Gender and culture: challenges to the sociology of religion', *Sociology of Religion* 65, 391–402.

Niens, U. and E. Cairns (2005) 'Conflict, contact and education in Northern Ireland', *Theory into Practice*, 44 (4), 337–44.

Noll, M. (2001a) *American Evangelical Christianity: An Introduction*. Oxford: Blackwell.

Noll, M. (2001b) [1992] *A History of Christianity in the United States and Canada*. Grand Rapids, MI: Wm B. Eerdmans.

Northern Ireland Life and Times Survey 1998–2008. Data available at: http://www.ark.ac.uk/nilt/

Northern Ireland Statistics and Research Agency (NILTS) (2002) 'Northern Ireland Census 2001 Population Report'.

Orr, P. (2008) *New Loyalties: Christian Faith and the Protestant Working Class*. Belfast: Centre for Contemporary Christianity.

Orzorak, E. W. (1989) 'Social and cognitive influences on the development of religious beliefs and commitment in adolescence', *Journal for the Scientific Study of Religion* 28, 448–63.

Peterson, J. A. (1964) *Education for Marriage*. New York: Scribner's.

Pettigrew, T. F. and L. R. Tropp. (2000) 'Does intergroup contact reduce prejudice? Recent meta-analytic findings', in S. Oskamp (ed.), *Reducing Prejudice and Discrimination: Social Psychological Perspectives*, Mahwah, NJ: Erlbaum, 93–114.

Porter, F. (2002) *Changing Women, Changing Worlds: Evangelical Women in Church, Community and Politics*. Belfast: Blackstaff.

Raj, D. S. (2000) '"Who the hell do you think you are?": Promoting religious identity among young Hindus in Britain', *Ethnic and Racial Studies* 23 (3), 535–58.

Rambo, L. (1993) *Understanding Religious Conversion*. New Haven: Yale University Press.

Ranger, T. O. (ed.) (2008) *Evangelical Christianity and Democracy in Africa*. Oxford: Oxford University Press.

Reimer, S. (2003) *Evangelicals and the Continental Divide: The Conservative Protestant Subculture in Canada and the United States*. Montreal, QC: McGill-Queen's University Press.

Richardson, J. T. (1985) 'The active vs. passive convert: Paradigm conflict in conversion/recruitment research', *Journal for the Scientific Study of Religion* 24, 163–79.

Riesmann, C. K. (1993). *Narrative Analysis*. London/Newbury/Delhi: Sage.

Rokeach, M. (1960) *The Open and Closed Mind*. New York: Basic Books.

Rollins, P. (2006) *How (Not) to Speak of God*. London: SPCK.

Rollins, P. (2008) *The Fidelity of Betrayal: Towards a Church Beyond Belief*. London: SPCK.

Rollins, P. (2009) *The Orthodox Heretic and Other Impossible Tales*. Norwich: Canterbury Press.

Roof, W. C. (1999) *Spiritual Marketplace: Baby Boomers and the Remaking of Religion*. San Francisco: Harper and Row.

Rosen. C. (2005) *My Fundamentalist Education: A Memoir of a Divine Childhood*. New York: Public Affairs.

Scharen, C. (2006) *One Step Closer: Why U2 Matters to Those Seeking God.* Michigan: Brazos Press.

Sells, M. (1998) *The Bridge Betrayed: Religion and Genocide in Bosnia.* California: University of California Press.

Sells, M. (2003) 'Crosses of blood: sacred space, religion and violence in Bosnia-Hercegovina', *Sociology of Religion* 64 (3), 309–32.

Selmanovic, S. (2009) *It's Really all about God: Reflections of a Muslim Atheist Jewish Christian.* San Francisco: Jossey Bass.

Sherkat, D. E. (1997) 'The impact of Protestant fundamentalism on educational attainment', *American Sociological Review* 62 (2), 306–15.

Sherkat, D. E. (2003) 'Religious socialization: sources of influence and influences of agency', in M. Dillon (ed.), *Handbook for the Sociology of Religion*, Cambridge: Cambridge University Press, 151–63.

Shirlow, P. and B. Murtagh (2006) *Belfast: Segregation, Violence and the City.* London: Pluto.

Smith, C. S. (1998) *American Evangelicalism: Embattled and Thriving.* Chicago: University of Chicago Press.

Smith, T. B., M. McCullough and J. Poll (2003) 'Religiousness and depression: evidence for a main effect and the moderating influence of stressful life events', *Psychological Bulletin* 129, 614–36.

Smyth, C. (1988) *Ian Paisley: Voice of Protestant Ulster.* Edinburgh: Scottish Academic Press.

Somers, M. (1994) 'Narrative and the constitution of identity: a relational and network approach', *Theory and Society* 23 (5), 605–50.

Southern, N. (2005) 'Ian Paisley and evangelical Democratic Unionists: an analysis of the role of evangelical Protestantism within the Democratic Unionist Party', *Irish Political Studies* 20 (2), 127–45.

Southern, N. (2007) 'Paisleyism: an ideology in transition?' *Studies: An Irish Quarterly Review* 96 (382), 179–92.

Spilka, B., R. W. Hood and R. L. Gorush (1985) *The Psychology of Religion: An Empirical Approach.* New Jersey: Prentice Hall.

Staples, C. L. and A. L. Mauss (1987) 'Conversion or commitment? A reassessment of the Snow and Machalek approach to the study of religious conversion', *Journal for the Scientific Study of Religion* 26, 133–47.

Stark, R. and W. Bainbridge (1980) 'Networks of faith: interpersonal bonds and recruitment to cults and sects', *American Journal of Sociology* 85 (6), 1376–95.

Stark, R. and R. Finke (2000) *Acts of Faith: Exploring the Human Side of Religion.* Berkeley: University of California Press.

Stockman, S. (2005) *Walk On: The Spiritual Journey of U2.* Orlando, Florida: Relevant Books.

Straus, R. (1976) 'Changing oneself: seekers and the creative transformation of life experience', in J. Lofland, *Doing Social Life: The Qualitative Study of Human Interaction in Natural Settings.* New York: Wiley-Interscience, 252–72.

Straus, R. (1979) 'Religious conversion as a personal and collective accomplishment', *Sociological Analysis* 40 (1), 158–65.

Thomas, J. (2006) 'Conning or conversion? The role of religion in prison coping', *The Prison Journal* 86(2), 242–59.

Thomson, A. (2002) *Fields of Vision: Faith and. Identity in Protestant Ireland.* Belfast: Centre for Contemporary Christianity in Ireland.

Thumma, S. (1991) 'Negotiating a religious identity', *Sociological Analysis* 52, 333–47.

Tickle, P. (2005) 'Foreword', in B. McLaren, *A Generous Orthodoxy*, 2nd edn. Grand Rapids, MI: Zondervan.

Tickle, P. (2008) *The Great Emergence: How Christianity is Changing and Why.* Grand Rapids, MI: Baker Books.

Tidball, D. (1994) *Who are the Evangelicals? Tracing the Roots of Today's Movements.* London: Marshall Pickering.

Todd, J. (1987) 'Two traditions in Unionist culture', *Irish Political Studies* 2, 1–26.

Todd, J. (2005) 'Social transformation, collective categories, and identity change', *Theory and Society* 34 (4), 429–63.

Todd, J. T. O'Keefe, N. Rougier, L. Canas Bottos (2008) 'Fluid or frozen? Choice and change in ethno-national identification in contemporary Northern Ireland', *Nationalism and Ethnic Politics* 12 (3&4), 323–46.

Todd, J., T. O'Keefe, N. Rougier and L. Canas Bottos (2009) 'Does being Protestant matter? Protestants, minorities and the remaking of ethno-religious identity after the Good Friday Agreement', *National Identities* 11 (1), 87–99.

Tomlinson, D. (1995) *The Post Evangelical.* Marion, IN: Triangle.

Tomlinson, D. (2008) *Re-Enchanting Christianity: Faith in an Emerging Culture.* Norwich: Canterbury Press.

Tornstam, L. (2005) *Gerotranscendence: A Developmental Theory of Positive Ageing.* New York: Springer.

Travers, M. (2006) 'Postmodernism and qualitative research', *Qualitative Research* 6, 267–73.

Tucker, R. (2002) *Walking Away from Faith: Unravelling the Mystery of Belief and Unbelief.* Downers Grove: InterVarsity Press.

Varshney, A. (2005) *Ethnic Conflict and Civic Life: Hindus and Muslims in India.* Oxford: Oxford University Press.

Warner, R. S. (1997) 'Religion, boundaries and bridges', *Sociology of Religion* 58 (3), 217–38.

Watson, C. (2006) 'Unreliable narrators? "Inconsistency" (and some inconstancy) in interviews', *Qualitative Research* 6, 367-84.

Weber, M. (1958) [1915] *The Protestant Ethic and the Spirit of Capitalism.* Boston MA: Beacon.

Wellman, J. (2008) *Evangelical vs. Liberal: The Clash of Christian Cultures in the Pacific Northwest.* Oxford: Oxford University Press.

Wicker, C. (1999) *God Knows My Heart: Finding a Faith that Fits.* New York: St Martins Press.

Wink, P. and R. Helson (1997) 'Practical and transcendent wisdom: their nature and some longitudinal findings', *Journal of Adult Development* 4, 1–15.

Winston, H. (2005) *Unchosen: The Hidden Lives of Hassidic Rebels.* Boston: Beacon Press.

Wong, P. T. P. (2000) 'Meaning of life and meaning of death in successful aging', in A. Tomer (ed.), *Death Attitudes and the Older Adult.* Brunner/Mazel Publishers, 23–35.

Woodberry, R. D. and C. S. Smith (1998) 'Fundamentalism et al.: conservative Protestants in America', *Annual Review of Sociology* 24, 25–56.

Wright, F. (1973) 'Protestant ideology and politics in Ulster', *Archives Européennes de Sociologie* 14, 213–80.

Yeakley, F. R. (1979) *Why Churches Grow*. Oklahoma: Christian Communications.

Other Resources

http://www.brianmclaren.net/

http://www.davetomlinson.co.uk/

http://peterrollins.net/

http://www.phyllistickle.com/

INCORE's guide to internet sources on mixed marriages, http://www.incore.ulst.ac.uk/services/cds/themes/marriages.html

Northern Ireland Mixed Marriage Association (NIMMA) (http://www.nimma.org.uk/). 'Celebrating the Work – Evaluating the Impact, 1974–2007', Belfast: Northern Ireland Mixed Marriage Association, 2008.

'Seeds of doubt: Ikon's Peter Rollins', *The Christian Century*, 2 June 2009, available at: http://www.christiancentury.org/article.lasso?id=7087, accessed 15 March 2010.

Index